DISCOVER THE POWERFUL SECRETS OF TODAY'S BEST LEADERS . . .

WITH *SUPERLEADERSHIP!*

"In *SuperLeadership* Charles Manz and Hank Sims . . . focus on leaders who lead, not for their own edification and glory, not through command and authority, but through a subtle and ill-understood process that leads others to *lead themselves* to excellence.

"Manz and Sims's book has a further strength. The authors do a superb job of articulating specific behaviors and strategies that leaders can utilize to bring out excellence in others . . . *SuperLeadership* is action oriented — it proposes specific strategies for leading others to lead themselves."

—From the Foreword by Tom Peters,
author of *In Search of Excellence*

Winner of the 1989 Stybel Peabody Prize

SUPER-LEADERSHIP

LEADING OTHERS TO LEAD THEMSELVES

**Charles C. Manz
and
Henry P. Sims, Jr.**

BERKLEY BOOKS, NEW YORK

This Berkley book contains the complete text
of the original hardcover edition.

SUPERLEADERSHIP

A Berkley Book / published by arrangement with
Prentice Hall Press

PRINTING HISTORY
Prentice Hall Press edition published 1989
Berkley edition / November 1990

ISBN: 0-425-12356-1

A BERKLEY BOOK ® TM 757,375
Berkley Books are published by The Berkley Publishing Group,
200 Madison Avenue, New York, New York 10016.
The name "BERKLEY" and the "B" logo
are trademarks belonging to Berkley Publishing Corporation.

PRINTED IN THE UNITED STATES OF AMERICA

10 9 8 7 6 5 4 3 2 1

Dedicated to our children

Christopher and Katy
and
Jonathan, Amy, and Andrew

The persons who have contributed most to
our practical understanding of the challenges
of leading others to lead themselves

Acknowledgments

In the preparation of this book, we have been fortunate to have had many sources of inspiration and support. We recognize the continuing inspiration of our colleagues, including Dennis Gioia, Robert House, Fred Luthans, Dan Brass, Bob Marx, Richard Hackman, Ed Locke, Barry Bateman, Mike Mahoney, Art Bedeian, Hal Angle, and Ed Lawler. John Slocum, John Sheridan, James Farr, Rex Warland, and Richard Cherry provided important encouragement for our earlier work regarding self-managing teams. Also, we thank Tom Peters, who in early 1983 provided Hank Sims with a special source of inspiration by graciously allowing him to participate in his class while on sabbatical at Stanford University, and who has generously contributed the foreword to this book.

In addition, while we have both moved on to other organizations, we express our appreciation to the Operations Management Center at the University of Minnesota and the College of Business Administration at Pennsylvania State University for their support of our leadership research that helped provide a knowledge base for this book. Further, we gratefully acknowledge the support of Coleman Raphael and Jack Pearce at George Mason University; Brit Kirwan, Rudy Lamone, and Ed Locke at the University of Maryland; and the management department faculty at Arizona State University. And we offer special thanks to Richard Hackman, Ted Levitt, and the other faculty members who provided very motivating reinforcement of the work of Chuck Manz by making possible his recent appointment as a Marvin Bower Fellow at Harvard Business School.

We also wish to thank the administrative and word-processing staffs at Penn State University and the University of Minnesota, especially to Judy Sartori and Barbara Apaliski for their significant energy and assistance in preparation of our manuscript. Likewise, we thank our agent, Jeanne Hanson, and our editors, Jeff Krames and Paul Aron, and all the other Prentice Hall Press staff members who provided us with invaluable guidance in completing our book.

We were assisted in preparing two of the SuperLeadership profiles by Joan Everett (the Dwight Eisenhower profile) and Craig Pearce (the Rene McPherson profile). Indeed, a large part of these profiles was originally written by these two individuals. We thank them for their support and their permission to use the fruits of their labors.

Finally, and most of all, we wish to thank our families, especially Karen and Laurie, for understanding the crazy, wacky life of a professor and author.

Contents

Contents

Contents

Contents

Foreword

BY

TOM PETERS

In the late 1970s when Bob Waterman and I were undertaking the research that ultimately led to our book *In Search of Excellence*, the evidence that "people" were the critical ingredient in excellent companies seemed overpowering. Eventually, our research led us to codify some of these "people-oriented" aspects in our "characteristics of excellent performing companies." For example, in our book, we articulated the importance of such characteristics as achieving productivity through people, decentralizing authority to allow autonomy and entrepreneurship, and relying on "loose-tight controls."

But where did these characteristics come from? It was obvious from our research that executive leadership was a powerful factor in developing corporate cultures that possessed these characteristics.

Later, stimulated by the success of *In Search of Excellence*, we continued our research, which led us to believe that executive leadership was of even more compelling importance. It was the executives who *did something* that were critical in creating this excellence in their corporations.

In fact, Nancy Austin and I recognized this "leadership difference" as so important that we made it the prime emphasis of *A Passion for Excellence*. Time after time, in my travels about the United States, I found examples of how leadership had been the critical factor in shaping excellent organizations. Many of these cases are featured prominently in *A Passion for Excellence*. And in 1987, with the publication of *Thriving on Chaos*, I've turned up the heat even more.

Thriving on change demands the empowerment of every person in the organization—no ifs, ands, or buts.

In *SuperLeadership*, Charles Manz and Hank Sims have added to this same theme. They focus on leaders who lead, not for their own edification and glory, not through command and authority, but through a subtle and ill-understood process that leads others to *lead themselves* to excellence. Indeed, in reading *SuperLeadership*, I recognized many of the characteristics that they articulate in the numerous executives I had encountered in researching my three books.

Manz's and Sims's book has a further strength. The authors do a superb job of articulating specific behaviors and strategies that leaders can use to bring out excellence in others. While philosophy and abstract vision are important executive strengths, the actions that executives take to realize these visions are critical. *SuperLeadership* is action-oriented—it proposes specific strategies for leading others to lead themselves.

I remain convinced that executive leadership will continue to be the critical ingredient in the success or failure of American business and industry. Certainly, the corporate environment is becoming ever more complex and transitory, so the more we can understand about leadership, the more effective our business organizations can be. Understanding the SuperLeader moves us closer to this elusive goal.

Preface

A leader is best
When people barely know he exists,
. . . When his work is done, his aim fulfilled,
They will say:
We did it ourselves.

—LAO-TZU

When most people think of leadership, they think of one person doing something to another person. We call this "influence," and we think of a leader as one who has the ability to influence another. A classic leader—one whom everyone recognizes *is* a leader—is sometimes described as "charismatic" or "heroic." A popular current concept is the idea of a "transformational" leader, one who has the vision and dynamic personal attraction to generate total organizational change. The word *leader* itself conjures up visions of a striking figure on a rearing white horse, crying "follow me!" The leader is the one who has either power, authority, or charisma enough to command others.

We can think of historical figures who fit this mold: Alexander the Great, Caesar, Napoleon, George Washington, Churchill, Patton. Even today, Lee Iacocca's turnaround of Chrysler Corporation might be thought of as heroic leadership. It's not difficult to imagine Iacocca astride a white horse, and he is frequently described as "charismatic."

But is this heroic leadership figure the most appropriate image of the organizational leader of today? Is there another model? We believe there is. Well over ten years ago, we began our quest through empirical research for a sound theoretical conceptualization that effectively answers this question. What we discovered is that in many modern situations the most appropriate leader is the one who can lead others to lead themselves.

Our viewpoint represents a departure from the dominant, and we think incomplete, view of leadership. We begin with the position that true leadership comes mainly from within a person, not from outside. At its best, external leadership can provide a spark and support the flame of the powerful self-leadership that dwells within each person. At its worst, it disrupts this internal process, damaging the person and the constituencies he or she serves.

In this book, our focus is on a new form of leadership—one designed to facilitate the self-leadership energy within each person. This perspective suggests a new measure of leadership strength—the ability to maximize the contributions of others by helping them to effectively guide their own destinies, rather than the ability to bend the will of others to the leader's. We refer to this subtle, yet tremendously powerful, approach to leadership as *SuperLeadership—leading others to lead themselves*.

SuperLeaders marshal the strength of many, for their strength does not lie solely in their own abilities, but in the vast, multiple talents of those that surround them. In this sense, the word *super* has a different connotation than it does in comic books or in terms like *superman* or *supermom*. It does concern bringing out the best, but mainly in others, not just in the leader. The SuperLeader does not carry the weight of the world alone but shares this burden with others. Further, those others become stronger and stronger through the process of really contributing.

A *SuperLeader* is one who leads others to lead themselves.

It is not our intention to provide all the answers to effective leadership. To do so would seem a violation of our argument that the ultimate answers and potentialities lie within the private worlds in each person. Instead, we will provide ideas designed to help the reader look at the world a bit differently and hopefully to discover new possibilities for achieving excellence, mainly through the assistance of fellow human beings (self-leaders).

For the most part, we focus on leadership in organizations— sometimes called managerial or executive leadership. We conceive of managerial leadership as a *practical* set of strategies designed to bring out the self-leadership capabilities of subordinates. The initial, and perhaps most important, strategy is to set a personal self-leadership example for subordinates. This means that the leader will first be an effective self-leader in order to serve as a positive model. Then the leader teaches, encourages, and reinforces effective self-leadership in subordinates. At 3M Company, for example, many top-level executives have the hands-on experience of championing a major new product innovation at some point in their careers. In addition to serving as living examples of initiative and self-leadership, they have learned to encourage and reinforce similar behavior in their juniors.

SuperLeadership also involves facilitating positive organizational cultures that support the practice of self-leadership. For example, Wal-Mart Stores, Inc., a thriving company in recent years, attributes much of its success to an emphasis on employee initiative and autonomy rather than close supervision. Chairman Sam Walton has explained that its management philosophy is to simply get the right people in the right places and to encourage them to use their own inventiveness to accomplish the task at hand.[1]

Stories, examples, checklists, and cases will be used throughout this book to provide practical insight on how these SuperLeadership strategies can be used successfully by executives in the pursuit of excellence. Our underlying philosophy is optimistic. We are optimistic about the vast, often hidden, capability within executives and their subordinates. Unfortunately, excessive external controls can deprive potential SuperLeaders of the benefits of these capabilities. SuperLeadership taps the potential each person possesses for making the world a better place if given a chance.

A recent study of many of our nation's top artists, scholars, and athletes indicated that their success resulted more from determination and practice than from natural, inborn talent.[2] They had been encouraged early on to value hard work and to be inquisitive learners, and over time they blossomed into great performers. Individuals need to be provided with the chance to develop and exercise the capabilities that they truly possess (the chance to be effective self-leaders). If denied this opportunity, they are robbed of their most valuable treasures—their human dignity and the right to live a life that is meaningful, that counts for something. When a person loses these treasures, the world loses, too. And, of course, organizations lose a great deal when employee talent is wasted.

We are not so naive as to claim that SuperLeadership is *the* final answer to the issue of the competitiveness of U.S. organizations. Nevertheless, in today's fast changing world, the emphasis is on creativity, innovation, and, most of all, the capacity to respond to environmental shifts. We think that developing the self-leadership capabilities of each employee is a critical factor in promoting these important attributes for total organizational success.

Since facilitating self-leadership is so important, we devote a considerable part of this book to describing what self-leadership is all about. We especially draw upon the thinking that Charles Manz brought forth in his earlier book, *The Art of Self-Leadership*.

Practical self-leadership consists of both behavioral and cognitive strategies designed to enhance personal achievement and effectiveness. Strategies such as establishing self-goals and administering self-rewards help facilitate effective behavior. Also, monitoring and managing beliefs and assumptions, as well as using mental imagery and internal dialogues, help to establish constructive thinking patterns (habits).

SELF-LEADERSHIP—A philosophy and a systematic set of behavioral and cognitive strategies for leading ourselves to higher performance and effectiveness.

Many organizations fail to understand precisely how to go about bringing out the wealth of talent that each of their employees possesses. Many are still operating under a quasi-military model that encourages conformity and adherence, obedience to command and instruction, rather than emphasizes how leaders can facilitate the full potential of subordinates, that is, how they can lead others to lead themselves.

In this book, we will discuss some of the behavioral and cognitive strategies that we have identified and articulated for leading others to lead themselves. In order to capture this in a single frame of reference, we have characterized the leader who can do this as a *Super-Leader*.

Everyone has heard the expression, "Give a man a fish, and he will be fed for a day; teach a man to fish, and he will be fed for a lifetime." The logic underlying this book is similar. We might paraphrase that expression: "Be a strong, even a charismatic, leader, and followers will know where to go as long as you light their way; teach them to lead themselves and their path will be lighted always." And we would add, "and they will illuminate for you new paths of amazing growth and opportunity that you might never have seen."

SOME SUPERLEADERSHIP THEMES

- An important measure of a leader's own success is the success of others.
- What makes a leader successful at one level can be counterproductive at a higher level.
- "[This transition] is even more difficult for me than other people. . . . I started to realize that I better let some other people do some things and I better start looking at the big picture a little more." —Joseph Vincent Paterno
- The strength of a leader is measured by the ability to facilitate the self-leadership of others—not the ability to bend the will of others to the leader's.
- If a person wants to lead somebody, he must first lead himself.
- The best of all leaders is the one who helps people so that, eventually, they don't need him.
- Give a man a fish, and he will be fed for a day; teach a man to fish, and he will be fed for a lifetime.

SUPER-LEADERSHIP

1

The Need for SuperLeadership

Tom gripped his drink tightly. "I don't get it, Frank! Your division is always on top of things. With all the changes that are going on in the business I just can't keep up anymore. I work my tail off for the company and my division; I try to keep everyone pointed in the right direction and monitor their progress very closely, but I always miss something! It's like trying to juggle a hundred balls at once. I'm drained but you always seem so relaxed and fresh. And what's worse, my division just doesn't perform like yours. It seems like I'm always pushing harder than you but your team is always ahead."

Having blurted out this disturbing realization in an exasperated tone, Tom Barnes just stared at Frank Jennings as though searching for some mysterious and magical source of power. "I mean our business is changing so much that I never know enough, even though I'm watching and reading constantly. How can you know and do so much?"

"Actually, Tom you overestimate my abilities—I suspect you know more about the business than I do. And you certainly do more."

Tom Barnes, obviously surprised by this answer, responded in sincere bewilderment. "Well then how do you do it? How can you keep so on top of things? I try so hard but I never get everything done!" continued Tom in an exasperated and frustrated tone that surprised even himself.

"I think that may be your problem, Tom," responded Frank. "You see, I *don't* try to know everything and do everything. I figure that's why I've got good people working for me. I spend my time encouraging and helping them to keep up with the changes and demands. I sure

1

know I can't. I do my best to help the people in my division reach their potential. They're much less dependent on me than I think your people are on you and I think they're very capable and enthused. I've found them all to be terrific resources if given half a chance and belief in themselves. It takes work and time, of course, and a different kind of energy than you've focused on—a more rewarding kind, I think. If I tried to do everything myself, I'd waste that potential."

Tom paused, pondering that for a while. "It seems so simple, but I guess I hadn't thought of it that way. It may be that the harder I've been working and the more responsibility I've taken on myself, the weaker my department has gotten—and the weaker it got, the harder I worked. I always thought you were just luckier in getting good personnel assigned to you. But maybe I just haven't let mine grow. And they don't seem very committed. I feel like they resent my authority and the way I use it to make decisions," Tom muttered to himself. "Well, what do you know, maybe I don't have to keep on top of everything. And you don't know everything after all," Tom murmured in relief. Catching himself after the last statement, Tom apologized as he turned embarrassedly to Frank: "I didn't mean that the way it sounded."

"Don't apologize. You're absolutely right. But I do know one thing," Frank continued as he turned to face Tom. "I know that I really know very little, especially when you realize all there is to be known. But I guess *knowing* how much I don't know . . ." Frank paused for emphasis "is an awful lot in itself—and a good start."

This is a great time to be in business. Don't get us wrong—we've read the news, too. We know that employee productivity and product quality have suffered in recent years and that American business has declined in the world's perception. But opportunities for achieving great things and for experiencing fulfillment in work and life have never been greater. Medical advances and increased standards of living have enabled people to enjoy longer lives. Educational opportunities are fantastic, and the war on ignorance has had some victories—preschool, primary school, colleges and universities, continuing and adult education, home computers . . . whew. And scientific advances have provided new technologies such as automated factories, robotics, supercomputers, biotechnology, and so on that only a few years ago would have seemed impossible. If we take stock of the positive opportunities that exist for corporations and their employees, it is difficult to be blind to all of the potentials.

But the challenges obviously are great. It's highly unlikely that people can reasonably expect to learn everything they'll need to be successful in their careers during "school years." Lifelong learning is no longer a luxury; it's now a requirement for survival. Most people cannot realistically expect to possess themselves all the knowledge that they need to perform their work optimally at any point in time, so they need to be continually learning and benefiting from the knowledge of others if they truly aspire to excellence.

There's no question that our world has become very complicated and that it is changing at an unprecedented rate. Unfortunately, many of our management practices have not kept up with these changes. We believe one of the greatest opportunities for change and advancement *centers* on the meaningful mobilization of human effort and innovative behavior. In fact, many of these changes cry for innovative ways of leading and organizing people at work. The potential payoffs are immense. Today, people are better educated and demand more from their jobs than a paycheck. In a recent study of several thousand workers in a computer manufacturing company, younger workers (in the "baby boomer" age group) consistently reported a lower quality of work life than their older counterparts. [1] A general conclusion was that traditional management-leadership methods simply do not fit today's workers. Frequently, they are more committed to their profession than to their company. All this means that most people won't stand for being ordered around all the time, and they would probably be wasting their unique talents and capabilities if they would. In his book *The Gold-Collar Worker*, Robert E. Kelley emphasizes the deeper significance of this young, upscale, educated work force. He discusses a "new breed of workers" and calls for business to adapt to their special characteristics. [2]

Since our own experience relates primarily to business organizations, they will generally be the focus of our discussion. We believe, however, that these fundamental challenges stretch to nearly all aspects of our lives—our relationships, the way we raise our children, the educational process, and so forth.

3

> "I *don't* try to know everything and do everything. I figure that's why I've got good people working for me."

WHAT ARE SELF-LEADERSHIP AND SUPERLEADERSHIP?

Over the past ten years, through our consulting, research, and writing, we have developed a set of ideas that we believe can help meet the challenge of leading this "new breed of workers." We use the labels of *self-leadership* and *SuperLeadership* to characterize a different approach to leadership. Since these terms are the keystones of our ideas, it's worthwhile to briefly define them.

Self-leadership is an extensive set of strategies focused on the behaviors and thoughts that can be used to exert self-influence. Self-leadership is what people do to lead themselves. In some ways, self-leadership might also be thought of as a form of responsible followership; that is, if given the autonomy and responsibility to control their own lives, what *specifically* can followers who are becoming self-leaders do to respond to this challenge in a responsible way?

We have heard the employee who complains, "They say they want to use 'participative management' around here. As of today, I'm supposed to 'participate.' I don't understand what that means. What am I supposed to do that's different?" In answer, self-leadership provides a set of guidelines for how an employee can responsibly meet the challenge of so-called participative management.

> Self-leadership is an extensive set of strategies focused on the behaviors and thoughts that people use to influence themselves.

SuperLeadership applies to the manager and executive who have responsibility for leading others, especially subordinate employees.

More specifically, a *SuperLeader* is one who leads others to lead themselves. The SuperLeader designs and implements the system that allows and teaches employees to be self-leaders. The approach consists of an extensive set of behaviors, all intended to provide so-called followers with the behavioral and cognitive skills necessary to exercise self-leadership. The SuperLeader asks, "What can I do to lead others to lead themselves?"

**A SuperLeader is one who leads others
to lead themselves.**

In the pages that follow, we will develop these ideas in some detail. First, we will present the behavior- and thought-focused strategies that are the essence of self-leadership. Understanding self-leadership is a critical first step to understanding SuperLeadership. Then, we will present the skills that we call *SuperLeadership*. We hope these ideas will not be seen as a panacea—they're not—but as a carefully designed game plan, intended to capitalize on the long-term potential of each employee.

RECOGNIZING EMPLOYEE SELF-LEADERSHIP

We propose a fundamentally different approach to leading people that we believe will become increasingly important in the future. We refer to this approach as SuperLeadership: leading others to lead themselves. But first we need to cover some preliminary ground. Our ideas are based, in part, on the view that essentially all control over employees is *ultimately* self-imposed. Regardless of where controls come from (for example, from the boss or a company policy), the effect they have depends on how these controls are evaluated, accepted, and translated by each employee into commitment.

The illustration on page 6 depicts this point graphically. Just as organizations provide their employees with standards, evaluations, and rewards and punishments, employees themselves provide and

5

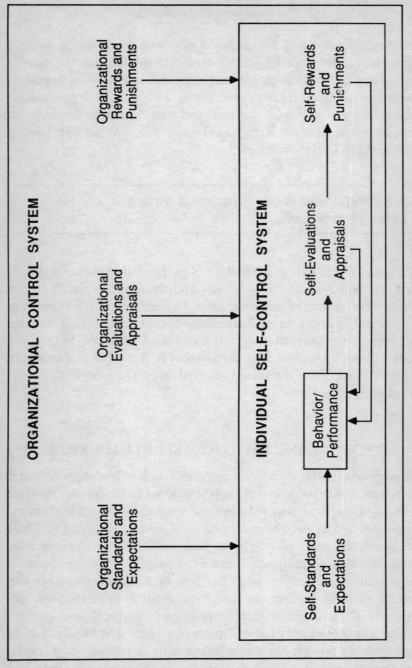

The Organization and Self-Control Systems

experience these same basic elements from *within*. Employees have expectations regarding their own performance, and react positively or negatively toward themselves in response to their own self-evaluations.

All control over employees is *ultimately* self-imposed.

This is a most important point to make. Typically, organizational attempts at employee control do not recognize the important role of the person's "self." Organizational standards will not significantly influence employee behavior if they are not accepted. Similarly, organizational rewards will not produce their desired effects if they are not valued by the employees receiving the rewards. Regardless of how employee performance is appraised, the performance evaluation that will carry the *most* weight will be the evaluations that employees make of themselves.

All this suggests that to be effective a leader must successfully influence the way people influence themselves. In fact, we believe the principal means of establishing the commitment and enthusiasm necessary to achieve true long-term excellence in an organization is to unleash the self-leadership potential within each person. A tight external control that undermines or displaces an employee's self-control system may produce compliance. Commitment to excellence, however, flows from the powerful leadership potential within.

To be effective a leader must successfully influence the way people influence themselves.

In addition, overreliance on external control that does not recognize a person's self-leadership capacity can produce some very dysfunctional outcomes. An external approach to control can result in bureaucratic behavior in which people focus their efforts only on what is measured and rewarded by the organization, neglecting many other important activities; the feeding of management information systems with inaccurate data that artificially enhances individual performance standings; compliance rather than commitment; and a number of other problems.[3]

A rigid performance-appraisal system for salespeople, for example, that focuses on established sales procedures and set standards for sales may be effective in producing short-term sales increases. But long-term performance can suffer because of a lack of attention to servicing existing clients. Moreover, this external-control process can interfere with the unique creativity and interests an employee needs to express to become committed to the job.

An overemphasis on external rewards at the expense of internal (or "natural") rewards can undermine important aspects of individual motivation:[4] If the emphasis is placed on what people will *get* for doing their work (money, promotions, and so on) rather than on the positive aspects of doing the task itself, the natural enjoyment of a job well done, then, we would argue, meaningful commitment to excellence is at risk. This suggests that the way control and leadership are typically viewed in this country may be too limited. We propose a new counterview that external controls should be designed mainly to stimulate and facilitate an employee's own *internal* influence and energy.

SUPERLEADERSHIP: A FUNDAMENTALLY DIFFERENT APPROACH TO LEADERSHIP

SuperLeadership is fundamentally different from traditional views of leadership. Its main objects are to stimulate and facilitate self-leadership capability and practice and, further, to make the self-leadership process the central target of external influence. Self-influence is viewed as a powerful opportunity for achieving excellence rather than as a threat to external control and authority. In fact, if leaders really want subordinates to develop into high performers, providing them with the autonomy and responsibility to be more in charge of themselves and their work is essential.

In our research, we have observed very significant contrasts in the way employees feel about their work. None has been more striking, however, than that between "traditionally" managed manufacturing plants and plants organized around self-managing teams.

In traditional, authority-based plants, we observed management-labor tension, alcohol and drug problems, and substantial worker apathy and discontent, all of which have a negative effect on employee performance. We especially noted the evident underutilization of employees. In contrast, in the plants using self-managing teams, we saw the workers themselves make many work-related decisions such as assignments to machines, the handling of quality and personnel problems, adjustments to work shift scheduling, budget recommendations, as well as many other concerns that are traditionally the responsibilities of management. We also noticed employees calling their work area "our business," actively striving to eliminate quality problems and to increase productivity, solving technical problems, and, most of all, working *with* not *against* management to make "their company" more profitable. Workers even did "crazy" things like staying after their shift was over to lend a hand if it was needed and dropping in on weekends, without pay, to make sure their machines were shut down properly. Most of all, these employees seemed to believe in and be committed to their work to a degree we had not previously thought possible. In chapter 9 we describe a plant using these teams in some detail.

A recent study at Honeywell, Inc., indicated the importance of delegation and allowing autonomy in developing good managers.[5] The study suggested that good managers are not born but can be cultivated within a company. Some of the study's recommendations include educating subordinates by delegating important projects to them and giving them autonomy, involving subordinates in long-range planning, and providing them with superiors who serve as good role models by displaying high standards and being open to the ideas and questions of subordinates.

We believe organized attempts to force people into some externally designed mold not only undermine individual potential but are likely to deprive an organization of its long-term opportunity to achieve excellence. One need only look at the track record of management-union relations in this country to recognize that something is wrong with traditional approaches. The reality is that no matter how strong or "right" the stance of management, commitment to excellence cannot be externally forced. This is not to say that all strong external influence is bad. Instead, it suggests that the goal of leadership needs to be redefined: a leader should strive to unleash the full talents of people by stimulating their own capability for self-leadership.

The unleashing of self-leadership is a very different way of viewing the process of leadership and control. Such an approach, however, is not entirely new in practice. In fact, several trends are apparent that suggest that such changes are already underway. For example, in his best-selling book *Megatrends*, John Naisbitt identified several trends for the future that are very consistent with an increased emphasis on self-control.[6] Four of the ten trends he identifies are moves from centralization to decentralization; from institutional help to self-help; from representative democracy to participative democracy; and from hierarchies to networking. These trends, which represent a move away from more formalized structures and institutions toward greater diversity and an emphasis on grass roots in our society, suggest a recognition of people as individuals and as uniquely valuable resources. We think learning to be a self-leader is consistent with Naisbitt's theories in *Megatrends*.

SuperLeadership is about a fundamentally different approach that stimulates and facilitates self-leadership in others . . . that recognizes self-influence as a powerful *opportunity* for achieving excellence, rather than as a threat to external control and authority.

As one example, the increase of people working autonomously in their homes (telecommuters) with the aid of computer terminals and other contemporary technologies suggests a significant trend toward increased reliance on self-leadership in organizational practices. In addition, many organizations, frequently the better performing ones, are increasingly emphasizing participation and various forms of autonomy as a means of increasing the capability and performance of their work force. Recent interest in quality circles, self-managed groups, Japanese management systems, and participative management generally indicate a growing realization that new management approaches are needed. In their bestseller, *In Search of Excellence*, Thomas J. Peters and Robert H. Waterman, Jr., argue that excellent companies develop environments where people can increase in self-esteem, and participate with excitement in the company and the whole of society.[7] Our intention is to develop specific strategies and behaviors through which this emphasis on people can be carried out.

D. Quinn Mills, a professor at Harvard Business School, discusses the consequences of presenting a corps of younger middle managers with a decision as a fait accompli.[8] When a new CEO issued his edict about the objectives of the company, Mills discusses how an observer could see ". . . the lights go out in many eyes. The same managers in whom [the CEO] had once sensed a seemingly genuine desire to have a bigger, better company suddenly appeared disaffected and sullen. Even when [the CEO] announced the chance of hefty bonuses . . . enthusiasm among the assembled managers was conspicuous by its absence."

Mills further describes the longer-term consequences of this action. "Within a year, several of the company's best managers had quit. Competitors were still gaining on the company, yet morale was so low that no one was pushing to turn the situation around." This CEO was no SuperLeader: he had forgotten the importance of gaining the commitment of younger managers as an important step on the road to success.

The time is not only ripe for, but indeed mandates, a new perspective on leadership, a view that recognizes the important role of employees' self-control systems and their potential to ultimately lead themselves. SuperLeadership—leading others to lead themselves—can help meet this challenge. At a time when Americans are bombarded with pessimistic reports on the fall of U.S. business in world standing, the depletion of the essential resources for our advanced society, and so on, we are nevertheless optimistic about our future because we realize that we have barely scratched the surface of what is probably our most powerful resource for economic and social progress—the vast potential for advancement and excellence within each person. The tremendous power of committed, motivated, self-led people can be the key to economic and social progress beyond what our world has ever seen.

Unfortunately, traditional control methods will not allow this potential to be unleashed. For several years, U.S. organizations have experienced employee compliance rather than commitment, mediocre productivity and quality, and dissatisfaction among their work force. Recent increases in international competition have made it all too apparent that such traditional controls can no longer be tolerated if companies are to survive and if the United States is to regain its world standing. Achieving the ideal of a commitment to excellence calls for a new era of facilitating, not snuffing out, the internal energy and potential of people. Striving to meet this challenge through SuperLeadership is at the heart of this important quest.

The time is not only ripe for, but indeed mandates, a new perspective on leadership. . . .
SuperLeadership—leading others to lead themselves—can help meet this challenge.

2

Self-Leadership: Behavioral Strategies to Influence Ourselves[1]

It was midafternoon when the limousine arrived at my hotel to take me to the airport. The driver was obviously harried and in a rather irritable mood. He told me he was running late and since my hotel was outside of his normal route he would have a hard time getting back on schedule. He apologized for almost knocking me out of my seat as he swerved around a couple of corners.

I was curious about his behavior (which was not all that different from the behavior I'd noted in other limousine drivers in other cities), so I asked him what happens if he's late for his next pickup.

"Three days' suspension without pay," was his curt response. He then explained that if he has an accident, no matter how minor (and even if it's not his fault), that also leads to three days' suspension without pay. As he attempted to make a left turn, he was forced to wait for some slow pedestrians. Impatient, he explained that if he hit a pedestrian, "that's twelve points, which is an automatic five days' suspension without pay." I could imagine the gears turning in his head. "If I'm late that's three days' suspension and if I hit a pedestrian that's five days' suspension." I almost wondered what his choice would be.

In an attempt to sound sympathetic, I said, "It sounds like a rather negative system."

13

"That's the problem with American companies," he agreed. "That's why Japan is killing us. Management and workers really work together there but, here, in this country, the right hand doesn't know what the left hand is doing. Often a problem will continue for weeks in U.S. companies because workers don't feel any incentive to tell management about it. Why should they if they think management is just out to screw them?"

"Well, if they removed the negative controls . . . ," I started.

"That's not it," he quickly interrupted. "It's just that we don't have a say, a real chance to contribute. They don't recognize that we need to have pride, too. They kick us in the rear without us having any input."

I mused to myself, "Even cab drivers are management philosophers these days—maybe we should be listening to them."

While this example is a bit extreme, our observations and experiences of the excessive control exerted over many U.S. employees have convinced us that this is an all-too-common problem. For decades, many American firms have used and still use excessive negative means to control their employees at all organizational levels. Unfortunately, this managerial approach—tight external controls, often punitive in nature, to assure that employee behavior is consistent with the organization's goals—overlooks perhaps the most powerful form of control: the control that comes from *within* a person. In this chapter, we explore this control that comes from within. We call this inner strength *self-leadership*—leading one's self to excellence.

Some might argue that Japanese firms recognize this issue better than we do, citing their emphasis on shared values and beliefs and maintenance of a familylike working environment. Japanese employees do not unwillingly comply with directives but instead seem committed to the well-being of the firm, internalizing the goals of their company to the degree that they require significantly less external control.

But Americans are not Japanese, and it's not appropriate to push this comparison too literally. It is unlikely, given the American emphasis on individualism, that the United States will soon establish the same kind of environment found in Japan. Yet, observing the Japanese is helpful in examining U.S. corporations and formulating questions about them. For example, when teamwork is required, what approaches are available to fill this void in a culture that often discourages cooperation and encourages competition and conflict? We believe that SuperLeadership offers an alternative to traditional top-down American management practices that have created this dilemma.

SuperLeadership means developing self-leadership in others. A SuperLeader's own effectiveness depends on the self-leadership practices of subordinates. The important twist in the leadership process is that followers are now treated like, and become, leaders. Since everyone is a self-leader, and frequently in need of improvement in his self-leadership patterns, SuperLeadership requires a great deal of power, although this power is often indirect and subtle. The main task of the SuperLeader is to help develop, encourage, improve, reinforce, and coordinate the self-leadership practices of others.

The apparent contradictions inherent in leading others to lead themselves require some mental adjustment. . . . This approach challenges leaders to rethink their fundamental assumptions about leadership practices and authority relationships.

The apparent contradictions inherent in leading others to lead themselves require some mental adjustment. For example, if subordinates lead themselves, then is the leader really leading at all? Our answer is an emphatic *yes*, although the specific leader behaviors are quite different. The leader is leading subordinates to be the best self-leaders they can be. The core of the difference is much less emphasis on command and instruction; the SuperLeader gets others to command and instruct themselves.

This approach challenges leaders to rethink their fundamental assumptions about leadership practices and authority relationships. In the long run, however, this effort can produce significant benefits in terms of increased performance, innovation, and fulfillment for leaders and followers (self-leaders) alike. Because the self-leadership of subordinates is so important, we will address this concept in some detail.

Self-leadership is the engine and provides much of the energy required for success. Self-leadership is the essence of effective followership. SuperLeadership provides a context for self-leadership, a means of coordinating it among individuals, and a support mechanism for its development. In short, SuperLeadership inspires and facilitates self-leadership in subordinate employees. The training case on the following page should stimulate thinking about what the concept of self-leadership means to each person and some of the issues involved in the process. We have used this case in many training settings and found it to be a useful way to get thoughts flowing on the idea of self-leadership.

TRAINING CASE
SELF-LED EMPLOYEES: WHAT DO THEY DO?

You are deeply settled into the conference room chair as you listen to Bart, the new division general manager (and your boss). This is the first meeting between Bart and his staff, and he is outlining some of his philosophy and ideas about how he expects the division to be managed. You are new yourself, having assumed the position of department manager only two weeks ago.

Both you and Bart have been brought into the division as part of an attempt to salvage an organization that has been in the red for the last three years. You haven't worked for Bart before, but you hear through the grapevine that he has a record as a top-notch performer.

"One of the most important attributes by which I judge managers," says Bart, "is how good they are at self-leadership. Are they able to lead themselves?"

As you sit, you wonder what he really means by "self-leadership."

1. Begin with yourself—*Are* you a self-leader? In what ways do you manage your own behavior? Do you use any specific identifiable strategies to lead yourself? Try to list *specific* behaviors or examples or both.
2. Can you think of other behaviors that might characterize a self-led employee?

Three basic assumptions, based on our years of studying self-leadership in many work settings at many organizational levels, underlie our ideas on self-leadership. First, everyone practices self-leadership to some degree, but not everyone is an effective self-leader. Second, effective self-leadership can be learned and thus is not restricted to people we intuitively describe as being born "self-starters," "self-directed," or "self-motivated." And third, self-leadership is relevant to executives, managers, and nonmanagers alike—that is, to anyone who works.

Self-leadership is the essence of effective followership.

We will address two classes of self-leadership strategies. The first focuses on effective behavior and action—behavioral-focused strategies; the second on effective thinking and feeling—cognitive-focused strategies. In this chapter we will concentrate on the behavioral strategies—specific actions designed to help lead ourselves. In the next chapter, we address the question of how constructive thoughts and feelings can develop self-leadership capabilities.

SuperLeadership inspires and facilitates self-leadership in subordinate employees.

SELF-LEADERSHIP: BEHAVIORAL-FOCUSED STRATEGIES FOR CONSTRUCTIVE BEHAVIOR

One self-leadership approach focuses on behaviors and is especially helpful to managers and employees in leading themselves to do difficult, perhaps unappealing, but necessary tasks. Several specific strategies are available, including self-set goals, rehearsal, self-observation, self-administered rewards, and self-administered punishment. The following case illustrates some of these strategies in practice.

17

The majority stockholder and manager of a small commuter airline found himself in a profit squeeze. Many of his competitors had already gone out of business. In addition to the countless duties involved in managing the firm on a daily basis, including personally flying some of the routes, he was convinced he needed a new, larger plane to operate more profitably. Somehow, he managed to juggle the details of his job while putting together a creative financing plan for acquiring the plane he needed. This plan, along with adoption of several other changes, including rerouting his flight patterns, kept his firm on a growth trend in the face of pressures toward decline.

How does he do it? How does he put out the daily fires and still manage to introduce new, innovative ways of doing business? Much of the answer lies in his behavioral-focused self-leadership practices.

First, he uses the strategy of self-observation by keeping a detailed log or record of how he spends his time. He also keeps a record of what he says to others over the phone regarding business matters to help him be consistent in his future dealings with these people. In addition, he has adopted various cueing strategies to help him manage his performance. He uses a chalkboard directly in front of his desk, for example, to record notes that serve as a reminder and a guide for his work efforts. He keeps a separate "follow up" file. He frequently rehearses what he will say during important phone calls before dialing. And he makes use of self-applied rewards. He enjoys reviewing his accomplishments against his goals and mentally rewarding himself for his achievements. As he put it, "Self-gratification—that's what it's all about."[2]

We have seen variations of these same strategies in use in many different work settings, including that of the energetic, self-led entrepreneur described above. To provide a clearer picture of the logic of the behavioral self-leadership strategies, we will discuss each in more detail. These strategies are available to assist in the quest for personal excellence. Some are invoked before a person actually starts a performance task and thus can be described as *antecedent* self-leadership strategies.

Several self-leadership strategies are available to assist in the quest for personal excellence.

Self-Set Goals

Self-imposed goals are an important ingredient for successful self-leadership. By establishing goals for both immediate work tasks and longer-term career achievements, an employee establishes self-direction and priorities. Limiting informal conversations to forty-five minutes of a normal workday might be a reasonable self-set goal for an employee who has a problem of talking too much. Similarly, making six sales calls a day or increasing sales by 8 percent for the fiscal quarter might be the self-set goals of someone in sales. Working evenings toward an MBA degree or becoming a vice-president is an example of a longer-term personal goal. Knowledge of the goal-setting process suggests that such goals should be challenging but achievable and specific in order to have an optimal effect.

In *Iacocca: An Autobiography*, Lee Iacocca talks about the importance of goals:

> What are your objectives for the next 90 days? What are your plans, your priorities, your hopes? And how do you intend to go about achieving them?
>
> [This] system makes employees accountable to *themselves.* Not only does . . . each manager consider his own goals, but it's also an effective way to remind people not to lose sight of their dreams.
>
> Every three months, each manager sits down . . . to chart his goals for the next term. . . . The manager puts them in writing. . . . There's something about putting your thoughts on paper that forces you to get down to specifics. That way, it's harder to deceive yourself—or anybody else. [3]

Management of Cues

By managing cues in the immediate work environment, desirable actions can be stimulated and undesirable actions can be eliminated. Having phone calls held during specific times of the workday, eliminating distracting noises by closing the door, or even an executive attempting to surround herself with talented people that bring out the best, all reflect different cueing strategies. An office, for example, can be decorated and equipped with things that stimulate performance.

Simple devices such as inspiring plaques or signs placed in strategic places can be helpful to some people. Posting the message "Are you using your time effectively right now?" in full view is a cue for effective time management. In fact, the popular time-management movement is largely based on cueing strategies.

David Packard, cofounder of Hewlett-Packard, described how, as a young man, he used a daily schedule as a cueing strategy to organize his own efforts. "I was resolved that I was going to have everything organized so, as a freshman, I had a schedule set for every day . . . what I was going to do every hour of the day . . . and times set up in the morning to study certain things. . . . You did have to allocate your time, because as you know, there are a lot of things to do."[4]

Don't get the impression that we advocate cutting off contact with people in order to get "work" done. In fact, we know that, for executives in particular, personal interaction often lies at the heart of the job. An executive who desires to improve information exchange with the lower ranks might, for example, adopt a practice of an informal monthly breakfast with employees (see the McKnight profile on page 47 for an example of this strategy). Bill Hewlett, cofounder of Hewlett-Packard, was noted for his "management by wandering around." Both of these actions are cueing strategies designed to provide opportunities to enhance an executive's informal information network.

The world does influence behavior with sights, sounds, and temptations that compete for attention. Employees can use cueing strategies to manage the immediate work and living environment, to increase desirable and eliminate undesirable stimuli, and thus, manage themselves more effectively.

Rehearsal

Rehearsal or practice is a useful antecedent self-leadership strategy. Practice is natural for improvement in golf or tennis—it should be just as natural in other parts of life, including work. Thinking through and practicing important tasks before they are done "for keeps" can contribute significantly to performance. Rehearsing a crucial formal presentation that will determine the annual department budget allocation *before* it is made to the budget committee is an obvious example of this strategy. But many less formal activities are potential occasions for practice. A few minutes of mental rehearsal before calling on clients, practicing sensitive parts of a subordinate's performance review, going over the key steps required to safely and efficiently start up a machine, and so forth are all appropriate ways of using a practice strategy. Role playing, for example, is commonly used in performance-appraisal training. Lee Iacocca recognizes the benefits of rehearsal: "Learning the skills of salesmanship takes time and effort. You have to practice them over and over again until they become second nature."[5]

Self-observation provides the necessary information for effective self-leadership.

Self-Observation

Other self-leadership strategies focus on the consequences of work performance, that is, what happens *after* performing a task. First, an employee needs information about how well the task has been done. Self-observation provides the necessary information for effective self-leadership. By observing what leads to desirable and undesirable behaviors, an employee can discover what needs to change and some cues on how to go about it. This strategy can be especially powerful if documented with information regarding specific behaviors that are the targets for improvement. A simple record of what leads to a behavior, its frequency, how long it lasts, and when it does or does not occur can provide a wealth of information.

For example, if an employee is dissatisfied with her own work productivity, she could observe and briefly record on a note pad nonproductive behaviors. These behaviors might include informal conversations, unnecessary busywork, and so on. Also she could keep a record of the frequency and duration of these behaviors and the events that distracted more productive efforts. If these observations eventually disclosed that an average of seventeen hours a week were spent on informal conversations, an obvious problem has been identified. Also if the records indicate that most of this chatting is triggered by trips to the department coffee machine, steps can be taken for self-limitation of this behavior—she can keep a pot in the office. (However, she should be careful: coffee-machine conversations are a form of "management by wandering around" and so can be an important source of information.)

Also, techniques of self-observation provide information for self-evaluations. By analyzing the information that she has collected, she sets the stage for personally assessing the effectiveness of her work efforts.

Here's an example of how self-observation can be used as a self-leadership strategy to control costs.

"We need to get the scrap down!" exclaimed the quality-control manager. He was talking about the line where the raw panels of glass went into the heat-treating system and emerged as hardened, tempered glass.

"How much do you have now?" I asked.

"I don't really know," he answered. "We don't get a report on that."

"Then how do you know it's a problem?"

"Just go out and look at the amount of broken glass. It's too much."

We talked about the problem in further detail. After some time, we concluded that a small programming change in the computer-generated weekly production report could give us the figures we wanted. It was mainly calculating the difference between the square feet into the line and the square feet out of the line.

"Let's try an experiment," I suggested. "How about posting the weekly scrap rate on a chart in the production area. Have the clerk post the weekly scrap rate every Monday morning. But don't make any big deal about it. Don't try to push them into doing better or make any promises. Let's just see if we provide the information whether there will be any change."

"OK," he agreed.

When I returned next month, I saw the chart near the tempering line. It showed the scrap for the previous three weeks—between 5 and 6 percent each week. I saw the chart again about six months later. It had shown 6 percent for about six weeks, and then had turned downward to about 4 percent. It stayed at about 4 percent for about two months.

Then, it went down again to about 2.5 percent and remained fairly steady. I asked the quality-control manager about it.

"Oh yeah!" he replied. "We really got that problem solved. I had forgotten about it. The crew did a terrific job without us saying a thing. I was surprised at how they used that information in such a responsible way."

Self-Administered Rewards

What is received in return for effort is an important factor in determining motivation and the choosing of future activities. Typically, the consequences received from the organization and others become the focus of attention, but self-administered rewards and punishments can be just as important. Self-administered rewards can be an especially powerful strategy in motivating employees to do tasks they find difficult or unappealing. These self-rewards can be concrete and physical, like a nice dinner out or a lazy afternoon spent reading in a hammock after completing an especially challenging task. Taking a weekend at the beach as a reward for finally working the bugs out of the new office computer system or after making a big sale can help motivate future successes. Sometimes self-rewards can be administered by withholding something until a particular task has been accomplished. The rewards can also be private, mental creations— imagining a favorite vacation spot or the future success and benefits accruing from successful work efforts. Purposefully self-administering both physical and mental rewards for high performance can help sustain motivation and effort.

Self-Administered Punishments

Self-administered punishment can also be part of the process, although generally it is not very effective. Actually, most self-punishment is mental, or cognitive, in nature. A mild degree of guilt can sometimes be useful, but when it becomes excessive or habitual, it can undermine motivation and effort. Habitual guilt and self-criticism can lead to depression and represent a problem that needs to be managed because it can seriously detract from a person's feelings of self-confidence and self-esteem. The key is to study patterns of self-criticism, by asking, for example, "How often do I get down on myself? Does my self-criticism help or hinder my performance?" Usually studying a failure, trying to learn from it, and refocusing energy on feeling good about accomplishments represent better alternatives. We discuss related ideas in more detail in the next chapter (see "Establishing Constructive Thought Patterns," page 36).

Again, Lee Iacocca offered some useful insight when he talked about mistakes: "Mistakes are a part of life; you can't avoid them. All you can hope is that they won't be too expensive and that you don't make the same mistake twice."[6]

In contrast, being too lenient when one is obviously behaving and performing in undesirable ways can be a problem as well. There are times when a good self-scolding is appropriate. Generally, however, concentrating on self-administered rewards for desirable behavior will be more effective than relying on self-imposed punishments.

Self-administered rewards and punishments are instrumental in this process just as are the consequences received from others.

EXAMPLES OF BEHAVIORAL-FOCUSED SELF-LEADERSHIP

In several work settings, behavioral-focused self-leadership strategies are already helping employees to improve their performances. These applications have involved managers in a variety of jobs in retailing, manufacturing, public service, advertising, and other settings, including both line and staff positions. In these various cases, specific behaviors targeted for self-leadership, such as time spent on the phone, timely completion of expense forms, and so on, can be identified. Consider the following case:

> The advertising manager of a newspaper identified several behaviors he needed to improve. One problem he targeted was his tendency to leave the office without remembering to leave word about where he was

going and when he would be back. It wasn't a matter of being controlled; he merely was forgetful about keeping his staff informed. A simple cueing strategy was used to solve the problem. A "checkout" board was conspicuously placed on the office door. He could easily move the magnetic disks on the board to indicate if he was out of the building, if he would return, and when.

He also had a problem getting himself to fill out expense forms on a timely basis. This problem was eliminated by having a secretary place an appropriate form on his desk in the evening, just before he went home. This strategy was adopted because he always tried to be back in the office just before leaving for home and he usually did not face many demands at that time. Thus, he could easily complete this task when cued by the form on his desk. In addition, he kept a chart of his progress for the purposes of self-observation. Soon the manager was filling out the form on a routine basis and the chart that indicated this performance improvement provided the occasion for self-praise. Further, by properly filling out the expense forms, the manager received the added benefits of avoiding personal financial loss by being reimbursed promptly for his expenses and of having a more accurate picture of expenses in his department.[7]

We have also observed behavioral-focused strategies used by blue-collar production workers for the purpose of self-leadership. In one particularly impressive high-performing plant organized according to a self-managed team concept (a system structured around teams of workers who are largely responsible for managing themselves), we observed countless scribbled notes pasted to machines to serve as self-established cues for guiding workers (for more details, see chapter 9, pages 186–189). And workers used other strategies such as self-observation, rehearsal, self-praise, and self-criticism readily within their groups. Consider the following example:

> "Hey Frank, you did a hell of a job in cleaning up our work area," Tom shouted with obvious sincerity over the hum of the machines. After giving Frank a quick pat on the back, Tom returned to his work location. He glanced at a note he had stuck to the front of his machine that described the new, more efficient welding procedure that he had helped to develop. After a moment of reflection, he began working again.
>
> A couple of hours later, as his team left for lunch, they noticed that

the previous month's efficiency ratings were posted on the bulletin board outside the cafeteria. "Yahoo!" shrieked Elizabeth, one of Tom's energetic peers, "we did it! We improved by ten percent!" The group stopped to give one another hardy handshakes, backslaps, and hugs before going in for lunch with their pride apparent in their strides.

Two o'clock that afternoon the team held a special meeting. "You know Bill didn't show up for work again today after being out twice last week," Tom started. "We agreed if it happened one more time we'd have to counsel him. That's why I invited Smitty [Smitty was the team's external supervisor though he served more as a coach and counselor than a foreman] to help us practice what we would say to him." Frank played the role of Bill while the rest of the team practiced what it planned to say. Smitty provided feedback and suggestions while the team worked out its plan.

The examples used in this chapter are a small sample of the many behavioral-focused self-leadership applications we have observed both white- and blue-collar workers use. Specific strategies such as these are especially useful for enhancing work performance on difficult and often unattractive tasks. SuperLeaders can promote employee self-leadership by modeling, encouraging, guiding, and reinforcing use of these kinds of tools by their subordinates. In later chapters, we discuss in more detail how SuperLeaders can enhance self-leadership in others. However, in the next chapter, we explore additional self-leadership strategies that have the potential of *naturally* motivating people to achieve excellence in their work, largely because they simply enjoy doing it. These cognitive strategies are designed to promote constructive thinking about work.

3

More Self-Leadership: Strategies for Productive Thinking and Feeling

Many years ago, we began our analysis of self-leadership by concentrating exclusively on behavioral strategies. It soon became clear, however, that the way a person cognitively perceives and processes information about work has considerable impact on self-leadership ability. Thus, our original ideas about self-leadership have been significantly extended to also include cognitive strategies.

Cognitive self-leadership strategies are mainly concerned with the issue of how individuals can constructively manage patterns of thinking, which in turn influence behavior.

For this chapter, we have divided the cognitive-based self-leadership strategies into two parts, although they are closely connected with each other. First, we examine how to use *natural rewards* that derive from the task itself to generate constructive thinking and feeling about one's own efforts. Then we examine the broader question of how individuals can develop productive patterns of thought.

BUILDING NATURAL REWARDS INTO TASKS

In truth, we have had some disagreement between ourselves as to whether building natural rewards into a task is a behavioral or a cognitive strategy. After all, this approach does entail specific behaviors that can be undertaken. But, the primary purpose is to define one's own job and task in such a way that it creates a desirable cognitive state.

The main point is that work, even the seemingly most monotonous kind, has at least some degree of latitude. Most work can be enjoyed to at least some degree and be performed with commitment, not just compliance, when the right approach is encouraged and accepted. We contend that the right approach usually involves seeking out and facilitating the *natural rewards* of tasks. The SuperLeader can play a critical role in modeling, guiding, and reinforcing subordinate discovery and management of natural rewards, which are the keys to constructive self-leadership of thoughts and feelings.

We contend that the right approach usually involves seeking out and facilitating the *natural rewards* of tasks.

What Are Natural Rewards?

"You sure seem to work hard at your new job, Bill. You must have really received a big pay increase when you took the position."

"Oh, a little one, Frank, but actually I don't make much more than I did in my old position."

"Really? That seems hard to believe. You seem to be working so much harder and have a lot more responsibility. You've never been a climber, Bill. Why did you take the job?"

"It's kind of hard to explain. It's just that I really like the kind of work I'm doing. I didn't really need more money to make the decision. I guess I'm getting a kick out of the work itself. I feel effective in what I'm doing and I have more freedom. When something gets done I know I've really made a contribution. I'm just plain motivated to do the work for its own value. Don't tell anybody, Frank," Bill sounded secretive but the playful smile on his face indicated that he was kidding around, "but I probably would do this job even if they paid me less than my old job."

An important distinction can be made between two basic types of rewards. The most obvious kind is the externally administered reward such as a pay raise, time off, a promotion, an award, a bonus, and so on. Even praise is a form of external reward. A second type of reward is generally less recognized and less understood but is no less important. We call it a *natural reward*.[1] It is so closely tied to a given task or activity that the two cannot be separated. For example, an individual who enjoys reading the newspaper or going to the race track is usually engaging in an activity that could be described as naturally rewarding. No externally administered or self-administered incentives are required to motivate this behavior. The incentives are natural; they are built into the task itself. Playing touch football on Saturday afternoon is another example.

Why Are Some Activities Naturally Rewarding?

In the discussion that follows, three elements of naturally enjoyable work that motivate employees to higher performance will be cited. These elements help promote constructive and positive thoughts and feelings about work. These are a sense of (1) competence, (2) self-control, and (3) purpose. Performance gains are possible when employees are given some latitude to essentially redesign their own work so that they can experience these feelings and thoughts. Our discussion is based on one simple idea: the desirability of using natural rewards (naturally motivating activities and tasks) to promote more effective self-leadership. We will address each of these features separately.

A natural reward . . . is so closely tied to a given task or activity that the two cannot be separated.

Feelings of competence. One common aspect of naturally rewarding activities is that they frequently make a person feel more competent; they provide a sense of "self-efficacy." People tend to like tasks that they perform well. Just as a couple of good shots on the last hole of the golf course can entice someone to play again, effective performance on the job can make work more naturally enjoyable.

Of course, activities that enhance feelings of competence are sometimes also tied to external rewards, but the natural rewards built into the task can be a potent motivating force in themselves. The feeling of being competent, and perhaps even the best, at *something* can be powerfully rewarding even if no praise and material rewards are received. This feeling is important whether the employee is a top executive or a production-line worker.

The SuperLeader will recognize this important need by providing subordinates with the opportunity to take on worthwhile challenges. A SuperLeader will also help subordinates to develop the confidence and master the skills necessary to really shine on the job by providing them with the autonomy as well as the guidance necessary for growth.

Feelings of self-control. A second characteristic of naturally enjoyable activities is that they make an individual feel more self-controlling. Most people have a natural tendency to want to control their own destinies. From the toddlers whose favorite activities seem to be the off-limit "no no's" to the adult who dreams of being his own boss, the desire for personal control as opposed to external control is readily apparent. Most people want at least some feeling of independence.

The combination of the desires to feel competent and self-controlling can lead to an interesting pattern of behavior. This pattern involves searching for challenges that a person is capable of mastering and then actually expending the effort to master them. Cutting a stroke off in a round of golf or striving to achieve a reasonable increase in task performance at work reflects this kind of pattern. Grappling with reasonable challenges can be naturally rewarding because successfully meeting them can contribute to feelings of competence and self-control.

A SuperLeader will be aware of this pattern and strive to provide subordinates with the freedom to seek out suitably challenging opportunities. The more success subordinates are able to experience, the more success they are likely to achieve in the future. Since subordinates can really get a kick out of performing well, the Super-Leader will let them do just that.

Feelings of purpose. One more important feature of naturally reward-ing activities is their ability to provide a sense of purpose. Even if a task makes an employee feel more competent and more self-controlling, it still may not be naturally enjoyable if the employee does not believe it is worthwhile. People yearn for purpose and mean-ing. The cigarette salesman who is obviously competent, who has freely chosen the profession, and who is otherwise self-determining still may not enjoy his work if he has ethical doubts about what he is doing.

But where do feelings of purpose and meaning come from? Many experts would argue that helping or expressing goodwill toward others provides a sense of purpose. In his well-known writings on human stress, Dr. Hans Selye has suggested that the best way to enjoy a rewarding life-style free of disabling stress is to practice what he calls "altruistic egoism."[2] In essence, this involves helping others and "earning their love" while at the same time recognizing our own needs and enhancing ourselves as individuals (egoism). The philoso-phy suggests that individuals can only enjoy a happy, meaningful life when they marry their innate self-centered nature as human beings with an altruistic effort to win the goodwill and respect of others. Furthermore, significant evidence from research in biology and psy-chology suggests that an altruistic motive may exist within a person apart from egotistic motives.[3]

Regardless of how altruism potentially adds purpose to a task or, more generally, to life, it should not be overlooked. It may be the key to achieving feelings of purpose and meaning. Interestingly, the manufacturing plant we discussed earlier that used a self-managed group approach and that displayed highly committed and motivated workers had as its motto, "People helping people." Examination of Japanese work organizations frequently reveals a similar concern with purposeful (altruistic) ends as well.

The challenge for the SuperLeader is to help subordinates discover what gives them a feeling of purpose and to provide them with opportunities to experience this sense of meaning in their jobs. It may well be that for most people some form of altruism is at the heart of this quest.

Activities that are naturally rewarding tend to enhance our feelings of competence, self-control, and purpose.

SELF-REDESIGN OF TASKS

Two primary ways of using natural rewards to enhance self-leadership effectiveness are (1) building more naturally enjoyable features into our tasks, and (2) making the naturally rewarding aspects of work the focus of thinking about our own jobs. First, consider Karen, who has an exceptional ability to redesign her own job.

> When Karen reported for work as the new office receptionist, she brought with her qualifications and abilities well beyond her narrow job description. In a tight job market, though, a paycheck was important, so she had to take what she could get. But over a period of weeks and months, her job changed dramatically until she had become a professional writer and assistant project director for a major project in the firm. She accomplished all this step-by-step by taking initiative and tackling challenges outside of her normal job responsibilities. She carefully identified and voluntarily pursued specific opportunities where help was needed. She would ask "Could I help you to ———?"
>
> Gradually, the managers began to realize that Karen could be depended on to undertake and accomplish tasks that were "falling between the cracks." And most of all, she did not act like a receptionist but instead like a key organizational employee ready to do whatever needed to be done. As Karen later explained, "I simply redesigned my own job."
>
> Through hard work and initiative, she had taken it upon herself to change her own work to provide opportunities for feelings of competence, self-control, and purpose. It wasn't too long before Karen's title, salary, and official responsibilities changed to reflect what she was actually doing. She knew the transition was complete when a new receptionist was hired.

Fundamentally, this approach to exercising self-leadership involves identifying aspects of tasks that are naturally enjoyable and trying to increase these as much as is reasonably possible. Karen's case admittedly is a bit extreme in that she essentially created a new position for herself. A key element in her success was taking on small chunks of greater and greater responsibility over time. Gradually, her initiative became obvious to her superiors.

But many strategies are available for making an existing job more naturally motivating. As a simple example, a business meeting can be held in an appealing location. Issues normally addressed in a formal conference room of a company building will take on a quite different flavor when they are addressed in a relaxed meeting room at a beautiful resort. Similarly, if an employee enjoys direct conversations with fellow employees, he may find that communicating a message face-to-face, rather than struggling to write a formal memo, may do quite well in many cases.

The point is that there are often several different ways and strategies to accomplish work tasks. By choosing to accomplish these tasks by means that they enjoy, employees build in natural rewards for their efforts. For example, if a woman runs around an oval track day after day through some force of will as a means of maintaining physical fitness, she is overlooking potential ways of making the task more pleasant. Running along an ocean shore or on a forest trail can be a more exhilarating experience. Running can be done in the early morning or at dusk while enjoying a brightly colored horizon. Running can be thus more naturally rewarding for those runners who choose to make it so, as can the work of employees in organizations.

In addition to choosing pleasant work contexts, an employee can increase the natural enjoyment of work by deliberately seeking out and building in activities that provide feelings of competence, self-control, and purpose. Karen accomplished this in her work, as have many others that we have observed. Work and life can be more naturally rewarding if people take them seriously enough to play at them and to build in enjoyment.

The timing or scheduling of work can also be important. For example, some people are "night persons" while others are "morning persons." One of the authors does about 90 percent of his productive writing in the morning and tries to schedule face-to-face meetings in the afternoon. The degree to which employees can schedule work to fit their own physiological rhythms and psychological preferences will enhance their personal productivity.

Clearly, there are limitations on how far people can redesign their own jobs. On occasion, it might even be necessary to implement the ultimate self-generated job redesign—resigning and going to work somewhere else. But we've seen too many people who begin by focusing on the reasons why "it can't be done." This is dysfunctional, negative thinking. A more productive and effective approach is to look for the simple, small next step by doing something in a more enjoyable way. Over the long run, step by step, it is possible to build enjoyment into work by seeking out desirable work contexts and activities that provide feelings of competence, self-control, and purpose.

Work and life can be more naturally rewarding if people take them seriously enough to play at them and to build in enjoyment.

Some readers may recognize that this discussion of self-designed tasks is substantially based on earlier theory and research on intrinsic motivation and enriched job characteristics. A major difference that we propose here is the employee's own responsibility and action in seeking out the naturally occurring rewards that stem from the task itself. Instead of depending on management or someone else to do it, every employee, if only in minor ways "at the margin," typically can find opportunities to redesign their own tasks.

MANAGING THE FOCUS OF ONE'S THOUGHTS

A second approach to tapping the power of natural rewards centers on the way people think while they perform tasks. To some degree, individuals have options about how to focus their attention. They can, for example, think about, talk about, and in general focus on the parts of work that they dislike, inevitably leading to negative feelings about their work. Alternately, an employee can focus on the rewards expected from performing work (such as money, praise, recognition, and so on) and thus be motivated by images of the future. This approach is a definite improvement over negative thinking. As a third option, employees can focus on the naturally enjoyable aspects of their work and enjoy the activity for whatever immediate value it might have: They can choose to "smell the roses." This last focus is the key to establishing natural enjoyment and being naturally motivated to higher performance.

The limousine driver cited in the previous chapter, for example, was not encouraged by the organizational system of control to focus his attention on the enjoyable, meaningful parts of his work, nor did he seem to have the capacity to do this on his own. For example, he was providing his passengers with an important service, and he had considerable responsibility for their safety. Most of all, he had an opportunity to meet a wide variety of people and was pretty much on his own. Instead, he was preoccupied with potential punishments.

Our experience is that almost all employees can identify several pleasant and unpleasant features of their jobs. We sometimes use the following procedure as a training exercise: "First, take a piece of paper and draw a line down the middle, forming two columns. Then list aspects of your work under the categories of pleasant and unpleasant. Which is longer—the pleasant or the unpleasant? [Participants are often surprised at how many pleasant features they can actually identify in their jobs.] Then later, when at work, you can focus your thoughts on the pleasant features for a time and then change your focus to the unpleasant features for a while." We have found that employees typically enjoy work much more when focusing on its more pleasant, rewarding features.

SuperLeaders will serve as models for and encourage constructive thinking among their subordinates. Tailoring jobs, to the extent possible, to the people that perform them can significantly enhance performance. For example, employees could carefully study their "unpleasant" work features in order to redesign or replace them with equally effective but more pleasant ways to get the job done. The

SuperLeader will help subordinates to manage their thinking about their work as well as their physical performance methods.

Consider the example of two managers in a large American company who had quite similar responsibilities. Manager A was constantly preoccupied with not only the difficulties of his job but the potential reprimands for his performance deficiencies: he engaged in excessive "obstacle thinking." Eventually, he became overwhelmed by his job pressures. Manager B focused his thinking much more on his accomplishments and seemed to thrive on the demands: he engaged in "opportunity thinking." He once announced jubilantly that he felt he lived "more in one day of this job than most people do in a week." Given virtually identical conditions, clear differences emerge in the degree of obstacle thinking and opportunity thinking.

Some might attribute the divergent ways in which people view their jobs to fundamental personality differences and thus consider them beyond influence. However, we think such an interpretation is too simplistic. While personalities can be important, a self-leadership view would argue that people can influence themselves and how they think about their jobs and, further, that they can learn to change patterns of thinking and behavior. An important part of the SuperLeader's role is to help subordinates do just that.

In summary, strategies are available for making work more naturally rewarding. These include (1) building natural rewards into tasks by choosing desirable work contexts and emphasizing activities that provide a sense of competence, self-control, and purpose; and (2) focusing on the naturally rewarding aspects of tasks while performing them. Part of the SuperLeader's role is to help subordinates learn and effectively apply these strategies.

ESTABLISHING CONSTRUCTIVE THOUGHT PATTERNS

"Kathryn, how do you always seem to manage to have such an optimistic outlook? You always seem to find something good in every problem we face. You turn them into opportunities. How do you do it?"

"I hope you won't be offended, Dave, but I could talk to you about the idea of developing more constructive habits in your thinking. I think it might help you reach your full potential," Kathryn, Dave's boss, suggested helpfully. They were in the early stage of a relaxing lunch away from the office.

"Habits in my thinking? I *was* able to quit smoking, but my brain just thinks without me telling it to. Habits of *thinking*? You've got to be kidding."

"Really, I'm not, Dave," Kathryn continued in a more serious, concerned voice. "For example, you have a habit of looking for the problems in things . . . seeking out reasons *not* to move ahead. It's really interfering with your capability to be creative and bring innovation to your department. My viewpoint is that we can manage our thinking just as we can our behavior. We just have to pay attention to our thoughts and choose to substitute new, more constructive ways of thinking when we discover destructive habits or patterns. We can develop new thought habits with persistent practice. Instead of always looking for obstacles, we have to look for opportunities."

Dave was deep in thought for a long time. Finally he responded, "You know my first gut reaction was to say what you're saying makes no sense. It can't work. Thinking is just automatic and we can't change it. But I stopped myself and I thought about what you said about me— that I look for reasons not to move ahead. And for a moment there I tried to think about the possibilities of what you said. And then it occurred to me that maybe you're right. I used to smoke, but I chose to change that behavior and I was successful, although it was damn painful. And normally I would have thought you're full of it and dismissed your comments at that. But I chose to think a little more and a little differently. A habit, huh?" Dave nodded his head slightly and continued to think deeply. "Yeah, maybe, just maybe, you've got something there. I guess I need to think about it."

Ultimately, a complete treatment of the self-leadership process requires a significant emphasis on thought. While behavioral strategies are useful and important, thinking is the core of the core; that is, individual thought processes might be considered the core of self-leadership, which in turn might be considered the core of effective SuperLeadership. An especially powerful way to view this crucial component of self-leadership is to rely on the notion of thought patterns. Just as people often develop habitual behavioral tendencies, over time they also develop habitual patterns of thinking. The challenge is to manage habitual thought patterns in such a way that personal effectiveness in work and life in general is increased.

Of course, this is no easy task. In fact, a major issue in the field of psychology is how to deal with something that can't be seen or fully understood. Indeed, telling one's self to "think differently" or trying to change patterns of thought through force of will is generally not very productive. On the other hand, some tools (some levers to pull) can facilitate this objective. These tools are especially appropriate for a long-term effort directed at altering established, and establishing new, patterns of thinking. Moreover, SuperLeaders can help subordinates to acquire these tools, but first they must learn them themselves. Specifically, they include managing beliefs, imagined experience, and self-talk.

Just as people often develop habitual behavioral tendencies, over time they also develop habitual patterns of thinking.

Beliefs

Beliefs or assumptions are fundamental to thinking. An especially powerful characteristic of beliefs is that they frequently become self-fulfilling. What a person believes can happen frequently does happen. Likewise, what a person believes is not possible is often doomed from the start. Rational Emotive Therapy, an approach to psychotherapy pioneered by Dr. Albert Ellis, maintains that beliefs can serve as a basis for change.[4] The theory behind it is that when a person has difficulty coping with certain situations, this ineffectiveness can often be traced to irrational beliefs; for example, a fear of speaking traceable to a belief that listeners will respond with rejection. This is a form of obstacle thinking. Only by challenging these dysfunctional beliefs, so the reasoning goes, can a person successfully deal with the problem.

Perhaps one of the most important beliefs that influence an employee's self-leadership capability is self-expectation. Do I really believe I can do it? Research shows that individuals' expectations become self-fulfilling prophecies; that is, positive expectations enhance the probability of actually *doing* it. Conversely, negative expectations decrease the probability. The state of mind about oneself has a clear impact on ultimate performance.

Purposefully establishing and altering beliefs is a difficult process. Beliefs are often so ingrained into personality that often a person has a difficult time recognizing them and the way they influence actions. As a result, identifying and challenging dysfunctional beliefs is a useful first step.[5] Ultimately, the goal should be to improve patterns of thought, a fundamental component of which is one's own set of beliefs.

The state of mind about oneself has a clear impact on ultimate performance.

Imagined Experience

Another important component of thought patterns is imagination. Specifically, mental images of the world, such as visions of the likely outcomes to problems, can influence subsequent actions and orientation toward work and life. Indeed, people carry unique worlds around in their heads. An especially vivid form of these psychological worlds consists of imagined experiences. These images occur naturally and can have a constructive or destructive influence. Imagining a klutzy performance and utter embarrassment in front of others in a first attempt at some activity (water skiing, golf, speaking in front of a group, and so on) can be a sufficient deterrent to keep a person from trying it. Or if he does try, dysfunctional mental images can undermine his confidence, detract from his enjoyment, and ultimately contribute to the very failure he feared.

Here again, however, one is free to challenge mental habits by purposefully choosing to form constructive mental images. One can, for example, sit back in a chair and imagine a beautiful white sand beach bordering a deep blue, sun-speckled ocean. Similarly, with practice, it is possible to use constructive mental images when faced with problems or challenges. Positive mental imagery can be used to rehearse an activity or to challenge those destructive imagined experiences that enter the psychological world. Again, this is no easy task, but it is possible to establish these positive thought patterns. Ralph Waldo Emerson put it well: "A man is what he thinks about all day long." Over time a person can improve by purposefully managing habitual patterns of thought. Mental images are a powerful ingredient in introducing such changes. Consider the following incident, which is reconstructed from an interview that actually took place on a TV sports-news program:

> The sports announcer was interviewing the high-jump star who had just broken the world high-jump record. The performance of this athlete was quite remarkable in that his own height was only about five feet eight inches, but he had high-jumped over seven and one-half feet. "What do you think about just before you make your jump?" asked the announcer.
>
> "Well," replied the young star, "I just have this picture of myself in my mind, and in this picture, I slowly run up to the bar and just float over the bar. When I can get this image fixed in my mind, I know I can make the jump."

People at work often do similar mental rehearsals before undertaking a task. Frequently that rehearsal is based on some model that they have observed in the past. Consider Charlie, the young new salesperson, who is about to make his first sales call:

> Charlie waited in the lobby of the purchasing department. He was about to make his first solo call on the national account buyer. Charlie was excited and he wanted to do well. He knew the characteristics of his product fairly well by now, and he also knew that they would meet the specifications of the buyer. In his thoughts, Charlie went over the things that he planned to say. As he did this, he thought about the sales calls that he had made with Marian, the senior salesperson in his department, and he also thought about the role-playing that he had done with his boss. Although he was nervous, Charlie was confident that he would be able to do the job.

Self-Talk

Perhaps the aspect of thought patterns most amenable to change is internal dialogues. Though they may try to deny it, people do talk to themselves. Usually these conversations take place at an internal, unobservable level. The employee that botches a work assignment and finds himself engaging in internal self-critical speech—"You dummy! Why did you do that? Can't you get anything right?"—is a representative example. Of course it's easy to recognize that this kind of internal verbal abuse is not going to provide much benefit. Instead, a more constructive, analytic approach—"What went wrong? I know I can do better than that. What can I do to improve my performance next time?"—is likely to reap more positive benefits.

Most people are very careful about how they talk to others. . . . They apparently are much less considerate of themselves.

Most people rarely think about self-conversations nor do they consider the possibility of changing them. Ironically, however, most people are very careful about how they talk to others, especially in sensitive situations. They apparently are much less considerate of themselves. Psychologists Donald Meichenbaum and Roy Cameron have suggested a powerful idea related to this issue. For years, psychological therapists have been working to change how clients speak to therapists, but Meichenbaum and Cameron believe it's time to help clients change how they speak to themselves.[6] Self-observation of patterns of internal dialogue and efforts to replace dysfunctional with constructive self-statements are useful ways to help effectively manage thinking. Perhaps it's time you had a talk with yourself on this subject. We doubt you'll find anywhere a better listener, or one that could benefit more from what you have to say.

Again, a piece of paper divided into two columns can be helpful in managing patterns of thinking (that is, beliefs or assumptions, mental images, and self-talk). First a person can identify disturbing situations that seem to negatively affect his thinking. Then he can list his dysfunctional thoughts about the situation in one column and list alternate, more constructive thoughts in the other. For example, after a disagreement with a subordinate at work he may find himself thinking, "He is directly challenging my authority and is a problem employee who could undermine performance in my work unit." But after careful examination of the situation, he may realize that he can substitute more constructive thoughts, such as "Actually, he is expressing initiative and creativity. By disagreeing with me, he is displaying motivation, which is preferable to apathetic compliance. What can I do to help him constructively channel this energy? This is actually a positive performance opportunity." Through such systematic analysis, an individual can actually begin to manage his immediate thoughts and to establish new, more constructive patterns in his thinking.

Perhaps it's time you had a talk with yourself.

Substantial research concludes that patterns of thinking can influence health, longevity, success, and scores on achievement tests, among other aspects of life. This research is a refinement of earlier work on self-fulfilling prophecies. According to Edward E. Jones, a psychologist at Princeton University, "Our expectancies not only affect how we see reality but also affect the reality itself."[7]

Dr. Martin Seligman, a leading researcher in this area, agrees: "My hunch is that for a given level of intelligence, your actual achievement is a function not just of talent, but also of the capacity to stand defeat."[8] For example, in a study of insurance agents, Dr. Seligman found that the manner in which agents dealt with their failures to make a sale often directly affected whether they became outstanding salesmen or quit the company. Salesmen with an optimistic outlook sold 37 percent more insurance in their first two years than agents with pessimistic views. Furthermore, pessimists were twice as likely to quit in their first year. What seems to be important is whether an individual will keep going when things get frustrating.

"Our expectancies not only affect how we see reality but also affect the reality itself."

In a nationwide study of more than 3,000 managers working for *Fortune* 100 corporations, a significant relationship was found between managers' performance levels and how they viewed performance obstacles. While higher performers concentrated more on external obstacles in their work environment, lower performers tended to dwell more on personal-skill deficiencies. A conclusion reached in this study was that recognizing obstacles is OK but dwelling on personal shortcomings, in self-leadership, for example, can undermine a person's sense of efficiency and ability to perform. [9]

While styles of thinking are generally stable over a person's lifetime, Dr. Seligman believes that styles can be changed. In one research study, he found that changes made in the thinking styles of individuals from pessimistic to optimistic persisted for one year after the change took place.

In summary, an important part of self-leadership centers on the management of thought patterns. In order to succeed at this difficult process, each person needs to analyze, challenge, and manage his or her beliefs, imagined experiences, and self-talk. A SuperLeader can be instrumental in helping subordinates to acquire the skills necessary to deal with the core of SuperLeadership—internal patterns of thought. First, SuperLeaders can model effective thought patterns themselves. Further, the SuperLeader can encourage, guide, reinforce, and otherwise facilitate subordinate self-leadership through constructive thought patterns. Specific SuperLeadership strategies for facilitating these and other self-leadership skills in subordinates will be addressed in detail in the chapters that follow.

The self-leadership capability of employees . . . is the greatest untapped natural resource in our country today.

CONCLUSION

There is growing realization in the United States that traditional management methods are inadequate. One of the primary weaknesses of these methods is the neglect of the self-leadership capability of employees. Perhaps this capability is the greatest untapped natural resource in our country today. In fact, knowing that this powerful resource is available offers a great deal of hope for the future of American companies.

SuperLeadership can help subordinates learn and effectively practice self-leadership. First, a SuperLeader must recognize what self-leadership is all about. The specific self-leadership strategies presented in this and the previous chapter are summarized in the table on page 45. By mastering behavioral-focused self-leadership strategies, such as self-set goals and self-administered rewards, people can work through difficult and sometimes unattractive tasks. Furthermore, by building in the natural rewards of work that promote feelings of competence, self-control, and purpose, workers can motivate themselves to achieve higher performance through natural enjoyment. Finally, the establishment of effective thought patterns through the management of beliefs, imagined experience, and self-talk can contribute to progress toward excellence. By modeling, encouraging, reinforcing, and otherwise facilitating these self-leadership processes in subordinates, a leader can become a Super-Leader.

In many ways, learning self-leadership skills is the essence of effective followership, especially under an overall system of so-called participative management. It helps to answer the employee's typical question: "So we have participative management here, and I'm supposed to be involved. How do I do that?"

We would wager that even the limousine driver cited in the previous chapter could provide a more comfortable, efficient ride if he were given a chance to participate with management in deciding how best to do it. We also believe that the performance of American workers at all levels can be improved tremendously if they are given

BEHAVIORAL FOCUSED STRATEGIES

Behavior	Strategy
Self-Set Goals	Setting goals for your own work efforts.
Management of Cues	Arranging and altering cues in the work environment to facilitate your desired personal behaviors.
Rehearsal	Physical or mental practice of work activities before you actually perform them.
Self-Observation	Observing and gathering information about your own specific behaviors that you have targeted for change.
Self-Reward	Providing yourself with personally valued rewards for completing desirable behaviors.
Self-Punishment	Administering punishments to yourself for behaving in undesirable ways (this strategy is generally *not* very effective).

COGNITIVE FOCUSED STRATEGIES

Building Natural Rewards into Tasks	Self-redesign of where and how you do your work to increase the level of natural rewards in your job. Natural rewards that are part of, rather than separate from, the work (i.e., the work, like a hobby, becomes the reward) result from activities that cause you to feel: • a sense of competence • a sense of self-control • a sense of purpose
Focusing Thinking on Natural Rewards	Purposely focusing your thinking on the naturally rewarding features of your work.
Establishing Constructive Thought Patterns	Establishing constructive and effective habits or patterns in your thinking (e.g., a tendency to search for opportunities rather than obstacles embedded in challenges) by managing your: • beliefs and assumptions • mental imagery • internal self-talk

Self-Leadership Strategies

the chance to practice self-leadership and the encouragement and guidance for doing it well.

The performance of American workers at all levels can be improved tremendously if they are given the chance to practice self-leadership.

PROFILES IN SUPERLEADERSHIP:
WILLIAM L. MCKNIGHT OF 3M COMPANY

William L. McKnight, former CEO of 3M Company, embodied many qualities of SuperLeadership. During the company's most crucial years, he established the trajectory of success that carried 3M to its current high levels of performance. McKnight, a shining leader indeed in the corporation's history, helped 3Mers believe in themselves and their company. In many ways, he served as a catalyst for the dynamic employee self-leadership that established the foundations for success.

Today 3M is a model organization. Among the most profitable *Fortune* 500 firms, 3M is especially recognized for its innovativeness, production of quality products, and respectful and dignified treatment of its work force. All the current lists of "Excellent companies," "Best companies to work for," "Best managed companies," among others, include 3M. Much of the company's success can be attributed to its style of management, one that emphasizes autonomy and entrepreneurship in creating and developing new ideas into useful, high-quality, and profitable products. As one 3M executive put it, "At 3M we don't talk about controls but working outside control."[1]

Visits to 3M's headquarters in St. Paul, Minnesota, and interviews with many of 3M's executives reveal several clues about management beliefs that are embedded in its culture. Employees of 3M talk of "champions" who spearhead the development of new products and the "new venture teams" who follow through on these new product ideas. The system itself is characterized by a host of nontraditional organizational practices that allow people to "work outside the boxes" in order to facilitate the advancement of new product innovations. Where necessary, employees "bootleg" the funding support that's needed to nurture the seeds that may spawn the backbone of tomorrow's profitable line of products. The word "lawlessness" is used to describe the work atmosphere at 3M that keeps things loose enough to allow creativity to bubble up from the rank and file. As one manager explained, "At 3M people try to bend the rules and redefine their authority . . . and they get a lot done."

When looking at an exemplary company such as 3M, the question invariably arises, "How did the organization come to operate the way that it does?" In the history of 3M, one element that stands out clearly in contributing to the unique character of the company is its leadership. One executive pointed out the need for leadership at the top that allows employee ownership. Then employees will take care of the "little [but so important] things." And 3M does indeed have a history of people-oriented leadership that has continued with its current leaders. One employee summed up the leadership of 3M's recently retired CEO, Mr. Lewis Lehr: employees, he said, could "just feel it."

It all started, 3Mers point out, with William McKnight's faith in people: he gave his subordinates freedom early in their careers, and that example has been passed on. Among other things, that translates into a chance for young entrepreneurs to make mistakes on the way to tomorrow's great discoveries. Indeed, no leader in 3M's history stands out so strongly in shaping the company's emphasis on achieving excellence through the unleashing of the vast capabilities of its people as William McKnight.

William McKnight knew after high school that he did not want to follow the family tradition of farming. He studied penmanship, business-letter writing, and bookkeeping at Duluth Business College before being hired by 3M Company as an assistant bookkeeper at $11.55 per week on May 13, 1907.[2] By the time he was twenty-four, McKnight had risen to the position of national sales manager. His approach to this job was rather unique, foreshadowing the exemplary leadership style he would later display in his career as a 3M executive. He rejected the usual approach of visiting the front office of potential customers and leaving a sales catalog. Instead, McKnight reasoned that the workers who actually used his product (sandpaper) would be more capable of providing first-hand knowledge of their needs.

"Those men and woman to whom we delegate authority . . . are going to want to do their jobs in their own way. These are characteristics we want and should encourage."

McKnight proceeded to train his salespeople to act according to this philosophy. They carried out his ideas by getting into the work areas to discover the kinds of abrasive material most needed by their customers. His salespeople were consequently able to communicate quality problems directly and precisely to 3M's factory. Even at this relatively early stage of McKnight's career, it was apparent that he sensed the critical need to rely on the knowledge and resources of others—in this case workers and customers who used 3M's products—to achieve enhanced performance. Later, as CEO, McKnight was to indelibly stamp on 3M's culture his belief in the potential of 3M's work force. His remarks in 1948 became the cornerstone of the 3M organization. They represent his own brand of SuperLeadership:

> As our business grows, it becomes increasingly necessary to delegate responsibility and to encourage men and women to exercise their initiative. This requires considerable tolerance.
>
> Those men and women to whom we delegate authority and responsibility, if they are good people, are going to want to do their jobs in their own way. These are characteristics we want and should be encouraged as long as their way conforms to our general pattern of operation.
>
> Mistakes will be made, but if a person is essentially right, the mistakes he or she makes are not as serious in the long run as the mistakes management will make if it is dictatorial and undertakes to tell those under its authority exactly how they must do their job.
>
> Management that is destructively critical when mistakes are made kills initiative and it's essential that we have many people with initiative if we're to continue to grow.[3]

McKnight's view on how employees reach their full capability has also left its mark on the thinking of management. As several 3M executives explained, the legacy that he left behind concerning employee development was that "all development is self-development." Again, McKnight's emphasis on the integrity and value of individual employees was apparent.

McKnight was also instrumental in establishing a promotion-from-within stance toward individual development. One story suggests that McKnight once lost a promotion to the office manager's son. McKnight and succeeding members of management were convinced that employees on the firing line should be encouraged and recognized. He believed that the success of the work force should be translated into opportunity—a crucial part of which was the chance to be promoted. And individual initiative and performance, not favoritism, was what McKnight wanted to reward.

McKnight seemed to have a keen awareness that workers should receive encouragement and reinforcement for work well done. Of course, encouragement can take many forms, and in many ways McKnight appeared to be a master in its personal delivery. For example, McKnight adhered to a weekend breakfast ritual that left a striking image of his ability to acknowledge the worth of 3M's employees. Those 3Mers who took part in those breakfasts still talk about them today. On Saturday mornings he would visit the employee cafeteria for an elbow-to-elbow breakfast with the workers he thought so highly of, a tradition that was carried on for many years.

Another interesting story revolves around a McKnight visit to a 3M tape factory. A newly hired plant guard would not allow McKnight to enter because he wasn't carrying his employee pass. An employee accompanying McKnight was astounded. "Don't you know that's Mr. McKnight?" he whispered. "I'm sorry, but he still has to have a pass," the guard replied. McKnight made no comment. Later he returned with his pass and complimented the guard for performing his duties well.[4]

"... we need a healthy appreciation of those who exercise the free man's option for excellence."

The 3M Company can generally be characterized as one that encourages participation and acknowledges the right to make mistakes and to transcend job descriptions in the pursuit of innovation and excellence. McKnight is described as the legendary leader who fostered this culture. Most of all, he instilled a lasting appreciation for the crucial contribution made by each member of the work force. In many ways, 3M continues to mirror and enhance his leadership philosophy in its contemporary management and organization approaches. Perhaps McKnight described his perspective best when he reflected on his sixty-five-year relationship with the company:

> It is proper to emphasize how much we depend on each other. Our challenge, while stressing this important lesson of humanity, lies in maintaining, at the same time, a proper respect for the individual. We lose something valuable if we uproot all notion of personal self-reliance and the dignity of work. . . .
>
> To continue our progress and service to America and the world, we need a healthy appreciation of those who exercise the free man's option for excellence, permitting the creation of something for all of us, enriching lives with new ideas and products.
>
> The best and hardest work is done in the spirit of adventure and challenge.[5]

In these words, and through his many exemplary actions, McKnight openly acknowledged his reliance upon the capabilities and strengths of others in the pursuit of excellence. And in this way especially, he captured the spirit and power of SuperLeadership.[6]

4

SuperLeadership: Leading Others to Lead Themselves

The teacher . . . does not bid you enter the house of his wisdom, but rather leads you to the threshold of your own mind . . . so must each one of you [develop your own] knowledge and . . . [your own] understanding.

—FROM THE PROPHET BY KAHLIL GIBRAN[1]

How can SuperLeaders guide followers to discover their own potential? How can SuperLeaders help their subordinates to become positive and effective self-leaders? How can SuperLeaders lead others to lead themselves?

This chapter will begin to introduce the fundamentals of Super-Leadership. We will first present an approach to leading others to lead themselves that provided much of the foundation for our ideas. We will also address some basic issues regarding problems of implementing these ideas and will identify when this leadership approach is most appropriate. In subsequent chapters, we follow up by describing in more detail the specific components of SuperLeadership. Most of all, SuperLeadership is *not* leadership in the way people have typically understood it. Overall, the main purpose is to define a strategy by which a SuperLeader can influence subordinates to engage in the self-leadership behaviors we have previously described.

SHIFTING TO SELF-LEADERSHIP

Few employees are capable of "perfect" self-leadership the moment they start a job. Especially at the beginning, the SuperLeader must provide orientation, guidance, and direction. The need for specific direction at the beginning stages of employment stems from two sources. First, new employees are unfamiliar with the objectives, tasks, and procedures of their positions. They will probably not yet have fully developed task abilities. But more pertinent to our discussion, new employees may not yet have an adequate set of self-leadership skills.

Note that we do not presume that all leaders should either relinquish complete influence over subordinates or rely on a premise that every human is endowed with fully developed self-leadership skills. On the contrary, we generally believe that only a minority of individuals in our society have had the natural opportunity to fully develop their self-leadership skills. Indeed, many institutions (family, schools, military service) inadvertently promote and encourage *dependence* rather than self-sufficiency. In other words, individuals become accustomed to authority figures making decisions and influencing their behavior in even the smallest details.

Self-leadership must be *learned*. It is a rare employee that comes to positions of employment with an adequate repertoire of self-leadership skills. Thus the role of the SuperLeaders becomes critical; they must play the pivotal role of leading others to lead themselves.

How is this done? We recommend a procedure that consists of (1) initial modeling, (2) guided participation, and (3) gradual development of self-leadership.[2] The SuperLeader approach that we will more fully develop in the following chapters will essentially expand upon these ideas. So let us begin with a brief discussion of each of the phases of this procedure.

Self-leadership must be *learned.*

Modeling

The importance of modeling cannot be underestimated. Those who are currently effective self-leaders can serve as a model from which others learn self-leadership. Even if unintentional, the SuperLeader's self-leadership behavior inevitably serves as a model to subordinates. For example, an executive who is overdependent on superiors would serve as a poor self-leadership model. We would likely find a similar pattern of overdependence in such an executive's subordinates. As Warren Bennis has stated, "Management of self is critical; without it, leaders and managers can do more harm than good."[3]

Thus the first step in teaching self-leadership to others is to practice self-leadership—to *be* a self-leader. As we previously mentioned, this means practicing behavioral and cognitive self-leadership and doing so in a vivid and recognizable manner that can serve as a model for others. Employees will tend to adopt the standards that they observe in exemplary models and then evaluate their own performance according to those standards. Thus, as one example, the executives who "stretch" themselves with challenging goals are likely to evoke the same sort of achievement-oriented behavior in subordinates. Conversely, executives who are satisfied with mediocre accomplishments are likely to see mediocre achievements by subordinates.

Even if unintentional, the SuperLeader's self-leadership behavior inevitably serves as a model to subordinates.

Guided Participation

In this phase, the verbal behavior of SuperLeaders is critical. For example, they can attempt to evoke self-leadership among their subordinates through a series of directed questions. To facilitate self-observation, questions such as "Do you know how well you are doing?" or "How about keeping a record of how many times that happens?" are appropriate. To facilitate self-set goals, the Super-Leader might ask: "How many will you shoot for?" "When do you want to have it finished?" "What will your target be?" To promote self-evaluation leading to self-reinforcement: "How do you think you did?" "Are you pleased with the way it went?" "Why don't you try it out?" and "Let's practice that" are appropriate remarks to stimulate rehearsals. To spur cognitive-focused self-leadership, questions to ask might include: "How do you like your job?" "Have you thought about trying different work methods that you might enjoy more?" "What opportunities do you see in the current problem you face?"

Questions such as these when combined with constructive suggestions, instruction, and coaching on effective self-leadership behavior and thinking can provide the necessary guidance to nurture and then ignite the self-leadership flame in others. The aim, of course, is to give the employee practice in thinking about and then implementing self-leadership behaviors.

The special implications of this process are that the direction, evaluation, and reinforcement functions are gradually shifted from external sources to the individual; the progress made in self-leadership is reinforced; and a shift is made from external rewards to self-administered rewards.

The verbal behavior of SuperLeaders is critical.

Gradual Development of Self-Leadership

Finally, the most important requirement is that SuperLeaders change their reinforcing functions and patterns as the subordinate becomes more and more capable of self-leadership. Initially, the SuperLeader reinforces specific performance-related behaviors by the subordinate. As time goes by, the reinforcement shifts from the performance-related behaviors associated with the task to the process of self-leadership itself. In other words, the SuperLeader reinforces self-leadership rather than specific task-related behavior.

The primary function of the SuperLeader becomes one of encouraging, guiding, and reinforcing processes such as self-imposed goal setting, self-reinforcement, employees' building of natural rewards into tasks, and their developing constructive thought patterns rather than that of *directly* providing instructions and reinforcing subordinate performance. Some executives may resist this shift because on first impression it gives the illusory appearance of less control over subordinates. Over the long run, however, this shift from direct (short-term) control to a subordinate's self-leadership is desirable. In the long term, the overall effectiveness of subordinates will be improved as a result of their increased self-leadership ability, and the executive will enjoy such rich benefits of SuperLeadership as more time, more committed employees, an increase in innovative ideas from subordinates, and a newfound strength or power for progress that flows from working with more fully developed self-leaders.

In this phase, it is particularly important that social reinforcement be given when employee self-leadership behavior does occur. Consequently, establishing a culture in which each employee supports and believes in self-leadership behavior is crucial (see pages 161–172 for more details). Unfortunately, reinforcement from other sources might detract from the development of effective self-leadership; reinforcement by peers, for example, can encourage overconformity. Thus, verbal encouragement and other forms of support from the SuperLeader are critical in establishing incentives for initiative and an environment that encourages self-leadership.

The SuperLeader reinforces self-leadership rather than specific task-related behavior.

PROBLEMS OF IMPLEMENTATION

Some words of caution are important. Attempts to encourage self-leadership can fail because of vague instructions or expectations. Self-leadership entails *specific* behaviors and strategies, and the more these self-leadership strategies are spelled out, either through models, verbal coaching, or a well-developed culture, the more successful the employee is likely to be in adopting them.

Another typical problem is that the short-term expectations of the executive can be too demanding; an executive embarking on a program of self-leadership for subordinate employees is likely to expect too much too soon. In fact, we have often observed an initial *decrease* in personal productivity while the employee adjusts to this new leadership concept. Also, the employee must be provided with the opportunity to learn from failure, and these failures sometimes are perceived as more important than they really are. If self-leadership is to effectively take hold, employees must be given some reasonable opportunity for failure without reprimand. Overall, short-term expectations should be extremely modest when moving employees along the road to self-leadership. It's the long term that really counts.

In addition, employees like to "test the water" and will sometimes do seemingly outrageous things to "see if the boss really means it." When they are convinced that the leader is sincere about wanting self-leadership from followers, then the foundation for employee excellence is established—and the leader can begin to take on the glow of a SuperLeader that is fed by shining, self-leading subordinates.

The short-term expectations of the executive can be too demanding. . . . The employee must be provided with the opportunity to learn from failure.

WHEN SHOULD EXECUTIVES ENCOURAGE EMPLOYEE SELF-LEADERSHIP?

Overall, we strongly believe that moving employees toward self-leadership is advantageous to an organization. Nevertheless, it is naive to assume that relying on self-leadership is *always* appropriate. Indeed, external executive control will always play an important role in any organization. Also, it is incorrect to assume that self-leadership and external control are mutually exclusive. Even in the most intensive external-control situations, employees always exercise some degree of self-leadership. Conversely, even when self-leadership is deliberately encouraged, some external control, primarily focused on output measures or at the task boundary, is commonly found and typically wanted by employees. In addition, external reinforcement of the self-leadership process itself will always be necessary to make it work.

Several important situational factors influence the appropriateness of attempts to develop self-leadership in subordinate employees: (1) the nature of the task, (2) the availability of time, and (3) the importance of subordinate development.

The Nature of the Task

The nature of the task itself has some connection with the potential applicability of self-leadership. For example, technology can be a constraint upon how much subordinate discretion is possible. An assembly-line technology will generally allow less discretion than several other approaches to performing work. Clearly, a managerial decision to "enrich" a job usually is concerned directly with the issue of self-leadership in one form or another (see chapter 9 on the design of sociotechnical systems). Also, it seems clear that when the task is largely creative, analytical, or intellectual in nature, greater self-leadership would be appropriate.

Self-leadership might be viewed as falling on a participative-decision continuum. Managers must make decisions as to how much self-leadership to encourage in subordinate employees, and some types of problems are more appropriate for self-leadership than others. In general, more participative decision methods are appropriate when

1. The problem is unstructured.
2. Information is needed from subordinates.
3. Solutions must be accepted by subordinates to ensure implementation.
4. Subordinates share organizational goals.[4]

Another task situation that calls for self-leadership is one where employees are supervised remotely because they are out on their own with minimal contact with the manager or supervisor, as in the case of salespersons in the field or employees working on computer terminals out of their homes. In this situation, self-leadership skills are clearly appropriate.

The Availability of Time

The time available for decision making or problem solving is another element that has a bearing on whether self-leadership should be encouraged. In crisis situations, the time simply may not be available to develop self-leadership capabilities. When the building is on fire, it's no time for a participative decision-making session. However, if an employee is likely to encounter a future crisis situation in the absence of a leader, then self-leadership training *now* would be appropriate if at all feasible.

The Importance of Subordinates' Development

At opposite extremes are the "development" mode and the "short-term efficiency" mode. In the "efficiency" mode, self-leadership will be deemphasized in order to speedily carry out the task in the most efficient manner possible. Conversely, in the development mode, subordinates' self-leadership will be emphasized, encouraged, and regarded as an investment for the future. This stance might be termed *leader investment behavior* from which a later return is expected. Note that we do *not* equate efficiency with long-term effectiveness.

Most executives operate in some zone between these two extremes. In the end, each executive must evaluate the specific situation. Factors such as the individual employee's eagerness and present capacity for self-leadership are important.

SELF-LEADERSHIP AS AN INDIVIDUAL CHARACTERISTIC

How much of an employee's self-leadership skill can originate from within? Are self-leaders born, or are they made? Can self-leadership skills be taught by an organization?

Certainly, genetic predisposition, family background, schooling and professional training, and the general social environment all have some impact on the self-leadership capabilities that individuals initially bring to an organization. Each leader would generally prefer to hire people who come from a background that teaches strong self-discipline. Consider Robert and Ben:

> Robert and Ben came to work for Harry during the same week, after they had both graduated from the College of Engineering at the state university. Within three months, Harry was able to observe substantial differences in the way Robert and Ben handled their jobs. Robert had developed his own project control system. He used a "current status" book that listed all the important target dates for his projects, along with his coded notations of the work that had been completed on each project. In addition, Robert kept a weekly "tasks to do" list that planned most of his work for a week in advance. Whenever Harry asked Robert about a specific project, Robert usually had the answer within a minute or so after looking at these records. And Robert really seemed to thrive on his work. He really seemed to be motivated to perform well and enjoyed expending the effort to do so.
>
> Ben was just the opposite. While Ben was as capable an engineer as Robert, Harry had difficulties keeping track of Ben's progress on his projects, mainly because Ben himself was so sloppy about target dates and keeping track of the work he had accomplished.
>
> In discussing his subordinates with his boss, Harry remarked: "Robert is excellent at controlling his own activities. He sets his own goals, he is aware of his progress, and he displays obvious commitment to his work. He learns from his mistakes. Ben on the other hand is having problems. He has very little self-control and I have to keep on top of him. I question his commitment to reaching his full performance potential. One of my main projects over the next six months is to teach self-leadership skills to Ben. His technical skills are just too good for us to lose."

Robert E. Kelley believes that business must adapt to the special needs and demands of the new employees. He emphasizes that the new workers deal in knowledge, not just physical labor or goods and services. He says of the new generation:

> They are imaginative and original. . . . They engage in complex problem solving, not bureaucratic drudgery or mechanical routine . . . and

have little tolerance for boredom. [They demand] interesting work and satisfying emotional relationships . . . [and] psychic and social stimulation on the job. . . . Taking orders . . . insults their intelligence and often results in a creative shutdown. . . . [they prefer to] manage themselves.[5]

We recognize that individuals come to an organization with different degrees of self-leadership skills. Nevertheless, our basic theme is that self-leadership can be taught, encouraged, and maintained by a SuperLeader. Furthermore, we believe that this objective can be approached in a systematic, proven way; *there are specific actions that organizations and leaders can take to develop the self-leadership capabilities of employees.* The key, of course, is SuperLeadership. How does a manager become an effective SuperLeader? How do organizations systematically encourage and develop SuperLeadership skills in those who have authority positions? Desiring self-led employees is not sufficient. Widespread self-leadership needs to filter down from the top to be ingrained in the culture of the organization. Learning to be a SuperLeader is the key ingredient in teaching self-leadership to employees.

Our basic theme is that self-leadership can be taught, encouraged, and maintained by a SuperLeader.

A NOTE OF CAUTION ABOUT TOO MUCH CAUTION

While we strongly believe that different situations call for different actions on the part of leaders, we would like to make our overall conclusions clear. There is a danger in being overly cautious in diagnosing the need for self-leadership.

It's all too easy to underestimate the capability of seemingly ordinary people. Lincoln Electric, the highly successful welding manufacturing firm, found some special capabilities among its employees when it found its sales sagging in 1982. Faced with a no-layoff policy, it asked its factory workers for some help. Fifty of its production factory workers volunteered to help out in sales.

After a quickie training course in sales, the former production workers started calling on body shops all over the country. They concentrated on small shops that would be able to use the company's Model SP200, a small welder. The end of the story is that their efforts brought in $10 million in new sales and established the small arc welder as one of Lincoln's best-selling items.[6]

Lincoln Electric was relying on the idea of the self-fulfilling prophecy. *Real* SuperLeaders will be willing to bet on their subordinates if there is even a little evidence that they can handle situations without imposing external constraints. Since they are willing to *take a risk* on people, success frequently becomes self-fulfilling. Such choices will not always pay off. But in the long run, most subordinates will become stronger if they are given plenty of opportunities to try out their own ideas, and sometimes fail, in their work. Invariably, they will come up with different ways of doing things, including some that the leader may not feel totally comfortable with. In the end, however, the team will benefit from more committed, innovative employees who have been given the chance to shape their jobs to their own unique perspectives and capabilities and to grow in the process.

Real SuperLeaders . . . are willing to *take a risk* on people.

Perhaps this is the most crucial question to ask in the short run: "Can my subordinate benefit from a reliance on self-leadership in this situation without causing significant performance problems for the organization?" If the answer is yes, the burden of proof ought to be on why she *shouldn't* be allowed the freedom and given the guidance to be a self-leader. The default decision should be to move toward self-leadership. By acting this way, leaders are instilling a sense of confidence in their subordinates and introducing forces that can ultimately lead to self-fulfilling employee excellence. After all, they are being treated as though the leader feels they are dependable, excellent people. If this approach is adopted, in the long run executives will more often find themselves saying "wow" and asking "what will these people think of next in moving toward new levels of outstanding performance?"

There will always be so-called rational reasons for not allowing employees to practice significant self-leadership. A SuperLeader will nevertheless be willing to take the risks necessary to let subordinates grow—and they will respond in remarkable ways. Our advice is straight and simple: when there is a *reasonable* potential for Super-Leadership, it should be tried and, most important, given some time to work. In the long run, the results will be rewarding.

The default decision should be to move toward self-leadership.

A BACKDROP FOR SUPERLEADERSHIP

The SuperLeadership approach we present in this book did not materialize out of thin air. Rather the strategies we present are founded on a strong theory backed by years of research and validation.

It is useful to introduce at this point some of the basic concepts that underlie our ideas. First, our thoughts are based on a reciprocal view of influence: persons and their world influence each other in a reciprocal manner.[7] The world influences who each person is and what he does; conversely, each person helps create the world that is relevant to him. In this sense, a leader is part of the relevant world for subordinates, and vice versa. Leaders can help subordinates to become more effective, and subordinates are the key to a leader's success. Only together can they achieve excellence. In order to articulate this mutual influence, we use an A $\rightarrow$ B $\rightarrow$ C model.

This model is relatively simple—we often say it's as simple as ABC. It describes the relationship between the behavior of individuals and the events (both preceding and following) that influence their behavior. The figure on page 64 shows the three parts of the model:

```
┌─────────────────────────────────────────────────────────┐
│                                                           │
│  ANTECEDENT ──────► BEHAVIOR ──────►CONSEQUENCES          │
│                                                           │
│  (e.g., instructions,  (e.g., task performance,  (e.g., contingent │
│  goals, models)        self-leadership           reward, contingent │
│                        behaviors)                reprimand)         │
│                                                           │
└─────────────────────────────────────────────────────────┘
```

Contingency of Reinforcement

the antecedent (A), the behavior (B), and the consequence (C). This is sometimes called a *contingency of reinforcement* or a *behavioral contingency*.

Many readers will recognize this model as fundamental to the organizational behavior-modification approach. We use this primarily as a framework for organizing our ideas. There are substantial differences, however, in the way we apply this model. First, traditional organizational behavior modification is essentially a model of external control. As we have indicated, we recognize the mutual influence between the person and the external environment—people influence external sources of control, and vice versa. Also, as we will show later, we adapt the traditional model to focus on how the external environment can influence employees to control themselves. Further, we place considerable emphasis on the cognitive aspects of self-control.

Antecedents

The *antecedent* is an event that precedes an individual's behavior and establishes an occasion for the behavior. Antecedents frequently provide cues that inform individuals about what is expected or what kind of behavior is likely to be reinforced. Sometimes an antecedent is merely a specific occasion on which a certain behavior might be expected. It might simply be instructions on how to carry out a task. Another kind of antecedent is a behavioral model (an example that can actually be observed). Behavioral models are of special interest to a SuperLeader because they can provide cues to employees about expected behavior. In the next chapter, we provide details about how a SuperLeader can use behavioral modeling to develop subordinate self-leadership.

As another example, one of the most important types of antecedents for both executives and subordinate employees is goal setting. Goal setting can be long term, as in management by objectives, or it can be a simple "to do" checklist that a manager uses to organize everyday work. Because it's so critical to successful self-leadership, we will subsequently explore some of the details of effective goal setting. We will emphasize how the SuperLeader can encourage subordinate employees to use this effective self-management technique.

In addition, a SuperLeader can do a lot to encourage appropriate patterns of thinking. For the most part, this leadership behavior is an antecedent because it typically precedes the actual employee behavior. In a later chapter, for example, we discuss how the SuperLeader can facilitate positive self-expectation in a subordinate employee.

Consequences

The third part of the model, the *consequence*, is subsequent to, what happens as a result of, the behavior. An important point is that in order for a consequence to be effective in influencing behavior it should be *contingent* upon the behavior desired: the consequence should occur *only* if a specific employee target behavior occurs. For example, rewards should be given only if the appropriate behavior has been demonstrated. Both rewards and punishments can serve as consequences. While the former can strengthen and increase desirable behaviors, the latter serves to reduce or eliminate undesirable behaviors. Using rewards to reinforce positive self-leadership is an essential part of the SuperLeadership approach. Also, as we discuss later, punishment should be used cautiously since it can cause several undesirable side effects that can be contrary to the objectives of SuperLeadership.

Employee Behavior

The "B" refers to the employee's behavior and is typically best thought of as a *target behavior* that an executive or manager wishes to concentrate on or to change. Of course, managers want to increase desirable employee behaviors and to decrease undesirable behaviors. Consider the following training case:

**TRAINING CASE
DESCRIBING JOE'S BEHAVIOR**

Phil Oaks, the department manager, describes his subordinate, Joe Scott, as follows:

> Well, Joe is just not easy to get along with. He's so disagreeable and negative all the time. He's very aggressive and disruptive. When he's unhappy he just sulks a lot, and he daydreams. He's also insubordinate and doesn't follow the rules. I don't know if he's immature, not intelligent, or irrational. Overall, his motivation is very low. He lacks drive and is generally hostile. I suspect that there may be a home problem also.

Phil has not done a good job of describing Joe in terms of specific behaviors. Let's help Phil out. To do that, it is necessary to describe Joe in terms of specific target behaviors. A target behavior is one that can be *seen* and described.

Use your imagination and creativity—do not be afraid to make assumptions—to create a new description of Joe that includes only specific, observable behaviors. Write your own description.

Phil obviously has had no training in pinpointing target behaviors. Many of the labels that Phil attaches to Joe are not observable and, while they may be true, do not provide a useful basis for Phil to begin to influence Joe's behavior. More important, Phil should not include such subjective terms as "disagreeable," "aggressive," "daydreams," "hostile," and "low motivation." Usually when managers use the term "low motivation," they mean that employee behavior has not been contributing toward the goals of the organization. There is another problem with Phil's approach: if Joe were able to hear Phil's comments, Joe would not know *specifically* how to improve his performance. In contrast, if Phil had training in pinpointing behaviors, he might describe Joe as follows:

Well, whenever Joe is given some direction, he responds by immediately *telling you why it can't be done.* He frequently *threatens* other employees and has even been in one or two *fights.* He *leaves his own work area* to *tell jokes* to other workers. Sometimes he just *sits in a corner,* or *stares out the window* for several minutes.

He has violated several company rules such as *smoking in a non-smoking zone, working without safety goggles,* and *parking in a fire lane.* He can't seem to *tell right-handed prints from left-handed prints.* Also, he *arrived late for work* ten times in the last month, and *returned from his break late* on twelve occasions.

Phil now is quite adept at pinpointing employee behaviors. More important, he is now able to describe Joe's behavior in *specific terms that can be observed.* Once he's able to do this, Phil has a useful base from which to begin his attempts to manage Joe's behavior. Note that several of Joe's behaviors are undesirable:

1. Telling the manager an assigned task can't be done.
2. Threatening other employees.
3. Fighting.
4. Leaving his own work area.
5. Parking in fire lanes.
6. Working without safety goggles.
7. Arriving late for work.

However, at least one of the negative statements about Joe can be reformulated into a desired, or target, behavior: Joe needs to learn to tell right-handed prints from left-handed prints. Several of the other undesirable behaviors Phil singled out can also be redefined as desirable behaviors: Joe can improve his performance by

1. Agreeing that a task can be done.
2. Staying in his own work area.
3. Wearing safety goggles.
4. Parking in the assigned parking area.
5. Arriving for work on time.

Restating negative behaviors as desirable behaviors has a substantial advantage. It is much easier to use positive behavior-management techniques that emphasize *increasing* the frequency of *desirable* behavior than to focus on undesirable behaviors that may require aversive behavior-management techniques. Of course, Phil's next step will be to decide which of Joe's behaviors he wants to select as target behaviors, those behaviors on which he wants to concentrate his managerial attention. Further, if Phil aspires to be a SuperLeader, he will concentrate on developing Joe's *self-leadership* behaviors.

One of the major points a SuperLeader needs to consider is the nature of desirable target behaviors of subordinate employees: What is the target behavior that needs to be reinforced? Usually, leaders think of job-oriented behaviors or specific tasks that an employee should perform, such as those described above. But a true SuperLeader thinks beyond immediate performance-oriented behaviors. A major objective of the SuperLeader is to improve the *self-leadership* capability of employees. Thus an effective SuperLeader will focus on specific self-leadership capabilities of the employee. Modeling, goal setting, and reinforcement are especially useful in developing employee self-leadership. In later chapters, we explore these Super-Leadership strategies in some detail. Again, the point to emphasize is that a SuperLeader mainly attempts to concentrate on encouraging an employee's self-leadership ability.

Modeling, goal setting, and reinforcement are especially useful in developing employee self-leadership.

SHIFTING FROM DEPENDENCE TO INDEPENDENCE

Ultimately a SuperLeader is trying to make effective self-leaders out of subordinates. A SuperLeader follows a straightforward, underlying theme in attempting to develop the self-leadership skills of employees: shifting employees from dependence on external management to independence. The following lists give examples of specific ways traditional management functions can be shifted according to this theme.

FROM	TO
External observation	Self-observation
Assigned goals	Self-set goals
External reinforcement for task performance	Internal reinforcement plus external reinforcement for self-leadership behaviors
Motivation mainly based on external compensation	Motivation also based on the "natural" rewards of the work
External criticism	Self-criticism
External problem solving	Self–problem solving
External job assignments	Self–job assignments
External planning	Self-planning
External task design	Self-design of tasks
Obstacle thinking	Opportunity thinking
Compliance to the organization's vision	Commitment to a vision that the employee helped to create

The following chapters provide specifics on how this shift from dependence to independence can be undertaken. The methods discussed later are based in part on the procedure that was presented earlier in this chapter but also go further. Some of the more straightforward elements of the SuperLeadership process, notably encouragement and guidance, are fairly intuitive and don't require much additional explanation. Several other components, however, that are not so intuitive we will address in some detail. The following section provides a brief preview of what's to come.

A SuperLeader follows a straightforward, underlying theme . . . shifting employees from dependence . . . to independence.

Remember, a fundamental reason for shifting from dependence to independence is to improve bottom-line indicators such as productivity and quality, while the employee benefits tremendously as well. As one example, Lincoln Electric manages to produce the lowest-cost, highest-quality welders in its industry with a supervisor-to-worker ratio of 1 to 100. Yes, that's right: one supervisor for every 100 workers. Clearly, this would not be possible unless every employee was considered a true self-leader. At Lincoln, every employee is evaluated on the "ability to work without supervision."[8]

A PREVIEW OF SUPERLEADERSHIP

The overall SuperLeadership framework that we will develop in the following chapters consists of several basic components. First, self-leadership serves as the core and focus of the process. A SuperLeader depends on the self-leadership of subordinates to achieve excellence. The SuperLeader facilitates self-leadership through the following basic SuperLeadership elements, which correspond to our chapter topics:

- Modeling self-leadership.
- Facilitating self-goals and productive thought patterns.
- Reinforcing self-leadership.
- Reprimanding constructively, with an emphasis on self-leadership.
- Facilitating cultures that foster self-leadership.
- Designing sociotechnical systems and teams.

Each of these SuperLeader strategies, while not necessarily natural skills for most persons, can nevertheless be learned. SuperLeadership is not the province of a select few who were fortunate enough to be endowed with special skills. Anyone can be a SuperLeader to at least some degree. In the following chapters, we lay out the path toward more effective leadership and excellence for both leaders and subordinates. We will provide a means to discover how to lead others to lead themselves.

PROFILES IN SUPERLEADERSHIP:
JOE PATERNO

By any standard, Joseph Vincent Paterno has reached the pinnacle of success in American college football. As head coach at Penn State, Paterno is one of football's all-time winningest coaches. He was honored as coach of the year after his Nittany Lions won college football's national championship in 1983 and as Sportsman of the Year after they captured the 1987 National Championship.

But Paterno is respected for his philosophy and opinions as well as for his coaching achievements. Sometimes he seems prouder of the percentage of Penn State athletes who graduate than of his own winning percentage. His opinions on recruiting, the treatment of players, and especially the proper role of football in an educational institution are widely quoted and respected. He is a frequent speaker before executive management groups. Clearly, both his philosophy and his standing on the all-time major college winning percentage chart merit attention. How did Joseph Paterno come to such a position of leadership and respect?

THE ROOTS OF LEADERSHIP

It's a long journey from the streets of Brooklyn to head coach of a major football power. But leadership began early for Joe Paterno: "When I got into high school," he recalls, "John Hooper . . . the headmaster at the Jesuit school in Brooklyn, took five kids for leadership discussions maybe two hours every other week. We would meet in his personal office . . . talk about things that went on in the school. He would ask us . . . how would you handle it . . . what would your ideas be on this . . . why would you do it that way. . . . He felt his responsibility as an educator [was] to pick out some people who had potential to be leaders . . . in addition to the normal curriculum. . . . He was a very farsighted guy."[1]

Paterno was also influenced by his father. "Everyone came to my

71

father for advice. . . . He was the patriarch in his own way. [He] fed my inclination to have some kind of impact on [other] people."

PATERNO ON LEADERSHIP

Paterno has definite ideas on leadership. He is unusual in that he is one of the few coaches that encourages players to call him by his first name. This small but important philosophy is indicative of how he feels authority relationships have changed in society over the years. "In my day [as a player], you called 'em 'coach' or else. . . . Things change," he says. "I've never felt that a title in front of your name means very much. When I was a kid, you were trained to have deference [for the title]. I don't believe that works any more."

He recognizes that the old authoritarian approach is out of touch with contemporary times. Young men no longer accept authority blindly. "You just can't tell a kid today that he has to do something and expect him to do it. He wants to know why, and he is entitled to know. An athlete will no longer buy this business that they'll do something just because you have 'coach' in front of your name."[2]

Another critical ingredient is setting a proper example. "People accept you as a coach if they know you're working as hard as they're working . . . and you're not relying on [titles] such as 'coach' to do the job for you." He further emphasizes that "a coach has to be as demanding of himself as he is of his players. He has to believe in what he is doing and then convince his players, not merely by demanding, but by instruction and example."[3]

This includes sincerity and trust: "Whether a coach or a father, being a hypocrite . . . being a phony . . . literally destroys the relationship."

Positive patterns of thinking—enhancing self-esteem—are an important part of the equation: "When the staff is down . . . when the squad is down . . . when they are starting to doubt themselves . . . then it's *gotta* be a positive approach. The minute I have the feeling they have doubts concerning . . . [their] ability to do it . . . then I immediately want to jump in there and . . . talk about how good the kids are and what a great job they've done." He emphasizes confidence and pride: "A coach must be able to develop three things in an athlete: pride, poise, and confidence in himself."[4]

Inspiration goes hand-in-hand with his goal-oriented philosophy. "A coach has to set high goals," he says. "He has to aim high, think big, and then make sure that his players aspire to the highest goals they can achieve. He has to be able to get people to reach up. As Browning wrote, 'A man's reach should exceed his grasp, or what's a heaven for?' "[5]

Risk taking is also part of his philosophy. "I try to get across to the staff and the squad all the time," he says, "you can't be afraid to lose. I think that's part of the problem that we have in this country sometimes. . . . We're not innovative enough because . . . we're afraid to take a chance. . . . We're afraid of the bad consequences. . . . We're not going to do something because we think of all the bad things that can happen, even though deep down . . . we say 'boy oh boy—we oughta' do it!' [Then] we talk ourselves out of it because of the bad things."

Paterno's temper is known to flare occasionally, but he seldom criticizes others publicly: "It's a foolish coach who criticizes his staff publicly . . . [but we] can criticize in the staff meeting." More frequently, Paterno is known to take the rap himself for a failure. A typical example was the 1970 season, when the team seemed to falter a bit. Referring to his own shortcomings, Paterno commented, "We had a 9–1 team with a 7–3 coach."[6] That's why it was surprising to read newspaper accounts of Paterno criticizing his players after the loss to the University of Pittsburgh in 1984. "We played like babies," he complained in a widely circulated quote.

When I asked him about this quote, he expressed his unhappiness with what he felt was inadequate reporting of that situation. "After the Pitt game, I *did* say we played like babies, but there's only one person you can blame for that and *you're looking at him*." He assumed the blame himself.

"If there is success," he continued, "that's the time to give it to other people. If there's a failure, you've got to be ready to take the blame."

Paterno frequently takes the heat when his quarterbacks don't play as well as the press and public want. But, as an ex-quarterback, he has almost a passion for standing by his signal callers. "I try to assure them that I'm not going to do anything because the crowd wants something done. . . . If I decide I'm not going to play them . . . take them out of a game, it's because *I* think it should be done."

RELATIONSHIPS WITH PLAYERS—TAKING THE LONG VIEW

Paterno seems to place considerable importance on developing a holistic relationship with players that transcends the playing field. "A coach has to be able to . . . help his players gain character qualities which will help them toward a successful life. He has to show them and prove to them that hard work, discipline, quality and ability will pay off, not only in football, but in later life."[7] He emphasizes life beyond football by encouraging them to ". . . have a little impact on society."

He stresses these lifelong values in recruiting. "When I recruit a kid, I tell him where we're coming from . . . so that there's no misunderstanding. I think it's important that he knows what I'm going to demand of him when he comes here."

Paterno admits to some introspective doubt when it comes to the broad criteria he uses when he evaluates his players. "If I have a kid that's not doing as well as he should academically, it influences my judgment of him. . . . Whether I'm right or wrong, it does. . . . That's the way I am."

He talks about the importance of teaching values as well as teaching athletic skills. "I had a meeting with one of the kids and I said my problem is that I cannot look at you and just evaluate you on your football ability. . . . I look at you and I know your grade point average, I know your living habits . . . and I know your abilities as a football player. I may be wrong in making judgments about your character, I may be wrong in going to your parents and saying that you've got to do better academically. Maybe I ought to just sit here and say how good a football player you are . . . but I can't."

Paterno recognizes that "[Sometimes players] are critical of me . . . because I'm assuming a teacher/father role in an area [outside the playing field] . . . but ten years from now, the things that I'm saying to them are going to have a great deal to do with how well they do in another profession. . . . Too many have come back . . . even those who were most bitter . . . and said 'you know I never thought I'd see the day . . . how many times I've sat down and didn't want to do something and made myself do it. . . .' So, I know." Richie Lucas, a former player and quarterback under Paterno, bears witness to this philosophy: "As a player, I learned so much from him. He has ideals and standards that many other people do not have. Everyone who comes in contact with him has to be just a little better for the experience . . . not so much for his success as a coach, but for the kind of man he is."[8]

The graduation rate of Paterno's athletes, one of the highest in the country, seems to confirm the wisdom of his philosophy. Generally, the longer it has been since a player has left the Paterno fold, the more he tends to recognize the benefits of playing under a Paterno philosophy. Charlie Pittman, one of Paterno's All-American players, said, "Some coaches try to get you to love and respect them so you'll do anything for them. . . . Joe's not loved, but he is respected for the type of person he is. He's really tough and he's intelligent."[9]

ON GROWING HEAD COACHES

As we sat in his office, I suggested the potential of a particular assistant coach to move on to a head coaching position. "No question," he agreed, recognizing the aspirations and abilities of this individual. He elaborated on the process of growing head coaches. "You know what he's going to have to be able to do to be a successful head coach, and you try to put him in situations where he gets experience. You can't do that all in one year. . . . Give him this [assignment]—let him do it awhile—coach the backs—work with the freshmen—all the things he's got to have experience with.

"There are certain areas where [he does] just about what he wants to do. . . . I let him go almost completely. . . . There are other areas where he is developing new expertise where he has not had a lot of experience . . . where I don't give him as much freedom. . . . [Knowing which is which] that's really what *my* job is all about.

"He'll be able to jump from this place—as Dick Anderson or George Welsh did [Anderson and Welsh are former Paterno assistants who have moved on to head coaching positions]. There will be very few things that he will not have been exposed to . . . administrative work, public speaking, alumni relations, recruiting, offense. . . . In a year or two he'll be ready."

When I asked Paterno whether a void is created when a highly qualified assistant (such as Anderson) moves on, the reply took an interesting turn. "Yes," he agreed, "[but] I miss Dick Anderson as a friend more than I do as a coach. . . . Dick was ready—I knew Dick would do well."

According to Paterno, having the opportunity to fail—making mistakes—is part of the learning process. "You can't grow [if you don't make mistakes]. . . . I've got to give them a chance to do some things [on their own]."

Paterno recognizes the value of mistakes in his own development. "Rip [Engle] allowed me to make a lot of mistakes. . . . Many times, I would go in there with the 'greatest idea in the world' [when] it may have [already] been tried three different times, [and] it didn't work. . . . I do the same thing. . . . [An assistant coach] will come in with a 'great idea.'. . . I saw the same thing twelve years ago. . . . [They] do some things I'm sure are not going to work."

However, Paterno recognizes a limit to this strategy, mainly revolving around whether a mistake will have severe consequences or not. "Ordinarily, [when] a guy comes in and wants to try something . . . you let him do it . . . but [in] a big game, if he wants to try something you know won't work . . . I can't afford that kind of luxury."

THE PARADOX OF CONTROL—ON MOVING FROM LEADERSHIP TO SUPERLEADERSHIP

Perhaps one of the most interesting aspects of Paterno is his ability to be introspective about the dilemma of overcontrol and undercontrol. "I'm not the kind of person who is reserved about his ability to do certain things. I have very positive ideas about how to do it." Further, he candidly admits, "I like the idea of being in charge."[10]

"It's difficult," he also admits, "for me to handle people in the way I think they want to be handled . . . because I have a tendency to want *complete* control. . . . In the early part of my career when I had boundless energy . . . I was literally getting up at four in the morning and working until twelve o'clock . . . and called all the offense and all the defense." Further, "I would plot every offensive and defensive move we would use in a ball game and try to devise the game plan by myself. . . . I felt that I had to have input on everything that went on every minute of the day and every day of the week."[11]

But Paterno also recognizes the benefits of getting others—especially assistant coaches—involved in the action. "I'm cognizant that people will not work two extra hours at the film projector if they're going to come in the next day and be told exactly what to do. . . . That's not going to work. . . . You destroy any ingenuity . . . any satisfaction they get out of the job itself. I'm aware of that. . . . I have to fight like hell to constantly remind myself of it."

Paterno seems destined to deal with the classic dilemma between his natural hands-on activist leadership style and the behaviors required of a SuperLeader. This seems to be a conflict between his emotional or "natural" self, which has a strong desire to control—perhaps overcontrol—the situation, and his intellectual self, which realizes the necessity and benefit of providing more opportunity for his assistant coaches. The "natural" self seems to be saying, "Hey, I gotta get in there and do it myself," while the intellectual self says, "I have to stand back and give them an opportunity to do it."

In the end, he says the important thing "is still keeping control but knowing when you don't have to have control. . . . A head coach should make each of his assistants feel that his job is the important one. . . . He has to hire people who can do the job, have confidence in them, and then let them do it. Each assistant has to have a pride . . . to be made to feel that it is a challenge . . . that he is an integral part of a leadership team.[12] . . . The whole thing is a partnership."[13]

But carrying out this philosophy does not always come easily. When asked about this dilemma, Paterno agreed: "Maybe this is even more difficult for me than other people." Nonetheless he seems to realize the benefits and necessity of developing his assistant coaches. He contrasted his present style to his earlier days as a head coach:

"Later I started to wind down a little bit. . . . I can't tell you when it happened, but I started to realize that I better let some other people do some things and I better start looking at the big picture a little more. I've done it, and I've done more and more of it." This is emotionally difficult for any leader to undertake because the first feeling is that of losing control. Nevertheless, Paterno recognizes the benefits: "I made the switch from that thirty-year-old coach who was involved in everything to where I can handle . . . my program better than before. . . . I have made my own personal adjustment."[14]

SOME CLOSING THOUGHTS

In many ways, Joe Paterno's introspection about the dilemma of moving from leadership to SuperLeadership can be a lesson for many executives in America today. In a typical success story, a high-energy individual achieves early success and attracts the attention of superiors. An important reason for this success is a "perfectionist" philosophy—acceptance of responsibility, preoccupation with detail, making sure that every fine point is covered. Typically, success at this early stage comes about through personal attention, a style in which she personally makes sure everything is done and done right.

Then, a promotion or two. Now, the scope of the responsibility is considerably expanded. The skills and behaviors that led to previous success are no longer sufficient. The newly promoted executive no longer has sufficient hours in her day or sufficient knowledge to personally accomplish all aspects of the assigned responsibility. Others *must* be involved, if only for the reason that the executive needs that extension of herself.

Some executives make this transition with little trouble, but others find the transition emotionally difficult to handle. No longer capable of carrying out the total task themselves, these executives find difficulty in depending on others and sense a "loss of control" as delegation becomes more and more necessary. A philosophy of "leading others to lead themselves" does not sit comfortably with those who have formerly depended mainly on themselves. Yet, this transition is necessary, especially at higher levels of the organizational hierarchy.

Like Joe Paterno, many executives might say to themselves that "this [transition] is even more difficult for me than other people." Yet, the most successful of these executives, those who are truly successful in redefining their roles as SuperLeaders, might later look back and reflect that they took the same course as Joseph Vincent Paterno: "I started to realize that I better let some other people do some things and I better start looking at the big picture a little more. I've done it, and I've done more and more of it."

5

Developing Self-Leadership through Modeling

As Mr. Herndon, the division manager, walked to the front of the room to address the assembly, the room quickly became tensely silent. "Information received in my office indicates that despite our massive efforts to the contrary, managers in this division are still using a directive punitive style of management. You know of our instructions from upstairs to be supportive and participative in our leadership orientation to help improve employee productivity.

"You mark my words," the division manager said, shaking his finger at the group of managers for emphasis, "You will be more supportive and participative or, dammit, heads are going to roll!"

The preceding ironic example is a bit extreme, but most executives are familiar with situations where leaders express expectations that contradict the way they themselves behave. In fact, to be honest, we are not always personally immune to the same kind of problem. Indeed, considerable evidence indicates that often the management philosophies a person claims to believe are frequently contradicted by the way that person actually behaves. This division manager knows the way he wants his managers to behave, but his own behavior contradicts the mandate he has issued. And he continues to be ineffective in facilitating the changes he desires. What is the problem? Why has the division manager been unsuccessful in achieving his objectives?

LEARNING THROUGH MODELING

This, of course, is a complicated question that is not easy to attribute to a single cause. Indeed, management styles in general can be very difficult to change. One problem with the division manager's approach, however, is especially obvious. He is relying on an old (but false) premise: *Do as I say—not as I do!* This premise doesn't seem to be working for Mr. Herndon, and it's not likely to work in other situations. The fact is that managers in the division are probably being influenced by Mr. Herndon's behavior: the influence can be subtle, perhaps not entirely conscious, yet extremely powerful. They are influenced (unintentionally in the wrong direction) by a learning process called *modeling*. Other terms for this process are *imitation, copying, matching, observational learning*, and *vicarious learning*.

The fundamental characteristic of modeling is that learning takes place, not by actually experiencing the target behavior, but by observing or imagining another's behavior. Over time, managers in his division see how Mr. Herndon acts and (perhaps without knowing it) associate the behavior with appropriate leadership and success in the company. Mr. Herndon is less effective because of his inability to counteract the years that he has been, and still is, modeling a directive punitive style of leadership.

Learning takes place, not by actually experiencing the target behavior, but by observing . . . another's behavior.

Generally, modeling can be considered a positive or constructive form of learning. Robert Waterman, coauthor of *In Search of Excellence*, recognized this:

> As humans, we seem to learn in two ways: First, by analyzing our shortcomings and trying to correct them and, second, by observing those who do things best and trying to imitate them. Our perspective is that for too long the teaching of business has focused on the problem-solving side: "What's wrong, how do we fix it?"
>
> Recalling dimly my days as a ski instructor, I would look at it like this: When I took my class on the hill and said, "You're falling down too much and here's why," they would learn something. But they would learn only half the lesson. They'd learn the rest when I showed them what it looks like when it's done right. It's that second half that we are searching for in management. [1]

MODELING AND SUPERLEADERSHIP

Modeling is an essential part of SuperLeadership. Executives can make deliberate and productive use of modeling in their quest for effective SuperLeadership.

One fundamental role of the executive is that of teacher, specifically, teaching others to become self-leaders. Teaching and coaching can be carried out in many ways, including providing task direction and goal setting, reinforcement, and criticism, but perhaps the most important teaching technique of all is modeling, especially the vivid modeling of appropriate self-leadership behaviors. Most of all, executives should avoid putting into practice, "Do as I say—not as I do."

In the development of subordinate self-leadership, modeling can be used on a day-to-day basis in two ways. The first use is in establishing new behaviors, especially self-leadership behaviors in subordinates. The second involves strengthening the probability that employees will continue to use previously learned positive behaviors. This is facilitated through subordinate observation of positive rewards received by others for desired behaviors. We develop both of these ideas in detail below.

But, in addition, modeling can be used in a more formal, deliberate manner through training. We will also present several ideas on how modeling-based training can be used to develop SuperLeadership skills in managers.

The most important teaching technique of all is the . . . vivid modeling of appropriate self-leadership behaviors.

LEARNING SELF-LEADERSHIP THROUGH MODELING

The boy watched the man carefully as he walked out of the village. The man was his mother's brother and had watched over the boy since his father had been killed in the raid of the hill people. More than anything else, the ten-year-old boy wanted to be like the man—to be the best hunter in the village.

Suddenly the man stopped and gazed for a long moment at the boy. Without saying a word, he motioned, and the boy knew he meant, "Come with me." With tremendous excitement, the boy followed the man out of the village. They hunted all that day and were very successful.

This day established a pattern for the next few years. On the days that the man would hunt, the boy would follow. At first the boy would only watch. The man spoke very little. Even when the boy asked a question, the man seldom answered, so after a while the boy asked fewer and fewer questions. They just hunted together in silence, with the boy watching carefully.

But the man was an excellent teacher. He knew that the boy was very bright and very quick. Before long, the boy was imitating the man and contributing to the hunt.

The boy also watched the man in the village, especially the way he prepared and planned for the hunt. He watched the man carefully tend to his weapons and equipment. In a short time, he was preparing his own equipment in the same way.

Within three years, they were known as the best hunters in the village. They no longer hunted as leader and follower, but as a team.

Without speaking, they knew what each would do in the hunt, and together, they were more successful than either of them alone could be. Day by day, the man noted the growing confidence, skill, and strength of the boy. The man knew that the boy was destined to be a leader of the Valley People.

How do leaders learn to lead? Most people recognize some developmental value in reading or classroom-oriented learning. But for managers in organizations, leadership is mainly learned through observing others—as "the boy" observing "the man." Thus, executives have a special responsibility to pass on the appropriate "lore" and "culture" of organizational leadership. As in ancient tribes, this knowledge is mainly transmitted through modeling.

Typically, learning through modeling is unsystematic and haphazard. It occurs without conscious direction and effort. Nevertheless, because of its pervasiveness and power, it can be very useful if managers understand more about the modeling process and use it in a deliberate manner.

Unfortunately, modeling can also create negative results if it is not well understood and managed. Consider the following case, which is based on events that occurred in a U.S. department-store company.

Tom, the new assistant buyer, was uncomfortable and confused about the punitive management style of Jim, the department buyer. Jim's behavior seemed inconsistent with his otherwise friendly and pleasant personality. Tom began to understand the situation only after witnessing several instances over a few weeks.

One day, when Jim was on a buying trip, a newspaper ad ran with the wrong information for his department. Tom was called into the division manager's office the first thing that morning. "Where's Jim?" the division manager demanded. "He's on a buying trip," Tom responded nervously.

"Well, you tell him to get his fanny in here as soon as he gets back!"

"Uh, OK," Tom said timidly.

"What the hell do you think you guys are doing anyhow, giving advertising the wrong information?"

The chewing out continued for about five minutes. What struck Tom was that the division manager didn't really seem that mad; he just seemed to be acting like he was. He seemed to be intentionally raking Tom over the coals as a conscious leadership strategy.

A few weeks later, a division meeting was held with the group vice-president to go over department plans that would be presented to the president in a couple of days. The vice-president was very critical in his feedback. When Tom finished presenting his material, he was informed that the president would "tear him apart." Interestingly, when the division made its presentation, the president found another target, the vice-president.

"Didn't you tell them to address the impact of our new strategic plan on their departments?" he snapped. "How in the hell do you expect us to make a profit if you don't manage your people?"

At this point the picture was becoming much clearer for Tom. Having now seen the entire chain of punitive command in action, he could understand Jim's leadership behavior a little better. A punitive management style was being passed down, by example, from level to level and from one management generation to the next.

The final blow came one day after lunch when Tom was standing in front of a company bulletin board with a couple of friends he had been trained with.

"Look at this. Smith was promoted to divisional manager in hard goods," one of the friends commented. "I think that was a real mistake," he continued. "I don't think he can be tough enough and get on his people the way he'll have to to get the work out in that division. He's just too nice of a guy."

Tom stared at his friend uncomfortably.

"This guy wouldn't have thought that way a few months ago," Tom thought. "He was really friendly and supportive in training, but he's changed." It seemed clear that a punitive leadership philosophy was being modeled and learned throughout the entire company. In that moment the whole organization looked different. Tom left the company a short time later.

Executives have a special responsibility to pass on the appropriate . . . "culture." . . . This knowledge is mainly transmitted through modeling.

MECHANISMS OF MODELING

Up to this point, modeling has been treated as a rather simple procedure—essentially copying or imitation. Actually, the process is a bit more complicated than first meets the eye. It essentially involves four distinct parts, technically called *attention*, *retention*, *behavior reproduction*, and *motivation*.[2]

For learning to be passed on through modeling, an observer must first give *attention* to the key behaviors of the model. The world is full of potential models, each of whom displays thousands of behaviors each day. What is it that causes an observer to single out a specific person as a model or to select certain behaviors to give particular attention to? In general, selected behaviors are those that have been vividly displayed in a detailed, understandable way and performed by a credible individual. Executives usually meet the latter criteria.

Once the behaviors are observed, the learner will generally need to repeat or rehearse what was observed in order for *retention* to occur. This can be done by physically working through the modeled behavior (for example, practicing a new golf swing that Arnold Palmer has used on TV) or sometimes by merely mentally rehearsing the behavior.

Retention then enables the observer to *reproduce the behavior* when faced with an appropriate situation (for example, trying out a new sales technique when calling on a customer). Part of the Super-Leader's role is creating opportunities for others to practice self-leadership and encouraging them to use the new behaviors that they have learned. Effectively reproducing the behavior in appropriate situations requires a mental model of the details of the desirable behavior to guide action. If this mental model is faulty, chances are that the immediate performance will be faulty as well. Of course, this emphasizes once again the need to display behaviors that are vivid, detailed, and understandable.

Even if the modeled behavior has been accurately retained and can be effectively reproduced, performance is still not likely to occur without the proper *motivation*. The most effective model of self-leadership will do little good if observers do not perceive any incentives to be effective self-leaders. These necessary incentives come in three forms: rewards or reinforcements received externally (for example, praise from a SuperLeader for effective self-leadership), rewards observed being given to others for a desirable performance such as effective self-leadership, and rewards that are self-administered (for example, self-congratulations).

Each of the components of modeling provide valuable insights for fulfilling the SuperLeader role. The primary objective is to provide an effective self-leadership example for others that is capable of facilitating self-leadership development. When these components are analyzed together, several specific guidelines become especially clear. The checklist summary provided below is a guide for the use of modeling in the SuperLeadership role.

CHECKLIST FOR USING MODELING AS A SUPERLEADER

1. Capture the attention of others. Establish yourself as a credible self-leadership model: if you want others to be effective self-leaders, be a credible example of self-leadership yourself. Display self-leadership behaviors in a vivid, detailed, and understandable manner.
2. Facilitate the retention of modeled self-leadership behaviors. Encourage others to rehearse both physically and mentally self-leadership behavior.
3. Facilitate behavioral reproduction of self-leadership. Provide opportunities and encourage others to use self-leadership behavior when appropriate.
4. Provide motivation to perform self-leadership behaviors. Facilitate the availability of external, vicarious, and self-generated incentives.

These guidelines are useful for assessing the immediate effectiveness of SuperLeadership and should become a permanent part of the thinking of the SuperLeader. These points should be kept in mind as we address the challenge of establishing new, and facilitating previously learned, self-leadership behaviors.

ESTABLISHING NEW BEHAVIORS

Perhaps the most important result of modeling is learning new behaviors by observing the behavior of someone else. The main point is that an employee can learn an entirely new behavior, especially self-leadership, without actually performing it.

"How about a break?" asked George. "Let's get some coffee."

"Sure, I'm ready," replied Art. "I think we're making a lot of progress." Art was visiting George at the Apex home office, and they were working out details of the Everflo project together.

As they sat down in the cafeteria, Art broached a new subject. "I'm curious about something, George. Would you mind if I asked you about that project-information system that you've developed? I saw you working with it this morning, and it really seemed to be helpful. How did you come up with an idea like that?"

"I wish I could take credit for it," replied George. "You're right, it really is helpful. I call it my 'checkpoint' system. The beauty of the system is that it's so simple, yet it really does the job. I've really gotten myself organized since I started using this system. As you know, in this job, I have a million deadlines and little checkpoints that need to be taken care of every day. Before I got this system, it was driving me crazy, and I didn't know if I was going to make it on this job or not."

"Well, if you didn't develop it yourself, where did you get it?" asked Art.

"Actually, I stole it from Charlotte, my boss. I'd been here several weeks, just long enough to be confused, when I noticed Charlotte using a system to organize her own activities. I got curious after she referred to it a few times in meetings we had. Finally, I asked her about it, and she offered to share it with me. I feel like it saved my job. I tell you it absolutely amazed me how that woman could keep so many details together at the same time. She's a real self-starter. She is really organized. After observing her for a while, I knew that I wanted to be as effective as she was."

"How come she didn't offer it to you when you first came in?"

"You know, I asked her that later. She said you have to really *want* to use this system and to make it your own. When I saw how effectively she used the system, believe me I wanted it. Of course, I made some adaptations and improvements on my own since I've started using it. And now Charlotte and I are working together to get it onto our office network."

"How do you feel about sharing the system with me?" asked Art.

"Sure," replied George. "We'll get the background materials together at the end of the day before you go. But you have to really *want* to use it to make it work!"

"Don't worry. I'm convinced. I *want* to use it!"

This story illustrates some of the more important points about learning through modeling, and especially about learning self-leadership through modeling. First, because of their position and status in an organization, executives have a special responsibility to show exemplary behavior. This behavior serves as a model to subordinates and to less-experienced employees.

Leaders need to recognize that employees are very likely to imitate their behavior, even if that behavior is unintended or undesirable. Furthermore, leadership behaviors, including self-leadership, are among the most likely to be copied and imitated.

Executives that are self-starters and well organized are likely to have subordinates who, in turn, are self-starters and well organized. George and Charlotte, for example, had obviously developed a system of self-observation, goal setting, and cueing strategies to organize their own activities. This way of "doing things" fit the needs of their work, their environment, and, most important, themselves.

George learned this new set of self-leadership behaviors because Charlotte passed down the knowledge by serving as a model. The story of George and Charlotte is much the same as the story of the boy and the man: only the specific circumstances and behaviors are different.

Executives that are self-starters and well organized are likely to have subordinates who, in turn, are self-starters and well organized.

MODELING AND REINFORCEMENT

Reinforcement can also play an important role in the development of self-leadership capabilities in others. First, the direct reinforcement of self-leadership skills is necessary and appropriate (see chapters 6 and 7). But reinforcement can also be used to establish and highlight models to send a message about what behavior is desirable. Consider the following example, which is based on an incident observed at a Tandem Computer manufacturing facility:

> I sensed that the weekly team meeting was nearing its end. Mary, the team leader, had conducted the meeting, which mainly consisted of informal reports from various members of the twenty-three-person team. The commitment of the team members to improvement was obvious.
>
> But from my viewpoint, the most interesting aspect of the meeting was the evident pride of several production workers as they stood and made their reports. Obviously not experienced public speakers, they were somewhat uncomfortable with this new role. Nevertheless, they stood, "spoke their piece," and were very pleased to have conquered this small but important personal challenge. Each speaker was reinforced by the nonverbal behavior of those sitting nearby.
>
> Mary turned the meeting over to Fred, the assistant team leader. As Fred stood, the broad smile on his face and his special manner hinted at a pleasant surprise. Curiosity and attention in the room picked up. "As you know," said Fred, "Tandem has a quarterly 'outstanding-performer's' club. Last quarter, there were thirty-five winners, and you may remember that the winners (with friends and spouses) attended Mardi Gras in New Orleans. This quarter, the winners will be taking a four-day, group-escorted trip to the Calgary Stampede.
>
> "I'm very pleased to announce today that our plant has its first member of the outstanding performer's club." The anticipation in the room was electric. "Of course, this award is for all-around performance, but in this case, special consideration was given because the candidate, on her own, had developed the special pretesting procedure for the XXX subassembly. As you know, this short pretest reduced the reject rate on this subassembly from 35 percent to less than 2 percent." Fred ceremoniously tore open the large envelope he was holding.

"Mrs. Louise Newman, would you please come up and accept your certificate and your tickets to the Calgary Stampede!"

I was amazed at the intensity of the spontaneous applause as a small, grandmotherly, grey-haired lady rose to accept the award. Afterward, she was surrounded by other team members whose kisses and congratulations were natural and sincere. It occurred to me that the Academy Awards must be like this!

This incident exemplifies public reinforcement of self-leadership behavior. In Louise's case the specific behavior was the development of a pretesting procedure. In self-leadership terms, this is a *cueing strategy*, because it sets the stage for a smooth and proper subsequent action. In general, any cueing strategy establishes an environmental cue that facilitates and supports a subsequent target behavior. And just as important, she developed this procedure using her own initiative—she acted as a self-leader.

There were several rewards in this incident; first, of course, the paid vacation trip to the Calgary Stampede. In addition, the certificate is a symbolic reward. But perhaps the most important reward of all was the public recognition that Louise received from the organization and her peers.

Another important point is that Fred went out of his way to link the rewards to specific behaviors, in this case the self-initiated development of the self-management cueing strategy of the pretest innovation.

But how does this incident serve as a model? Through this incident, management made clear that initiating the development of innovative cueing strategies is desirable and that it wishes to encourage and reward these types of actions. For Louise, the rewards were dramatic and public. The hope and intention is that other employees will perceive innovative behavior to be desirable and potentially rewarding. Over time, the objective is to encourage and stimulate widespread incidents of innovative self-leadership.

The lesson from this story is straightforward. Employees learn from and are motivated by rewards they observe given to others for the performance of self-leadership behaviors. Indeed, executives can learn to use this principle by remembering the often quoted "praise in public" approach. Public praise can be a powerful motivating force for others to initiate self-management actions.

Reinforcement can also be used . . . to send a message about what behavior is desirable.

TRAINING SUPERLEADERS WITH MODELING

In recent years, modeling has become much more widespread as a training and management-development technique. Advances in knowledge and the availability of low-cost video technology have aided in the diffusion of this approach. Leadership development has been one of the most widely used applications of formal modeling training.

In a traditional training approach such as the lecture method, the trainer concentrates on transmission of knowledge and attitudes as a means to change behavior. The modeling approach, however, focuses on behavior. It relies on observation and rehearsal to evoke changes in behavior. Changes in knowledge or attitudes or both are generally considered to be outcomes of rather than preconditions for changing behavior.

In modeling-based training, the trainees usually observe a short film or videotape of a *model* demonstrating effective behavior in a leadership situation. An effective trainer will point out the specific desirable and undesirable behaviors.

Also, modeling-based training typically uses *rehearsal*, in which trainees act out leadership behaviors in a simulated leadership situation. Rehearsal is a form of role-playing, but is more structured and less free-flowing. Of course, one significant advantage of rehearsal is that trainees are allowed the luxuries of making mistakes and learning from those mistakes in a sheltered situation.

The final components of the modeling-based training process are *social reinforcement* and *transfer of training*. Social reinforcement involves feedback to trainees regarding their rehearsal performances and learning progress. The feedback comes from the trainer and other trainees. It also includes reinforcement (for example, praise) of effective performances of desired behaviors. Transfer of training consists of applying those elements of the training process that will enhance actual performance on the job. For example, target behaviors are frequently arranged from less difficult to more difficult to facilitate learning progress. Also follow-up sessions are typically scheduled for trainees to continue meeting with the trainer and other trainees as they attempt to actually apply learned behaviors back on the job. In these sessions unexpected difficulties that trainees have encountered and new questions can be discussed.

We suspect that problems with transfer of training are the most frequent reason why training fails. In the case of modeling, behaviors can be learned in the training laboratory, but individuals may encounter additional problems in using these behaviors back on the job. Perhaps the most salient issue is demonstrated by the following conversation between a department-store training manager and a young manager of one of the store's departments.

> I ran into Michelle as she was coming out of the sports equipment department. "How's it going?" I asked. "OK," she replied. "I'm managing to survive."
>
> I was a little surprised at this less-than-optimistic answer since I knew that Michelle is one of the most confident young executives in the store. She had been one of the best participants in the managerial leadership program I had conducted for the young managers about five months earlier.
>
> "How are you doing with your people?" I asked. "Did our leadership program make any difference?"
>
> "You know our program was built around the use of positive reinforcement. I really try to recognize my people when they do something well. But every time I do that in front of Blowhard, the vice-president of merchandising, he gets on my back. He says I'm being too soft on them, that I need to get tough, and that I really won't get anywhere until I do. You know his idea of getting tough is to yell and scream if something goes wrong. Frankly, I'm afraid I've created the wrong image with Blowhard and it may cost me a promotion."
>
> "So what are you doing about it?" I asked.

"I'm being selective in my behavior. When he's not around, I behave like we talked about in the training program. Whenever he comes around and is watching things, then I get tough. I feel I'm being two-faced, but I don't know what else to do. I thought for a while that it would have a detrimental effect on my department, but my people are no dummies. They know what's going on and are fairly understanding."

The moral of this story is that behaviors learned in a sheltered training environment must be reinforced if they are to be successfully transferred to the job situation. Reinforcement, of course, can come from different sources. Perhaps reinforcement from superiors is the most critical. The greatest potential for conflict exists when one layer of management is trained in concepts that are alien to a higher level of management. Behaviors learned in training must be reinforced by organizational superiors if the behaviors are to endure.

MODELING-BASED TRAINING CAN EFFECTIVELY PROMOTE SUPERLEADERSHIP

The primary elements involved in modeling-based training correspond closely with the fundamental mechanisms of modeling-based learning (see the figure on page 95). Specifically, the presentation of a model corresponds with the attention process, rehearsal with retention, social reinforcement with motivation, and transfer training with motor reproduction. This correspondence emphasizes that this training process is based on sound learning principles.

The effectiveness of modeling for leadership training has been evaluated extensively. The study conducted by Dr. Gary Latham and Dr. Lisa Saari, which is perhaps the best known, involved a controlled evaluation of a behavioral-modeling program designed to improve organizational leadership skills.[3] The training intervention included modeling and role-playing rehearsals of several leadership situations.

The training produced highly favorable results in terms of subordinate reactions, scoring on learning tests, performance in behavioral simulations, and subsequent managerial performance ratings. The

Components of Modeling-Based Training			
Presentation of Modeled Behavior (usually via video-tape or film)	Rehearsal	Social-Reinforcement	Transfer Training

Mechanisms of Modeling-Based Learning			
Attention	Retention	Motivation (Incentives)	Reproducing the Behavior

The Components of Modeling-Based Training and Their Correspondence with the Mechanisms of Modeling-Based Learning results were repeated when an untrained "control" group was also trained at a later date. Overall, this study, along with several others, demonstrates the significant potential of modeling-based training for teaching leadership skills.[4] We believe this approach holds especially strong promise for training the SuperLeader.

SuperLeadership is a challenging process that requires a delicate balance between autonomy and direction. Communicating the key elements of SuperLeadership will likely require significantly more than verbal explanations. Providing effective models who vividly display important SuperLeadership behaviors is an essential element for transmitting the essence of SuperLeadership. The modeling-training principles remain the same; the main difference lies in the conceptualization and specification of the "target behaviors," which are the specific leadership behaviors that the trainees are intended to learn. To train the SuperLeader through modeling, the first step is to develop a thorough and precise understanding of what self-leadership is (see chapters 2 and 3). Then trainees are presented with the problem of how they can encourage or induce these self-leadership practices in subordinate employees. Usually, a thorough discussion of this problem will elicit very pragmatic suggestions from the trainees.

The next step is to present the step-by-step SuperLeadership procedure for aiding the development of self-leadership in others. We presented the primary components of this in chapter 4: the use of modeling, guided participation, and several other compatible elements to facilitate the gradual development of effective self-leadership.

In the next stage, a model of how a SuperLeader would use verbal behavior to introduce self-management to the subordinate is presented. Then rehearsals are conducted and critiqued to facilitate practical learning of the specific SuperLeader behaviors. Feedback and reinforcement provided by cotrainees are also important to the learning process. Finally, subsequent follow-up sessions for discussing problems that arise in applying this training back on the job are provided.

We believe, in fact, that modeling-based training is virtually mandatory to develop SuperLeadership skills in traditional supervisors and managers. At first, learning to be a SuperLeader may appear to be unnatural or contradictory because it sometimes implies that assistance or decision making would be deliberately withheld from a subordinate employee. The long-term purpose of this "holding back" is to reduce dependence and to encourage and enhance the self-leadership of the subordinate. SuperLeadership can reap significant future benefits in terms of enhanced performance and innovation.

Nevertheless, we have found that, in the short term, SuperLeadership sometimes runs against the grain with experienced, traditional supervisors. They must experience the long-term positive results that come from enhanced self-leadership of more self-confident and capable subordinates.

Modeling-based training is virtually mandatory to develop SuperLeadership skills in traditional supervisors and managers.

Jerry watched with some discomfort as Betty and Denny finished up the role-play exercise. The short simulation dealt with a technical decision that Betty (who played the subordinate) had brought to Denny (who played the supervisor). When they finished, Elizabeth, the trainer, looked at the other trainees and asked, "Any comments or suggestions? What did you think of that?"

Jerry just couldn't contain himself. "Yeah, I've got a question," he replied. "I just don't understand why Denny just didn't make the decision when Betty brought it to him. He had the experience and he had the information. It was no big deal. He could have made the decision with no problem and saved some time. Why does he have to ask her all of those questions?"

"How about it, Denny?" asked Elizabeth.

"Well," answered Denny, "I think the whole point of what we're doing is trying to get the subordinate to manage her own behavior. For me to always make the decision would seem to contradict that objective.

"I think it fosters her dependence on me and makes her less capable of doing things on her own. One of the ways I try to get her to act more on her own is by asking questions, mainly questions that will lead her to discover the best answers herself. In the short run, it does take more time, but I think it will have a long-term payoff."

"What if she makes the wrong decision?" asked Jerry. "It seems to me you have the experience and more knowledge to make that decision, and you should do it."

"I may have more knowledge about *this* particular decision, but I'm not always going to have more knowledge, and furthermore I just have to get her in the habit of using her own abilities as much as she can."

Elizabeth chimed in again: "One of the things we know from our experience, Jerry, is that employees on the road to self-leadership will indeed make wrong decisions and the supervisor will know the decision is wrong. This is perhaps the most difficult time for SuperLeaders. They have to give employees an opportunity to make mistakes on their own and to learn from those mistakes. Again, taking a long-term view, a SuperLeader realizes that employees will tend to make fewer mistakes in the future, and their dependence on the executive lessens. At some time, they *will make* a bad decision, but they *must be* allowed to make mistakes if they are to learn. Why don't we try this role-play again, with you in the supervisor's role, Jerry, and George, will you be the subordinate?"

"OK," replied Jerry. He was still somewhat skeptical, but he was willing to give it a try to see what happens.

SUMMARY: MODELING AND SUPERLEADERSHIP

Modeling is an important part of how employees learn new behaviors. Effective use of modeling includes gaining the attention of subordinates and helping them to retain what they learn. It also provides subordinates with opportunities and incentives to try out the new behaviors. In particular, learning self-leadership skills can be greatly facilitated when experienced executives and managers exhibit these behaviors to subordinate employees.

Executives, therefore, have a special responsibility to serve as an example that they wish subordinate employees to emulate. They cannot depend on *Do as I say, not as I do* to counteract poor examples of self-leadership. United Technologies apparently recognized this when they published the ad, "Let's Get Rid of Management."

Let's Get
Rid of
Management

People
don't want
to be
managed.
They want
to be led.
Whoever heard
of a world
manager?
World leader,
yes.
Educational leader.
Political leader.
Religious leader.
Scout leader.
Community leader.
Labor leader.
Business leader.
They lead.
They don't manage.
The carrot
always wins
over the stick.
Ask your horse.
You can *lead* your
horse to water,
but you can't
manage him
to drink.
If you want to
manage somebody,
manage yourself.
Do that well
and you'll
be ready to
stop managing.
And start
leading.

A message as published in The Wall Street Journal by United Technologies
Corporation, Hartford, Connecticut 06101

Modeling can also be useful in a more formal sense, for training in SuperLeader behaviors, for example, especially if used in conjunction with modern videotape technology. In a training program based on modeling principles, the critical elements are observation of models, behavioral rehearsal, feedback and social reinforcement, and transfer of the training to the work itself. Overall, modeling can indeed be a critical technique to facilitate the development of Super-Leadership and self-leadership capabilities throughout an organization.

Learning self-leadership skills can be greatly facilitated when experienced executives and managers exhibit these behaviors to subordinate employees.

PROFILES IN SUPERLEADERSHIP:
GENERAL DWIGHT D. EISENHOWER[1]

General Dwight D. Eisenhower, hero of World War II, is still regarded by many historians as one of the most effective military leaders in history. Indeed, Eisenhower—or "Ike"—displayed many of the characteristics typically associated with SuperLeadership. In this profile, we trace the development of Ike as a military leader to show how he displayed many leadership characteristics that were consistent with the basic concepts of SuperLeadership.

EARLY INFLUENCES: LEARNING SUPERLEADERSHIP FROM OTHERS

Eisenhower was born the third of seven sons in a strict, religious, and relatively poor family. His father's aloof discipline was balanced by his mother's cheerful nature, and most accounts detail a happy childhood. Undoubtedly, Ike's strong sense of self-discipline was rooted in those early family years.

But it was after his graduation from West Point that his style of military leadership began to take form. His first assignment was at Fort Sam Houston, in Texas. There he became the "power behind the throne" of Colonel Daniel Moriarity, "a fine old fellow who didn't like to bother much with the details of training and administration. . . . As I look back on it, it was one of the valuable years of preparation in my early career. . . . The arrangements made by the Colonel gave me the feeling of personal authority . . . of training, disciplining, and equipping such a large command."[2]

Clearly, in his first command experience, whether it was intended or not, Ike was given the encouragement and latitude to develop significant self-leadership skills. More important, he found a model of leadership who provided younger officers with full opportunity for self-development.

Later, while serving under Douglas MacArthur in the Philippines,

Ike found a similar arrangement. Though he found MacArthur eccentric, Ike also thought him rewarding to work for: "When he gave an assignment, he never asked any questions; he never cared what kind of hours were kept; his only requirement was that the work be done."[3] The two men initially held one another in high esteem, though their relationship deteriorated through World War II as Eisenhower's fame and popularity eclipsed MacArthur's.

In the years prior to World War II, we can trace the development of Eisenhower's leadership style. As he absorbed the military environment, he learned to be delegated to and, in turn, to delegate authority. Through his role models, he came to value the role of communications and personal magnetism in dealing with superiors and subordinates. He understood the significance of autonomy, of "owning" a job and doing it well in his own style. Ike learned leadership through exposure to models that strongly facilitated his own self-leadership skills.

He understood the significance of autonomy, of "owning" a job and doing it well in his own style.

A Special Relationship: Eisenhower and Marshall

One of the greatest influences and most important models in Eisenhower's life and career was General George C. Marshall. Their relationship has been described variously as being like that of a father and son, a leader and protégé, and partners. Undoubtedly, Eisenhower learned much from Marshall.

From the very start, Marshall let it be known that he wanted no yes-men in his camp. On Eisenhower's first day at the War Plans Department at the beginning of World War II, Marshall called him into his office and asked Ike what the United States' Philippine strategy should be. Eisenhower spent the day at his desk, then returned with an analysis of the Philippine situation and a recommended strategy. Marshall was pleased with Ike's response to the task:

"Eisenhower, the Department is filled with able men who analyze their problems well but feel compelled always to bring them to me for final solution. I must have assistants who will solve their own problems and tell me later what they have done."[4]

As he had done under other commanders, Eisenhower completed his own tasks with a minimum of supervision. When his time came to command, he expected the same from his subordinates. "What General Marshall wanted most . . . were senior officers who would take the responsibility for action in their own areas of competence without coming to him for the final decision; officers who in their turn would have enough sense to delegate the details of their decisions to their subordinates."[5] Learning to lead from those above him, Ike carried this sense of delegation and control over into his own leadership style.

Marshall groomed Eisenhower for the rigors of the high command of troops. He could do this only because of his exceptional ability to delegate "headquarters" authority. Prior to the D-Day invasion, Eisenhower realized that, no matter how much work and planning he did, the soldiers held the keys to the operation's success. According to Stephen E. Ambrose,[6] much of Ike's time before D-Day was spent visiting field troops. Most of the soldiers who went ashore on D-Day had the opportunity to at least look at the leader who was sending them into battle. He personally talked to hundreds of troops.

These visits had a tremendous impact on the soldiers' morale. "Wherever he went he talked, asked questions, listened, observed," Ambrose noted. "He was patient, clear and logical in his explanations to his officers and men about why things had to be done this way or that. He mingled with the men on an informal basis, got to know them, listened to their gripes, and, when appropriate, did something about them."[7] Of course, the interaction worked two ways: chatting with the soldiers seemed to restore his energy.

According to Ambrose, Eisenhower's personal magnetism and involvement seemed to be the key factors. "The officers responded to his personality, his encouragement, his good humor, his seriousness about his job and theirs, his professional competence, and most of all to his leadership. 'I was often astonished to see how much better they worked after they had unloaded their woes,' he later wrote, but astonished or not, he realized full well what a positive effect he was having. He made a sympathetic ear an essential part of his leadership technique."[8]

Teamwork. Ike considered athletics a metaphor for leadership. After an injury, Eisenhower coached the West Point junior varsity football team with as much enthusiasm as he had previously shown for playing the sport. He later coached at Fort Sam Houston, Camp Meade, and other army camps prior to World War II. The football coach is a perfect metaphor for Eisenhower's leadership style. Football places an emphasis on the team, not on star performers; it requires coordinated efforts, not flashy individual performances.

Peter Lyon wrote about Ike's North African operations. "Essential to leadership, in Eisenhower's view, was the team. First, the members of the team must be carefully selected and trained to work together, each man doing his own job: then all pull together, shoulder to shoulder, with a team spirit, an esprit de corps, a high morale, able to accomplish anything together, to win. The captain of such a team need only have their respect and affection: the team would follow him anywhere."[9]

Eisenhower discussed teamwork in a letter to his son, John: "the one quality that can be developed by studious reflections and practice is the leadership of men. The idea is to get people working together . . . because they instinctively want to do it for you."[10]

The self-management concept of guided participation enters into play here, as the coach-leader must first teach skills and teamwork behaviors, then guide the athletes as they develop these skills and behaviors, and eventually allow the athletes to control their own actions in the competitive arena.

". . . get people working together . . . because they instinctively want to do it for you."

The Common Man. Eisenhower had a high opinion of the potential of the common man. In 1967 he wrote: "In our Army, it was thought that every private had at least a Second Lieutenant's gold bars somewhere in him and he was helped and encouraged to earn them. . . . I am inclined by nature to be optimistic about the capacity of a person to rise higher than he or she has thought possible once interest and ambition are aroused."[11]

Since he thought well of others, he intuitively understood the advantage of sharing information with subordinates. For example, he wrote that "The Army . . . as far back as the days of von Steuben, learned that Americans either will not or cannot fight at maximum efficiency unless they understand the why and wherefore of their orders."[12]

Baron Friedrich von Steuben, a Prussian-born American general during the Revolutionary War, found that American soldiers required personal incentive to fight at maximum efficiency. In other words, these soldiers required leadership that matched their personal goals to reach the targets of the army. To that end, von Steuben modified his own European-based command practices, trying to understand the individual American soldier's role and motivation.

This positive viewpoint of man-in-general is a fairly common characteristic of SuperLeaders. They seem to have unlimited faith that, if given the opportunity to perform, most people will come through.

"Americans either will not or cannot fight at maximum efficiency unless they understand the why and wherefore of their orders."

Reward and Reprimand. Constructive criticism, at the appropriate time and place, was part of Eisenhower's style. Ambrose compared Ike's critique of his own and his troops' performances after the North African campaign as analogous to the successful football coach studying the movies of the preceding week's game.[13] Ike's self-criticism was searching and positive, designed to eliminate errors and improve performance.

But he had a good sense of balance between reward and reprimand. As he explained about war games in preparation for World War II, "After each stage of the maneuvers, we tried to assemble the principal officers for a critique. In these morning chats, we emphasized everything that went right; encouragement was essential to the . . . men. At the same time, we had to uncover and highlight every mistake, every failure, every foul-up that in war could be death to a unit or an army. With every one of these critiques, the self-confidence of each participant seemed to grow."[14]

Clearly, Eisenhower emphasized the positive. "He preferred to praise and encourage, to give a man a task and then leave him alone, resisting the temptation to look over his shoulder or to guide him to the correct solution."[15]

Developing Others. Ike was highly concerned about the development of others, especially subordinate officers. In writing to General Prichard, he gave this advice: "While you are doing your stuff from day to day, constantly look and search among your subordinates for the ones that have these priceless qualities in greater or lesser degree. As the War Department moves you on up, you will find greater and greater need for people upon whom you can depend to take the load off your shoulders. The more you can develop and test these people now, the greater will be your confidence in them when you are compelled to thrust bigger and bigger jobs upon them."[16]

Deemphasis of Status and Rank. At some stages of his career, Ike commanded men who technically outranked him. For example, even though the British generals Arthur William Tedder, Andrew Browne Cunningham, and Harold Alexander all outranked Ike, Ambrose wrote that "Eisenhower was never awestruck by rank or title. He tended to work with his deputies, not by imposing his will on them, but through persuasion and cooperation, to draw on their talents by establishing a close personal relationship with them."[17]

Also, for the most part, Ike's way was not one of direct command.

As Ambrose says, "Eisenhower's method was to lead through persuasion and hints, rather than through direct action."[18]

"The more you can develop and test these people now, the greater will be your confidence in them when you are compelled to thrust bigger and bigger jobs upon them."

Loss of Control: Exceeding the Boundaries of Self-Management

As we have stated elsewhere, one of the risks of leading others to lead themselves is that occasionally they will exceed the legitimate boundaries of their self-controlled domain. With Eisenhower's highly delegative style, he occasionally suffered from this problem.

One of the more prominent incidents involved Major General Lloyd R. Fredendall, commander under Ike in the North African expeditions. Fredendall was apparently not interacting with his troops directly enough.

Ambrose tells the story in this way: "Eisenhower tried to lead through persuasion and hints rather than direct action, and although he was worried about Fredendall's burying himself outside Tebvessa, all that he did was to tell Fredendall that 'one of the things that gives me the most concern is the habit of some of your generals in staying too close to their command posts,' and asking him to 'please watch this very, very carefully among all your subordinates.' Eisenhower then gave a brief lecture on the advantage of knowing the ground, knowledge which could come only through personal reconnaissance and impressions. The lecture did no good. Fredendall did not change his habits, and within two weeks, the American forces would pay for it dearly."[19] Shortly afterward, Ike relieved Fredendall from command.

Another, more famous incident involved General George S. Patton, one of the most daring and aggressive combat officers of World War II. When confining his efforts to the battlefield, Patton performed brilliantly, and Eisenhower provided Patton with a lot of leeway.

Nevertheless, Patton occasionally went astray in noncombat situations. One of his indiscretions involved slapping a private in an army hospital during the battles for Sicily and Italy. Reports of the incident reached Eisenhower, who chose to discipline Patton personally rather than publicly. Patton was abashed and apologized to the soldiers, doctors, and nurses involved. The affair would have ended there had not an American newsman gotten wind of it and published an exaggerated version in the United States.

Unfortunately, that was not the end of Eisenhower's troubles with Patton. A public statement by Patton about Britain and America ruling the world received press attention. Again, Eisenhower chose to hang on to Patton because of his indispensability to the combat effort. But this time, he let him sweat it out for a few weeks before telling him that he could stay.

These incidents are useful examples of the risks of SuperLeadership and point out that, for even the best of leaders, perfection is not possible. Despite an occasional problem, Ike is still regarded as one of the outstanding military leaders in our history.

One of the risks of leading others to lead themselves is that occasionally they will exceed the legitimate boundaries of their self-controlled domain.

POSTSCRIPT: EISENHOWER AS PRESIDENT

Interestingly, earlier historians were not equally generous in evaluating the effectiveness of Eisenhower as president of the United States. To some, he seemed weak—a "do nothing" president. More recently, however, a new historical perspective has emerged that has placed Ike's presidency in a different light. Many of these more contemporary opinions are based on private papers that have only recently become available.

According to the newer viewpoint, President Eisenhower was a much more active and influential leader, albeit one who was content to lead through others and wield influence quietly behind the scenes, to give credit to others rather than worry about staying on center stage. In this sense, the presidency of Eisenhower takes on a greater similarity to his military leadership. Perhaps his greatest contribution as both a military and political leader was his quiet but effective ability to lead others to lead themselves.

6

Developing Self-Leadership through Goal Setting and Productive Thought Patterns

In this chapter, we discuss antecedents, which are events that precede employee behavior and can influence that behavior. Goal setting is one of the most important classes of antecedents. The term *goal* refers to *a desired end*, or, fundamentally, where a person wants to be at some time in the future. Also, later in the chapter, we address the issue of how SuperLeaders can encourage productive thought patterns. Both goal setting and constructive thought patterns focus on internal cognitive self-leadership issues.

GOAL SETTING AND PERFORMANCE

Goal setting in general has been one of the most actively investigated aspects of employee behavior and performance. Perhaps the best summary of this research was presented by Gary Latham and Edwin Locke in their article "Goal Setting: A Motivational Technique that Works."[1]

The purpose of all of this research has been to acquire knowledge of how goal setting can be more effectively used to enhance employee performance. The following general principles have been derived from this extensive research.

Goal Specificity

First, virtually any kind of goal setting seems to be better than none at all. The mere existence of a goal serves to focus employee attention and energy. This is one of the most pervasive findings of all organizational psychological research: the existence of goals serves to improve employee performance. Sometimes, however, writing self-goals can be a difficult step for some employees to take. Consider the case of Bill Minder.

TRAINING CASE
BILL MINDER

Bill Minder was hired as your new personnel manager about three months ago. You originally delayed *formal* goal setting with Bill in order to give him a few weeks to adjust to his new job. Time has passed all too quickly, however, and last week you asked Bill to write objectives for the next four-month period. This Monday, when you came into the office, you received the following informal memorandum from Bill:

Since I'll be at Corporate Staff all this week, I thought I would write to you regarding my views on MBO. I'm sure you will understand when I say that MBO seems to apply to production and sales areas very well, but really does not apply to the Personnel Department. Last week, our department was actively engaged in studying the new OSHA safety regulations, and collecting the attitude survey on our foremen. When I return, we shall begin our work with the controller to prepare for the upcoming contract negotiations. We also have to prepare for the meeting (scheduled for next month) to explain fringe benefits to our nonunion employees. On top of all that, continuation of the

---

monthly housekeeping and safety inspection is particularly important at this time because of the new OSHA requirements. Besides all this, I'm making a special effort to learn as much as I can about the behavioral aspects of bargaining.

I know you realize that all of these problems have placed extraordinary demands on the Personnel Department. In the past, Personnel was primarily engaged in hiring and layoffs. Now, the bulk of our time is taken up with governmental compliance, administration of fringe programs, and dealing with the union. At this point, we just don't have the manpower to handle all of these demands.

Do you agree with me when I say that, in a staff area like Personnel, our main objective should be to get new personnel specialists to handle the problems that already exist? I see two objectives for my department: (a) more personnel; (b) a bigger budget. It really is impossible to write any other objectives for a staff department like Personnel.

See you in a week,

Bill Minder

You are somewhat taken aback by Bill's casual response since you had felt he was working out well in his new position. However, you really believe it is important for staff areas to develop objectives. You suspect that Bill's flippancy may be a cover-up for his insecurity about *how* to write objectives, so you decide that you should actively suggest objectives to Bill and show him how to write the objectives. What might be some sample objectives for Bill Minder?

Specific goals seem to be better than ambiguous or "fuzzy" ones. Usually, in goal setting, "specific" means to be as quantitative as possible. Most goal-setting training programs place significant emphasis on how to write specific, concrete goals. Yet, qualitative goals that include firm time deadlines also seem to be effective, especially with tasks that are very complex, "professional," or "project" in nature.

The commonsense simplicity of MBO (Management by Objectives) can be misleading; some managers find it very difficult to write objectives when no direct cost, profit, or other unit of measurement is readily available. Staff managers, for instance, may never deal with an easily measurable objective (with the exception of their own departmental budgets).

Some MBO purists are militant about demanding quantitative measures for *every* objective. As a result, objectives frequently do not get written for some key areas, so MBO becomes a paperwork charade for some managers.

We believe it is important to recognize the legitimacy of qualitative objectives. The fact is that many key areas are not amenable to quantitative measurement, especially over shorter time periods. It is preferable to write activity-oriented objectives with a firm *time deadline* than to write no objectives at all. In the training case on pages 111–112, for example, Bill Minder might write qualitative objectives similar to the following:

- Submit report covering the impact of the new OSHA regulations . . . by February 15.
- Complete analysis of foreman attitude survey and prepare feedback report . . . by March 10.
- Complete research and preparation for contract negotiations. Have documentation completed by April 15 (joint objectives with controller).
- Conduct fringe-benefit meeting with nonunion employees during month of February.
- On first Monday of each month, conduct housekeeping and safety inspection (joint objective with production manager and plant engineer). Complete status report by the following Friday.

In some jobs like production and marketing, quantitative objectives have always been a way of life and represent nothing really new. In general, quantitative objectives are preferred because they are less ambiguous and provide a clear target to shoot for. Nevertheless, objectives should never be ignored merely because they cannot be quantified. Qualitative objectives should be recognized as legitimate and useful. In fact, the *real* improvements frequently come about because of the achievement of qualitative objectives, those that move beyond goals for the bottom line.

In addition, and of particular importance for SuperLeadership, employees should be encouraged to write *personal-development* objectives for themselves. These objectives are directed at the person, not the job. They may involve increasing a person's technical, managerial, or self-leadership skills to meet current objectives or preparing for future responsibilities. A personal-development objective for Bill Minder might be this:

- Read the book A *Behavioral Theory of Labor Negotiations* (or *Self-goal Setting: The Key to Improved Self-Management*) before May 1.

Thus three categories of objectives have been defined, although the "mix" will be quite different depending on the nature of the job.

Quantitative objectives provide a measurable standard against which results will be checked and refer to a specific time span or time deadline. These objectives are end-result oriented and are most common with line managers.

Qualitative objectives refer to whether an event has occurred or not by a specific deadline. The objectives are "activity" or "project" oriented. They are more common with staff managers.

Personal-development objectives refer to the development of skills of the individual rather than to the goals of the job itself. These objectives are also typically "activity" oriented and can have a special focus on the development of self-leadership skills.

Level of Difficulty of Goals

Some researchers have concluded that more difficult goals result in higher performance—provided the goals are accepted by the employee. We prefer to conclude that, in general, moderately difficult goals seem to result in higher performance than easy or extremely difficult goals. Easy goals do not sufficiently challenge the employee: the individual stops once the goal has been achieved. On the other hand, the employee considers extremely difficult goals to be "impossible" and is less likely to accept them. The best performance seems to result from a moderately difficult goal, one that "stretches" the employee but is seen as attainable if enough effort is given to it.

Participation in Setting Goals

Last but not least, many believe that participation in setting goals will also enhance performance. The logic is that if an employee sees the goal as her own, she is much more likely to give the effort required to attain the goal. Since the idea of participation is very closely connected with the essence of SuperLeadership, we will develop this idea in some detail later in this chapter.

Virtually any kind of goal setting seems to be better than none at all.

GOAL SETTING AND SUPERLEADERSHIP

In beginning this section, let us return to a basic theme of this book: the main objective of the SuperLeader is to improve performance in subordinates through the development of their own self-leadership capabilities. We know that a key element in self-leadership is self-goal setting (see chapter 2). Thus, one of the major efforts of an effective SuperLeader is to encourage subordinates to set their own goals.

An important point to note is that goal setting is a *learned behavior*, that is, a skill or sequence of actions that employees can develop over a period of time but one that is not necessarily an innate behavior that every new employee brings to the job. Since goal setting is something to be learned, the role of the SuperLeader is to serve as a model, coach, and teacher.

Teaching employees how to set goals can follow the general framework that we have established earlier: first, an employee is given a model to emulate; second, he is allowed guided participation; and finally, he assumes the targeted self-leadership skill, which in this case is goal setting. Note that we begin with modeling, which, as we previously discussed, is a key element in learning new skills. Because of their formal position of authority, SuperLeaders have a special responsibility to personally demonstrate goal-setting behavior that can be emulated by other employees. It's unrealistic to expect a subordinate employee to set goals when the executive is not setting them. Furthermore, goals need to be coordinated among the different levels of the hierarchy. Subordinate goals, even those that are self-set, need to be consistent with superior and organizational goals.

Goal setting by employees is a recurring theme in the general employee-participation literature. It is part of the idea that employees can be more motivated and achieve higher performance if they participate in decisions that subsequently affect their lives at work. But the concept of participation has remained somewhat ambiguous. Below, we focus on the factors of time and experience to help develop a model that addresses the question of how self-set goals might change as an employee gains maturity, skill, and experience.

Employees can be more motivated . . . if they participate in decisions that subsequently affect their lives at work.

Degree of Participation

First, we will consider the concept of participation in goal setting. Typically, the idea of participation refers to *subordinate* participation since it is normally assumed that the manager has the formal authority and power to participate. But the concept of participation involves both manager and subordinate. If the levels of managerial and subordinate participation in goal setting both range from low to high, then various combinations might be considered. The figure on page 117 graphically demonstrates this idea.

Note that the participation level of both manager and subordinate in goal setting can range from low to high. If the levels for both

		Participation by Manager	
		Low	High
		I	II
	Low	No Goals	Assigned Goals
Participation by Subordinate			
	High	IV Self-Set Goals	III Interactive Goals

Participation in Goal Setting

manager and subordinate are low, then the result is a "no goal" condition (Cell I). This is the situation when neither the manager nor the subordinate is interested in setting goals.

In Cell II, "assigned goals," the manager provides the main input for the goal-setting process. Generally, this is the traditional model of manager-subordinate relations, where the function of the manager is to give directions and make assignments and the function of the employee is to carry out the assignments, including complying with assigned goals.

In Cell III, "interactive goals," the level of participation by both manager and subordinate in setting goals is high. Both provide substantive input to the process and to the final outcomes. Classic management by objectives is generally considered to be an example of interactive goals.

David Packard, cofounder of Hewlett-Packard, describes how his company used interactive goal setting during the early days of his company. "These objectives were not things that [were] dictated, these were ideas that we generated working together with people . . . I believe it's very important that if people have some part in making the decisions that they're going to be involved with, they're going to be much more effective in implementing those decisions."[2]

Finally, Cell IV represents "self-set goals," where employees have the major responsibility for establishing their own goals within an overall organizational goal framework—the ultimate self-leadership condition. The SuperLeader's objective is to move employees toward this condition.

An executive can use these four cells to decide what degree of both executive and subordinate participation to aim for in the relationship with a specific employee. Perhaps the easiest and first rule of thumb is this: almost any way of setting goals is better than none at all. Nevertheless, Cell I is the least-preferred cell.

When considering the other cells, an executive should take into account the employee's time and experience on the job as well as the degree of the employee's skill and capabilities. For a new employee, whose job-related and self-leadership skills may yet be undeveloped, an executive may wish to begin with assigned goals, Cell II. Within a short period of time, the executive should endeavor to move toward Cell III, interactive goals. Usually, the best way to accomplish this is to begin by "guided participation," that is, asking the employee to propose his or her own goals. At this stage, the executive still retains substantial control over goal setting, actively proposing and perhaps imposing some of the goals. Usually, this is the give and take, sometimes regarded as "negotiation," that is typical of the traditional MBO technique.

Finally, for true self-leadership to develop and flourish, the Super-Leader will deliberately move toward Cell IV, employee self-set goals. In this situation, the executive serves as a source of information and experience, as a sounding board, and as the transmitter of the overall organizational goals. But in the end, in a true self-leadership situation the employee is given substantial latitude to establish his or her own goals.

Among the more interesting and extreme examples of institutionalized self-set goals is the "Research Fellows" program at IBM. These high-status, high-performing scientists have reached the peak of the dual-career ladder system at IBM. Each Research Fellow is awarded a research budget—reputed to be about $1 million a year—with little or no restrictions regarding its use. Fellows make their own decisions about how those research resources will be allocated. Obviously, IBM believes its investment in the self-leadership capabilities of these eminent scientists will pay off in the long run.

Difficulties of Transition to Self-Set Goals

Often, deliberate movement toward self-set goals creates a dilemma for the executive. Inevitably, the time will come when the employee seems to be making a mistake; perhaps the employee sets an inappropriate goal, an incorrect target level, or an "action plan" for goal achievement that is not well conceived. Recognizing the mistake, the executive faces the choice of whether to intervene or to allow the employee to proceed. Of course, the overall importance of the situation will have a bearing on the executive's final choice; the more critical the goal, the more likely the executive is to intervene.

But here are some guidelines. First, the executive should ask a lot of questions. Generally, questions are less intimidating and power oriented than outright rejection of the goal, and they typically deliver an implicit message to the employee that something might be wrong without making a direct challenge. Questions help the subordinate to clarify consequences of projected courses of action or to detail specifics of the "action plan." Questions provide the employee with opportunities to reconsider previously chosen courses of action without undue threat.

But questions don't always evoke a change of direction, and the subordinate employee sometimes remains committed to a course of action that, in the end, the executive believes is wrong. What next? Consider the following training case:

TRAINING CASE
MARY HANSON

You are a division manager in a large, American-based corporation. Your division has enjoyed very positive results in cost efficiency and profitability over the past few years following the introduction of an extensive employee involvement and development program. You are strongly convinced that a highly participative style of management within your division is largely responsible for these results. Consequently, you continuously attempt to extensively involve your subor-

---

dinates in important decisions and to encourage them to do likewise with their subordinates.

The process of facilitating the involvement of your subordinates has not always been easy. Since the rest of the corporation tends to be considerably more autocratic, your division sometimes seems to be a bit of an oddity within the company. When managers are transferred in, they sometimes express some initial discomfort with, and display some resistance to, the level of autonomy they experience in their positions.

Mary Hanson is a case in point. In her previous position, she worked in a highly structured environment for a manager who was very competent technically and who liked to maintain a tight rein on his unit's operations. Mary had become very comfortable with that environment, which afforded her little autonomy and responsibility, although she was a high performer in her previous system. Consequently, since entering your division she has struggled and resisted committing herself to her new responsibilities. Over time, however, you have been able to help her become a more independent, self-led manager. In particular, in the last couple of weeks she has taken obvious pride in developing a new service program, on her own, for your division's clients.

Mary has just entered your office to present her goals for the coming quarter. As you listen to her speak, you find yourself feeling generally uncomfortable. Based on your years of experience in the business, you believe her plan will require extra resources and will not provide an adequate added value to your product to justify the increased costs that will have to be passed on to your clients. At the same time, you are impressed with the creativity and effort that she has obviously put into developing her ideas. It is apparent to you that Mary has really done her homework and sincerely believes the added costs will be more than compensated for by increased demand for your products. Also, you have never seen her so enthusiastic about her work since entering the division.

She has just finished presenting her ideas and is eagerly waiting for your response. What will you say?

Generally, except under the most critical conditions, a Super-Leader will allow the employee to continue on her chosen course. We suggest that the executive's formal authority to change this course be used only when the decision has very serious consequences. In the long run, making mistakes is part of any learning process, and it is an inevitable and necessary part of learning self-leadership. Hopefully, having made a mistake, the employee will have gained a useful developmental experience and will be less likely to repeat the error.

An important factor is whether the type of culture exists where the employee can positively learn from mistakes. Organizations that encourage risk taking are much more likely to find significant improvements in employee productivity and performance. Most of all, employees need to feel that making a mistake is not a "capital offense," but is only one (perhaps unpleasant) milestone leading toward the full maturity of their capability to be self-leaders.

We have found that the goal-setting factor is frequently the most difficult for traditional leaders to understand and accept on their road to effective SuperLeadership. Good leaders intuitively understand the effects on performance of "knowing where they are going." During subordinate employees' critical transition from traditional external leadership to self-leadership, previous dependency on superior authority needs to be unlearned. In its place, employees must develop a strong sense of confidence in their own abilities to set realistic and challenging goals on their own.

But frequently this transition is not very smooth, leaving the employee wondering why "the boss" is not providing more help, and the executive biting his lip to avoid telling the employee to do the "right thing." Nevertheless, effective SuperLeaders sometimes *deliberately withhold* goals that, at other times, in other places, they would be more than willing to provide. Self-led employees must learn to stand on their own.

Once through this critical transition phase, the effects on the self-led employee's performance can be remarkable. Employees develop a much better understanding of the full range of their own capabilities and of the demands of their surroundings. Most of all, setting their own goals produces a motivation and psychological commitment that

energizes employees to greater and greater achievements. Super-
Leaders who have successfully unleashed the power of self-led employees understand the ultimate reward and satisfaction of managing
these individuals. Furthermore, they can see beyond the problem of
living with the difficult days of transition into self-leadership.

**In the long run, making mistakes is part of any
learning process, and it is an inevitable and
necessary part of learning self-leadership.**

DIFFICULTIES AND REWARDS OF TRANSITION

The process of change in becoming a SuperLeader is not easy.
Martin Berger, a corporate executive vice-president, described how
he felt and what happened to him as he underwent this change on the
road to SuperLeadership.[3] One of the first steps is to recognize one's
overinvolvement, compulsiveness, and unwillingness to let go. "I'm
involved in a great many projects in my company, and I can't do them
casually."

Berger is candid about his own motivation. "Thinking about this
compulsion, I realized I don't do it for the money, nor do I have
ambition any longer for promotion. It's something in me . . . ," he
explained. "I am sure that at least part of my problem is that I am still
seeking 'stroking' . . . approval. . . . I'm still anxious that my bosses
know when I do something well. I get especially upset if someone gets
credit for something that I believe I did."

But Berger has a plan for changing, one that sounds somewhat like
becoming a SuperLeader. "I think there is a way. I call it making
myself into a 'backroom person.' . . . Now I'm attempting to become
a person who makes things happen without appearing to be
there. . . . I work hard at making myself invisible.

"When someone says, 'Gee, we sure have been lucky getting this
done' and I know it got done because of my behind-the-scenes phone
calls, meetings, and reports, I am beginning to experience pleasure,"

he continued. "When I concentrate on my new role as éminence grise, my yearning to say 'Hey I did it' diminishes. This allows me to make contributions with less stress."

As Berger talked about his method, he became more indirect. "My way of dealing with it is to think of myself as a combination coach-spectator. What that means is that I spend a lot of time listening before I do anything. When someone describes a plan of action that I think is incorrect, I don't take the plan apart and substitute my own. I let the speaker finish and wait to hear what the others have to say. Usually, if I see something wrong, someone else will too.

"I recognize that this approach has its risks," Berger admitted. "I may hide myself so successfully that people will start to wonder what I'm doing and decide I'm not necessary. It is also possible that the effort to be silent and to relinquish credit may take more out of me than an excess of activity. So far though, that has not been the case." Berger further realized the benefits and described an incident where he ". . . learned a great deal. . . . I gathered information that I don't think I could have gotten any other way. I was more involved in what was [really] going on. . . . I was in an improved situation relative to the business."

GOAL SETTING AND SELF-LEADERSHIP

Goal setting is a critical part of SuperLeadership. Research and experience show that setting specific goals generally leads to higher performance than if no goals or ambiguous goals were set. Moderately difficult goals generally lead to higher performance than easy or impossible goals.

The major challenge to the SuperLeader is to develop the capability of subordinate employees to realistically set their own goals, including goals for their own self-leadership development. The transition from assigned goals to self-set goals can be very difficult, but employees need to have some latitude in making mistakes during this critical period. Sometimes, a SuperLeader may even deliberately withhold goals from a subordinate as a planned strategy to develop subordinate self-leadership. Perhaps the most critical factor of all is whether the SuperLeader sets a personal goal to encourage and facilitate a subordinate's own goal setting.

CREATING POSITIVE THOUGHT PATTERNS

In chapter 3 we addressed self-management of thought patterns for effective self-leadership in some detail, focusing especially on beliefs, self-talk, and imagined experiences as the primary building blocks for creating and maintaining constructive thought patterns. Throughout that chapter, we also touched on some ways the SuperLeader can, through modeling, encouragement, guidance, reinforcement, and so forth, facilitate employees' constructive thought patterns. Here we will address in more detail some important features of the Super-Leader's role in this regard. We will especially focus on the importance of facilitating positive self-expectations in subordinates.

Consider the following conversation between Anne and George:

"George, what are you doing for lunch today?"

"No plans. Do you have something in mind?"

"I sure do. I want to celebrate! I'm feeling great! Let's go to Alfredo's and pig out."

"What's the occasion?" George asked.

"I just sold my first computer system this morning. You know, I just might make it in this business!"

"Did you have any doubt?"

"Listen—a year ago, if anyone had told me I had the technical capability to understand a computer-system application, I would have laughed! But Fred has had confidence in me all along. He gave me the training I needed, and showed me how to do it. Most of all, he always showed confidence in my abilities—even when I had doubts about myself. He always told me I could do it. Now I've done it on my own, and I know I can do it again and again! Let's get Fred to go, too."

Perhaps Fred is a SuperLeader. He certainly has succeeded in creating positive thought patterns in Anne. Most of all, when Anne didn't seem to have confidence in herself, Fred was persistent in supporting Anne with a belief that she could do what was required. He also seemed to use rehearsal to bolster Anne's confidence.

Constructive thought patterns are an essential component of self-leadership. Sometimes, especially at the early stages of employment, employees do not have adequate natural habits of constructive thinking about themselves. They have doubts and fears—a general lack of confidence in themselves. At this stage, the actions of the Super-Leader are critical: his or her positive comments sometimes must serve as a temporary surrogate for the employee's own constructive thought patterns.

The SuperLeader creates productive thought patterns by carefully expressing confidence in the employee's ability to extend her present level of competence. Support and encouragement are necessary. In many ways, this expression of confidence is the essence of the guided-participation phase of teaching each employee to lead herself.

Here's another case where a sensitive manager helps an employee to use productive patterns of thought,[4] this time to overcome his anxiety about speaking before a group, a fear shared, according to some estimates, by perhaps as many as 85 percent of all people.

"Oh, Helen," exclaimed Keith, "I'm never going to be able to do it." Keith and Helen were talking about Keith's assignment to make his first presentation to the Finance Committee. Since Keith worked for Helen, she was particularly concerned that he do well—both for Keith's own sake and for the reputation of her department. She knew that the development of Keith's presentation skills was an important ingredient in Keith's career advancement.

"Public speaking used to bother me, too," replied Helen. "I thought I would die when I was assigned my first presentation."

Keith was skeptical because he knew that Helen was a highly regarded presenter. "I don't believe it," he said. "Everybody knows how good you are."

"I'm not kidding," said Helen. "I was shaking in my boots during my first presentation, but I managed to stumble through. I knew I needed to get help, so I attended a course at the university that was designed to relieve speech anxiety. I learned a lot, too."

"Like what?" asked Keith.

"Well, I learned some physical things, like using keyword notes, and not memorizing or reading. I learned how to use visual aids like transparencies. I learned how to make eye contact with the audience. I found that using a pointer helped relieve my anxiety about what to do with my hands. But the part that really helped me the most was the way I changed my thinking about making a speech."

"Changed your thinking!" exclaimed Keith. "What do you mean by that?"

"First, I tried to think of my presentation *not* as a performance that would be evaluated, but more as a communication. I even tried to think about it as ordinary communication, even though I knew, of course, that it wasn't exactly ordinary. Once you think of a speech as communication, you can think of it in terms of your normal everyday conversation rather than giving a big performance. This nonperformance way of thinking helped me realize that the real objective is to communicate.

"The next step followed rather logically. What I really tried to do was to speak the way I talk. I tried to think of my presentation as a casual conversation with someone I respected.

"My instructor used an exercise that was very effective. He would tell me to forget about giving a speech and to simply talk spontaneously. He and I would talk back and forth in a conversational mode, but I would use the outline notes that I had developed for my speech as a guide. What I found was that I was able to use natural language and to maintain this conversational style as the keynote of my presentation.

"Once I got onto this technique, I would practice this conversational style by myself. You find that you never say what you want to say exactly as you prepared it, and this preserves the naturalness of the presentation."

"So now you have no anxiety?" asked Keith.

Helen laughed. "Well," she said, "I still have some anxiety, but I'm able to keep it under control, and even use it in a positive way to keep up my enthusiasm and motivation. But most of all, I just keep thinking of my presentations as conversations, and this keeps my confidence up. After all, you know I *do* like to talk!"

"Do you think you could help me?" asked Keith.

"Sure," replied Helen. "First, let's work on your outline notes, so you're sure of your objective, your structure, and your content. But *do not* write the speech! Then we can use the technique of my instructor, rehearsing the presentation as a conversation between the two of us. After we've done it a couple of times, we'll invite one or two sympathetic friends to join us as we go over it again. You'll see. You'll end up being a pro. It's all in the way you think!"

Of course, this SuperLeadership behavior is well founded in the results of research on the self-fulfilling prophecy: if a person believes something can be done, that belief makes it more likely that it *will* be done. Perhaps Helen was playing "Professor Higgins" to Keith's "Eliza." She was creating the positive conditions that were just right for Keith to learn and achieve on his own. In particular, she served as a credible model since she had faced the same difficulties and had succeeded in overcoming them. Also, she provided encouragement and guidance for Keith to accomplish the same result.

The SuperLeader creates productive thought patterns by carefully expressing confidence in the employee's ability to extend her present level of competence.

Most of all, through her expression of confidence in Keith, she was helping him to create productive patterns of thinking—new constructive thought habits. Through a step-by-step process, she was helping Keith to reexamine his beliefs about and images of what public speaking really is. In the end, Keith will likely find himself speaking more effectively to himself (constructive self-talk) as well as to his audiences.

PROFILES IN SUPERLEADERSHIP: DR. RUTH RANDALL[1]

Dr. Ruth Randall, Minnesota's state commissioner of education, originally captured the attention of Governor Rudy Perpich with her creative and dynamic leadership during her short term as superintendent of an independent school district in the Twin Cities metropolitan area. As superintendent, she involved all kinds of people—teachers, administrators, parents, and students—to an amazing degree. She initiated a commitment to and eagerness for progress and excellence in education.

Dr. Randall appears to have been a strikingly successful leader. First, following her term as superintendent, the district demonstrated significant academic success: students in the district were ranked above the national average in every area and at every level tested using the California Achievement Test. Parental involvement in the district was also strikingly high, ranging from 70 percent parental attendance at high school conferences to over 90 percent attendance at the elementary school conferences. Under Randall, the district's impressive guiding philosophy was established: "to treat each learner as a unique individual with unique potential, whose limits only he or she will ultimately determine." That philosophy rests heavily on recognizing the importance of self-leadership.

In many other ways, Randall's leadership was exemplary. When the district was faced with serious budget cutbacks in 1981, for example, Randall expanded her programs to revitalize the district rather than acquiescing in the retrenchment. She used the budget crisis as a means of galvanizing people throughout the district into action rather than allowing it to be a source of demoralization. To accomplish this, she helped create a vision of a greater purpose for the district and solicited vast participation by collecting the opinions and tapping the energies of everyone who was willing to contribute—staff, students, parents, and citizens—in determining how to make the budget reductions. In the end the budget cuts were made without alienating district members from one another or from Randall. The budget also was unanimously approved by the school board. The teachers rewarded Randall with a standing ovation for her efforts. Even several community members sent unsolicited letters to Randall thanking her for providing them with a say in the process.

Randall's innovative introduction of school-based management (see page 132) into her district was perhaps her most impressive leadership contribution. It moved the district structurally toward a strong self-leadership orientation. And the district's efforts in this regard were rewarded with a sizable multiyear grant from the Northwest Area Foundation.

Innovation was rampant throughout the district during her tenure. At the end of her two-year term, the district had received and recorded more than three hundred suggestions from staff employees for innovative ventures. In the end, Dr. Randall, singled out for admiration by the governor, was appointed to the prestigious position of state commissioner of education.

Dr. Randall, like no other school superintendent we are familiar with, has exemplified effective SuperLeadership. By the time she was appointed commissioner of education, she had already established a legacy of leadership that encouraged and helped many to realize their fullest potential. She was indeed very effective at leading others to lead themselves. Dr. Randall's people-focused style illustrates in some vivid and unique ways the characteristics of SuperLeadership in action.

FACILITATING PARTICIPATION OF LARGE NUMBERS OF PEOPLE

Perhaps one significant measure of effective SuperLeadership is effective personalized involvement of subordinates, even when they represent huge numbers of people. This can largely be accomplished by modeling SuperLeadership behavior, facilitating and reinforcing it in immediate subordinates, and encouraging them to practice the same type of leadership with the ranks below them. But in addition to encouraging a focus on self-leadership down through the ranks, the SuperLeader establishes a model for every worker in the organization by her own example. This can be particularly true when dramatic events or ceremonies thrust the SuperLeader into the spotlight for all to observe.

On the morning of February 18, 1983, Dr. Ruth Randall, then superintendent, conducted a meeting involving all of the several hundred staff members employed under her jurisdiction. She had recently initiated a major shift in her school district from a centralized management approach to "school-based management"—essentially self-management at the school level. This innovative approach was designed to more fully exploit the capabilities and commitment of teachers, administrators, parents, and, ultimately, students of the district. The first agenda of the meeting, originally to include some twenty speakers, had been thrown out under the suggestion of a close associate. Instead, Randall focused on the reasons behind the dramatic changes and explored how staff members felt about these changes. Dr. Randall spoke for about forty minutes and then announced a break—but no one would leave the auditorium. Sensing their unusual interest, she promptly began to answer questions that her staff members had been invited to write earlier in the meeting and that had subsequently been collected. Thus her new agenda became a stack of unsorted and unscreened cards containing anonymous questions.

At 10:00 A.M. Randall had a previously scheduled appointment. She was besieged on stage by persons requesting that she change the agenda again and continue to answer the questions. She agreed to return at 12:30 P.M. to continue the meeting. When the meeting resumed, she proceeded to respond to every issue raised by the staff. Consequently, each person at the meeting was provided with an opportunity to contribute and to be personally involved in the agenda of the meeting that day. The level of interest during that meeting, which lasted for hours, was nothing short of amazing.

In a later interview, she commented that she felt she had actually achieved a dialogue between herself and some eight hundred people. Many who had attended described the meeting in charismatic terms—as a strange phenomenon in which the room almost seemed filled with a special power drawing the staff closer together and during which their superintendent won an unusual level of respect. Perhaps more important, Ruth Randall had dramatically and vividly provided a model of SuperLeadership in which the views of every individual were recognized as critically important to the success of the organization. Notably, in this case, she accomplished this with hundreds of people at one time. Clearly, the meeting served as a dramatic event in which self-leadership was encouraged and fundamental Super-Leadership ideals were transferred to subordinates through vivid example.

RANDALL'S SUPERLEADERSHIP APPROACH: SOME BACKGROUND AND PHILOSOPHY

Before becoming district superintendent, Randall held the position of assistant for personnel. Interestingly, many described her style in this previous position as rather authoritarian. The nicknames her associates coined for her, such as "ruthless," "Mother Superior," and "railroad," reflected this view. Upon her appointment as superintendent, many were concerned that her leadership style would justify those earlier impressions. It soon became apparent, however, that while Randall was a strong, even tough, leader, she wanted, encouraged, and expected others to contribute their own significant strengths.

As she explained it, much of the key is

> recognizing what the skills of people are and using those. Anything you do you need to set goals and strategies and tactics, and rely on people to get there. Sometimes you assign but other times you just say [the issues] and you have people coming up to you saying they would like to work on this or that. That's how you find out what the skill, or the talent, or what the interest is. If I have a regret, it's that there are so many people out there that would like to do things or work on something but you just can't get to everybody. . . . If only you [the leader] can do something that people need that's *help* . . . but if you reach the point where a lot of other people can do it that's *helpful*.

Much of Dr. Randall's orientation toward helping others reach their capabilities apparently resulted from a thorough self-analysis following her husband's unexpected death in an automobile accident several years ago.

It [her husband's death] helped me to crystallize what motivates me. I had to sort through a lot of things . . . in working through [the grief process]. I made a conscious decision to be happy, to do and be involved in things that make me happy. I had to sort through what is important—power, money, clothes, position—and I came down to it has to be people. If I'm to be living in this world it has to be doing with people, helping people with their whole potential. It is what we do with other people that is important . . . not doing for them; [again] that's only *help*, but giving them opportunity and wings for themselves—then it's *helpful*.

SuperLeadership in Action: Facilitating Self-Leadership in Individuals

Throughout her tenure as superintendent, Dr. Randall displayed an unusual talent for stimulating innovative change by drawing on the ideas and abilities of others. School-based management, the primary feature of the changes she initiated as superintendent, involved passing a great deal of control regarding primary issues such as budgeting, staffing, and curriculum to the school level. One might view school-based management as an ambitious and comprehensive form of participative management. A major theme of this approach is a relinquishing of centralized control at the district-office level in favor of participation and "ownership" for school district employees and residents.

Dr. Randall has a strong personality with a strong will, yet she displays an unusual adeptness at singling people out. She has a knack for discovering burning purposes and interests people hold deep inside and then simultaneously releasing and harnessing this energy for positive change. She often remarked that "teachers don't realize how powerful they are. I keep telling them that." She has had her share of disagreements with people but she has also displayed a remarkable ability for recognizing the value she saw in others. In one district meeting, for example, a teacher kept a tally of how many times Randall used specific names to acknowledge and praise the work and efforts of others—the final count came to 221. That is 221 specific incidents of verbal positive reinforcement in one meeting!

Randall pointed out that she saw a significant part of her role as helping others to see and acknowledge their own value, abilities, and contributions—positive patterns of thinking. She spoke with obvious conviction about how so many people just can't see the significant achievement of which they are capable. She frequently asked people throughout the district to serve on task forces and special assignments beyond their normal responsibilities—an apparent attempt to simultaneously tap the potential of others and to foster their individual development.

Dr. Randall also displayed considerable tolerance, even when going head-to-head with others who held widely diverging views. During a meeting at one school, a teacher was very vocal and abusive in his comments toward her. Randall made it a point to get the teacher's name and visited both his office and his auto shop class trying to understand his view. At the end of the class meeting, as he described later, she shook "his greasy hand" and obviously won his respect if not his support.

CONCLUSION

In many ways, Randall's style reflects the SuperLeadership model we develop in this book. She relied heavily on the involvement of others, and as a consequence they grew stronger and she became more effective. One school district member described her leadership style this way:

> Well it's the superintendent's style to get a lot of people involved. She brings the administration and teachers and people within the community all into task forces, and seminars, and workshops. . . . Her philosophy is involvement with the greatest number of people. . . . Many superintendents are locked in a chain of command sort of thing. She seeks out input from people that superintendents have traditionally ignored.[2]

A primary message that can be gleaned from Dr. Randall's leadership successes seems clear: no matter how capable and how strong and charismatic a personality a leader possesses, her chances for achieving excellence will be greatly enhanced by relying on and respecting the contributions of others. Dr. Randall has one of the strongest direct leadership personalities we have encountered. Yet her greatest asset seems to be her ability to allow and help others to be their own leaders. In doing so during her term as a superintendent, she helped herself to be a SuperLeader.

7

Developing Self-Leadership through Reward and Reprimand

Georgeanne was smiling as she emerged from Sam's office. As she sat down at her desk next to Frank, he remarked, "You look like the cat that ate the canary. What happened?"

"I wasn't sure how Sam was going to like my plans on the new advertising campaign," she replied. "My original assignment was to just do some research about the competitive product line. But the more I got into it, the more things fell into place."

"What do you mean?" asked Frank.

"Well, as I got into the competitive products, I could see an opening—a niche or opportunity for us. I could see how we could exploit our own distinctive competence. I was in the library, daydreaming a bit, when a whole new integrative theme just came to me. Before I knew it, I had the theme outlined and had started working on the details.

"I just couldn't stop myself," she continued. "Over the next few days, I did a complete thematic workup, along with some sample story boards, and then plotted out a fairly detailed timeline and schedule. I even did a preliminary budget. I know this stuff isn't my job, but I did it because I wanted to see if I could put it together all by myself."

"I see you're smiling," said Frank. "Sam must have liked it."

"He did. He really did. Oh, it wasn't perfect; he had a few suggestions here and there, and I wasn't much good on the budget. There were quite a few things that I didn't know about. But he was very complimentary. He said he was especially pleased with my initiative. I was surprised that he wants me to turn most of my research duties over to Judy so I can concentrate full time on this campaign. And you know what? He said I was a 'real self-starter'!"

In this story, Sam used verbal rewards to reinforce Georgeanne's self-leadership behaviors. More specifically, Sam used *contingent positive reward*, verbal praise, to encourage her initiative, creativity, and innovation. By saying the right thing at the right time, Sam has provided the proper environment to unleash Georgeanne's self-leadership abilities.

In previous chapters, we discussed how the SuperLeader could encourage subordinate self-leadership by providing an appropriate model with his own behavior. We also discussed how the Super-Leader could encourage self-leadership through goal setting. Now, in this chapter, we focus on more direct means that SuperLeaders can use to reinforce subordinate self-leadership.

REWARD AND REINFORCEMENT

One of the SuperLeader's most potent strategies in developing employee self-leadership is reward and reinforcement. Later, we discuss how rewards can be used specifically to encourage and maintain employee self-leadership. First, however, let us examine some more general ideas about rewards in organizations.

Typically, a reward is something that is pleasing or desirable to an employee. A reward becomes a reinforcer when it is given as a consequence of some desirable target behavior by the employee.

When an executive uses rewards to reinforce some desirable target behavior it is an example of *positive management of employee's behavior*. It is positive because the end result, or the consequence, is usually desired by the employee. From the extensive research on the subject of using rewards in organizations, several conclusions or guidelines have been formulated that help to increase the potential effectiveness of positive management.

First, and perhaps most important, is the idea of *contingency*: for a reward to have maximum effectiveness, it must be administered only if the target behavior is performed. In other words, the reward must be contingent upon the behavior of the employee. A reward loses its power to reinforce if it is given when the target behavior has not been performed. A leader should offer praise, for example, only when deserved.

For a reward to have maximum effectiveness, . . . [it] must be contingent upon the behavior of the employee.

It is also useful to classify the type of consequence as either positive or aversive. Positive consequences are desirable or pleasing to the employee, while aversive events are undesirable or displeasing. Also, a consequence can take the form of being either presented or withdrawn.

The particular combination of whether a positive consequence is presented or withdrawn, or whether an aversive consequence is presented or withdrawn, will have different results in terms of increasing or decreasing the future likelihood of the employee behavior. The figure on page 138 shows how these factors can be combined to produce various types of contingencies of reinforcement.

Note that reinforcement, whether positive or negative, always has the effect of increasing the frequency of the employee behavior, while punishment always has the effect of decreasing the behavior. Of course, *reinforce* means "to strengthen."

Second, the more immediately a reward is given after a target behavior, the more effective it is. It is important that the employee associate the reward with the specific target behavior; that is, the employee must perceive the contingent nature of the reward. Significant delays between the target behavior and giving the reward reduce

	Consequence Is Presented	Consequence Is Withdrawn
Positive Environmental Consequence	**I** Positive Reinforcement (Increases Employee Behavior)	**II** Punishment by Removal (Decreases Employee Behavior)
Aversive Environmental Consequence	**III** Punishment by Application (Decreases Employee Behavior)	**IV** Negative Reinforcement (Increases Employee Behavior)

Classification of Various Contingencies of Reinforcement

the likelihood of the employee perceiving the contingency. The following illustrates what can happen if the reward is seriously delayed.

> Chuck brought the "hot" report into Dan's office half a day early. He knew Dan had been anxious to see the report. Dan was distracted and so merely said, "Leave it on the desk." Three weeks later, Dan told Chuck that he appreciated receiving the report before the deadline. After working so hard, this was the first comment Chuck had heard about the report. Chuck thought to himself, "If it was so important, why didn't he say something when I delivered the report?"

Third, the amount or size of a reward can also have an effect. Generally, the larger the amount or size of a contingent reward (a bigger bonus, for example), the greater the likelihood that it will have a future effect. Of course, the amount or size of a reward is relative and has differing effects on different individuals. It is important to determine what amount is viewed as worthwhile by specific individuals.

Last, rewards tend to be more effective if the employee is to a degree in a state of deprivation since the more deprived a person is of the reward, the more likely is its presentation to have the effect of increasing future occurrences of the target behavior. If an employee has recently had his fill of a reward (for example, his den is already full of company award plaques), then the reward will have less effect.

ORGANIZATIONAL REWARDS

What types of rewards are used in organizations? The first answer that comes to mind is material rewards—money, salary, fringe benefits, and so forth. However, organizations offer a wide range of rewards, many of which are not immediately apparent. Included among these other rewards are such things as verbal approval, improved working conditions, and scheduling flexibility. By providing opportunities to perform tasks that offer these rewards, the SuperLeader can take an important step in facilitating employee self-leadership. Later, we will focus on verbal rewards as a special facilitating strategy for the Super-Leader.

In addition, an important class of rewards—sometimes called covert or private events—comes from the task itself or is self-administered. Indeed, a reward such as self-congratulations for accomplishing a particularly difficult assignment can be a potent reinforcer. In chapter 2 we discussed self-rewards in some detail. Also in chapter 3, we discussed natural rewards, those that stem mainly from the task itself or the employee's own sense of accomplishment, self-control, and purpose. Natural rewards are enhanced when a SuperLeader encourages an employee to redesign his own task. Consider the following case of Pam and her boss, Steve, at Pam's performance review.

> "I know I'm doing a good job, Steve, but to be honest, I just don't feel as motivated lately. At first, mastering my new job was enough, but now it's been a year and I'm not sure I like it, even though you do say I'm a top performer."
>
> "Maybe that's because you haven't redesigned your job yet," Steve responded in a matter-of-fact tone.
>
> "Redesign my job?" Pam shot back, looking suspicious. "I don't have the authority to do that."
>
> "Sure you do. In fact, if you don't redesign your job it will redesign

you, and probably in some less-than-desirable ways. No job fits us perfectly. And while we need to complete our assigned responsibilities, there are usually several ways to go about performing them. You need to seek out the rewards that are built into doing your job competently and in your own way. And don't ever lose sight of the needed service you are providing in your work, Pam. You deserve to enjoy your job more."

"Wow, redesign my own job as long as I still effectively perform my responsibilities. I never thought of it that way. I've had a lot of ideas about how I'd like to perform my duties differently for a long time but I thought I'm not supposed to make decisions like that. I can't wait to get started," Pam concluded as she rose from her chair to leave.

Steve smiled as he noticed that old look of motivation on Pam's face that he used to always see in Pam's early months on the job. And he couldn't help silently laughing to himself as he reflected that she never even mentioned the big raise he had given her a couple of minutes earlier. "I guess with some high achievers like Pam, there are some rewards that they carry with them inside that may be more effective than anything I have to offer," he thought to himself as he watched Pam walk off with newfound enthusiasm in her stride.

The figure on page 141 shows an extensive list of typical rewards from within organizations. SuperLeaders are adept at using a wide range of rewards, especially to reinforce subordinate self-leadership. And helping others to find natural rewards in their work will be high on their list.

SUPERLEADERSHIP: MOVING EMPLOYEES TOWARD SELF-ADMINISTERED AND NATURAL REWARDS

For the most part, conventional viewpoints about using organizational rewards tend to focus on target behaviors that are very task-related: behavioral management programs usually concentrate on specific tasks or parts of jobs that contribute directly to an individual's performance. Moreover, these programs tend to concentrate on so-called extrinsic rewards as a means of implementing contingent reinforcement. One example is incentive pay systems.

We are basically in sympathy with this behavioral-management

Material	Fringe Benefits	Status Symbols	Social/Interpersonal	Natural Rewards (e.g., from the Task)	Self-Administered
Pay	Medical plan	Corner office	Informal recognition	Sense of competence, self-control and purpose resulting from: a pleasant work environment, interesting, challenging tasks	Self-recognition
Pay raise	Company automobile	Office with window	Praise		Self-praise
Stock options	Insurance	Carpeting	Smile		Self-congratulations
Profit sharing	Pension contributions	Drapes	Evaluative feedback		Self-administered physical rewards (e.g., a break, a cup of coffee . . .)
Bonus plans	Product discount plans	Paintings	Compliments		
Incentive plans	Vacation trips	Watches	Nonverbal signals		
Christmas bonus	Recreation facilities	Rings	Pat on the back	Job with more responsibility	Self-administered cognitive rewards (e.g., imagining favorite vacation spot, imagining receiving recognition at an award ceremony . . .)
	Work breaks		Ask for suggestion	Job rotation	
	Club privileges		Invitations to coffee/ lunch	Output feedback	
	Expense account		Newspaper article		
			Formal awards/ recognition		
			Wall plaque		

Typical Rewards from Organizational Environments

viewpoint and generally believe that material rewards should indeed be used to reinforce job-related target behaviors. However, the idea of reward and reinforcement takes on a new perspective when seen through the eyes of the SuperLeader. If the purpose of the Super-Leader is to lead others to self-leadership, then an essential ingredient of SuperLeadership is to teach employees how to reward themselves and to build natural rewards into their work and then to encourage and facilitate their doing so. This philosophy is much less dependent on external reward systems to influence employee behavior.

The characteristics of SuperLeader reward systems are thus somewhat different than those of more traditional reward systems. The SuperLeader attempts to construct a reward system that emphasizes self-administered and natural rewards and, in a comparative sense, deemphasizes externally administered rewards. Thus, the focus of the reward system shifts from the left side of the chart on page 141 to the right side; from material and fringe types of rewards to a stronger emphasis on natural rewards that stem more from the task itself and from self-administration of rewards.

There is a different type of dependency relationship between superiors and subordinates under a traditional situation: even a high-performing employee is relatively dependent upon the power, authority, information, and ability of his manager. High performance is maintained through a leadership system that focuses on unambiguous directions and goals from the manager, with performance-contingent rewards clearly controlled by the manager. Overall, research has shown that this system is more than workable and can produce high-performing subordinate employees. Nevertheless, it is a system of hierarchial dependency that tends to produce task-focused conformists that frequently turn out a minimum of creativity and innovation. Such employees are good at following orders. A traditional leader tends to emphasize short-term task performance more than long-term effectiveness.

The SuperLeader, on the other hand, develops an entirely different system with subordinate employees, a system of independence rather than dependence. Within an overall system of goals and rewards, employees who have developed their self-leadership skills are much more focused on self-set goals, self-design of tasks, and self-administered rewards. These self-directed individuals are quite different from the high-performing conformists of the traditional leadership situation. While such independent employees can be distressing to more traditional leaders because they may seem less controllable, Super-Leaders will tend to appreciate them for their creativity, innovation, and productivity as they strive to unleash and maximize their self-leadership.

An essential ingredient of SuperLeadership is to teach employees how to reward themselves and to build natural rewards into their work and then to encourage and facilitate their doing so.

PUNISHMENT

When the new systems department was formed, Chris was appointed manager. This was Chris's first managerial assignment, although she had considerable experience in the technical aspect of the work and she had been considered a top performer by her previous bosses. She had always given a lot of attention to detail. Chris was resolved that the department was going to be "run right." Having had experience with weak managers before, she was determined that the performance of her department was going to be outstanding. Above all, she was not going to be tolerant of any subordinates who were not willing to do the work in the way Chris thought it should be done.

Within a month, Chris's subordinates knew she "meant business." The first week, she gave Mary a public dressing down because Mary had arrived five minutes late for work. Chris also became quite distressed and expressed her displeasure when one of her staff made an error in his work. When Skip made a special effort to complete the report that Chris wanted, Chris said nothing about his extra effort. In addition, within the first month, Chris had Skip transferred to a lower-paying job because "he couldn't do the work."

When a year had gone by, Dale Slobin, the assistant personnel manager, was called into the office of Chris's boss, the district vice-president. "I'd like you to take some special time to look at Chris's department," said the vice-president. "We thought that Chris had the potential to do an excellent job, and the first few months, the performance of her department got off to a good start. Lately, however, things seem to keep going wrong. First, the turnover and absenteeism in her department is terrible. Over 50 percent of her employees have quit or requested a transfer in the first year. In addition, we seem to have a great deal of trouble when something unusual comes up. Chris's department seems to be able to handle the routine things OK, but when we get special requests or when we have to develop a new procedure, we seem to have a lot of trouble. Her people don't seem to have the creativity and the 'get up and go' that I thought she'd be able to inspire. In addition, I just haven't seen any signs of loyalty and cohesiveness within her department.

"Most of all," he continued, "I'd like you to make an assessment of Chris's health and emotional stability. The launching of this new department has been stressful, and I'm beginning to worry about Chris herself and her ability to take care of herself under difficult conditions. The bottom line of what I'm asking you to do is to help me in my decision about whether I should replace Chris as manager."

Fortunately, Chris is probably not really an Attila the Hun, and with some guidance, counseling, and training, she might be able to adapt. But most employees have at one time or another encountered a disagreeable, aversive supervisor. From a technical viewpoint, this type of boss uses an excessive amount of punishment to impose his will upon subordinate employees.

For at least a short period of time, employees will accept this behavior because of the power that positions of authority typically hold. Nevertheless, we know that excessive amounts of supervisory punitive behavior can lead to poor morale, excessive absenteeism and turnover, and limited creativity and innovation. It may, in the short term, keep somebody's nose to the grindstone, but the long-term efficacy of this mode of behavior is limited. As author Ken Blanchard has said, "Most managers can get things done when they are around to nag and push. However, the real test of leadership is when management isn't present . . . which is about 70 percent of the time."[1]

Punishment or aversive control of employee behavior is not all that uncommon in organizations today. *Aversive* means "unpleasant";

aversive control is the use of something unpleasant or displeasing to control employee behavior. Sometimes punishment is formal, as in a disciplinary layoff. But informal punishment, delivered through the use of unpleasant, critical, or disagreeable verbal behavior, is more frequent. We typically think of this behavior as a reprimand.

A reprimand can be contingent on some actual undesirable behavior or omission on the part of an employee. Much more damaging is a noncontingent reprimand, one not delivered to reprimand any specific employee behavior. Noncontingent reprimand in particular leads to poor initiative and excessive turnover. Consider the following story.

> "My boss is an autocrat and a dictator," complained Mary. "Most of all, he likes to threaten and intimidate people and always to keep them on edge. Last month when I asked him why we were deemphasizing the Morrow account, he said it was none of my business. He said I should just do as I'm told."
>
> "Why does he act like that?" asked George.
>
> "I don't really know," replied Mary. "I overheard someone ask him once why he was such an SOB; he just laughed and said it kept people on their toes. I just know that I'm leaving as soon as I can find a new position."

From a behavioral viewpoint, reprimand *should* be easy to understand. When an employee does something wrong, the manager provides a contingent aversive consequence, and the undesirable employee behavior *should* be reduced or eliminated. In the short term, punishment usually works, which is one reason it is seemingly so attractive as a means to influence an employee.

"The real test of leadership is when management isn't present."

But in the long term, the efficacy of punishment is much more complex and leaves much to be desired. Several undesired side effects stem from overuse of punishment. First, the suppression of undesirable employee behavior is only temporary. As soon as the supervisor is out of sight, the bad behavior is likely to resume. Punishment leads to high turnover and absenteeism. Excessive use of punishment can be one of the leading causes of union-organizing campaigns that are fired by hostility toward management rather than cooperation.

Most of all, a complex and sometimes confusing set of emotions accompany punishment. Despite a supervisor's best intentions, punishment typically evokes a strong emotional reaction, sometimes even leading to aggressive and disruptive behavior. At the least, punishment is a leading cause of apathetic, noncreative performance. How many of us have heard an employee explain, "Just tell me what to do and I'll do it—but I won't do anything more." Frequently, "working by the book" can be a disaster.

Of course, we strongly recommend an emphasis on positive management techniques. Research has generally shown that the use of positive reinforcement as a dominant leadership practice is generally more effective in managing employee behavior in the long term. Yet, aversive influence occasionally has an appropriate place in a manager's repertoire, particularly when dealing with unethical or unsafe behavior that endangers others, when giving constructive feedback to newer employees, or when handling a particular employee who is chronically troublesome.

An executive might find it helpful to remember certain tips when using reprimand. Following these tips will help assure that the reprimand is constructive. First, a reprimand should follow the occurrence of the undesired target behavior as immediately as possible. If a supervisor waits an unnecessary length of time, the reprimand is likely to lose effectiveness. Consider the following example.

Ms. Frisch wondered why she was being called into the assistant manager's office. When she arrived, she knew from the serious look on Mr. Jenkins's face that the visit wasn't going to be pleasant.

"I just wanted you to know that I noticed it when you were discourteous to that customer last month," Mr. Jenkins began, "and I plan to remember it when your performance evaluation comes up."

Ms. Frisch was shocked. "Which customer are you talking about?" she calmly asked, even though she was trembling inside. After several minutes of discussion, Ms. Frisch still wasn't sure which incident Mr.

Jenkins was referring to. As she left his office, she thought about whether she should begin to look for a new job.

Aversive influence should be tied directly and obviously to the particular undesirable target behavior. Verbal reprimands should never be delivered about behavior in general and especially should never be delivered about a so-called bad attitude. An effective reprimand will pinpoint and specifically describe the undesirable behavior that is to be avoided in the future. In the last example, Mr. Jenkins could have handled the problem more effectively:

After the customer left, Mr. Jenkins waited a few minutes and then came up to Ms. Frisch and quietly said, "Let's talk about that last customer. First, your decision was correct; his requests were out of line and it was not appropriate to provide a service that was against company policy. But do you think you handled him the best way you could?"

Embarrassed, Ms. Frisch managed to reply, "No—I guess I muffed it."

"Now that we have a moment to think about it," said Mr. Jenkins, "what do you think might have been done?"

"Well," Ms. Frisch hesitated, "I guess I shouldn't have lost my temper."

"Right," said Mr. Jenkins. "More specifically, it's important to keep your voice at a normal tone. Even if someone annoys us, it's never acceptable for us to raise our voice to a customer. Also, we should always try to smile, especially at the end of the conversation. This way, we let him know that we are still friendly toward him and still value him as a customer.

"What if he's insistent and won't give up?" continued Mr. Jenkins. "What would be the best thing to do?"

"I guess I should ask him to see you," she replied.

"Right," said Mr. Jenkins. "If you refer him to me, I can take the time to explain the reasons for the policy or to see if I can find some special way to help him solve his problem. This is the kind of courtesy and friendliness that our company expects when we deal with our customers. Do you have any questions, or do you need any help?"

"No," Ms. Frisch replied. "I appreciate your suggestions and I'm sure I'll do better the next time I have that problem." At lunch that day,

147

she commented to a coworker, "You know, even when Mr. Jenkins gives me a little bit of the devil, he is an awfully good assistant manager."

It's always important to let the employee know specifically what *is* expected—for example, a smile and patient, courteous behavior toward customers. In this case, Mr. Jenkins showed some of the characteristics of a budding SuperLeader. Through his questions, he attempted to get Ms. Frisch to engage in self-criticism. Last but not least, the supervisor must strike an appropriate balance between the use of positive and aversive management incidents. When a manager has a practice of using contingent positive reinforcement on a regular basis, the use of an occasional deserved punishment can be quite effective. However, if a manager *never* uses positive reinforcement but relies entirely on aversive management, the long-term negative side effects are likely to counteract any short-term benefits. Most of all, a manager should try to avoid any negative emotion in a reprimand. Focusing entirely on the behaviors helps to reduce negative feelings about the person.

If a manager . . . relies entirely on aversive management, the long-term negative side effects are likely to counteract any short-term benefits.

PUNISHMENT AND SUPERLEADERSHIP

Punishment takes on special importance when an executive attempts to develop self-leadership in subordinate employees. Especially during the transition, when the superior-subordinate relationship becomes very delicate, careless use of reprimand can seriously set back the subordinate's transition to self-leadership.

The issue becomes especially salient when employees make mistakes—sometimes serious mistakes. In our experience, during the transition to self-leadership, some mistakes are inevitable and should be expected as an employee "reaches out." The way the executive responds to the mistakes can ensure or thwart a successful transition.

Consider the case of Stan Williams, who made a mistake when he was too eager to repair his machine on his own initiative. This case is based on an actual incident that we learned about in our research.

TRAINING CASE
STAN WILLIAMS

You are the general manager of a relatively small foundry owned by a large American automobile corporation. The plant has long had a strong reputation for having effective and highly motivated employees who display above-average initiative and innovativeness in solving problems and improving work methods. During your tenure as general manager, you have tried to reinforce this tradition by encouraging the work force to demonstrate independent, self-managed effort.

Among the many changes you initiated when you took the position was a more organized procedure for orienting new employees to the machinery they will operate in the foundry. This is a responsibility you have taken very seriously because you realized from the beginning that the effectiveness of the plant was directly dependent on how well the workers operated the machines to which they were assigned. You have also emphasized to new employees that, while initiative was highly valued in the foundry, new employees should seek help from more experienced operators when they encountered problems that they weren't sure how to deal with.

A few moments ago, Stan Williams, a new employee in the plant, entered your office and reported that he had made a mistake that had resulted in significant damage to his machine and would result in extended and costly production downtime. He explained that when his machine malfunctioned, no one in the plant, which was unusually busy at the time, was available to lend him a hand. In attempting to fix the problem on his own, he improperly grounded the electrical wiring, which resulted in the damage.

As you listened to him explain the situation, you realized that, although you had personally gone over the proper grounding procedure with him during the orientation a couple of days earlier, he had incorrectly performed an important step of the process. Stan has just finished his explanation and is waiting apprehensively and silently for your response. What will you say? What action will you take?

A traditional leader might well have been very punitive in this case. Here's one way a SuperLeader might respond to Stan Williams; it is essentially the way the actual foundry general manager handled the situation:

In the discussion following the grounding incident, the general manager simply asked Stan if he knew why the problem occurred and if he remembered the previous orientation regarding the proper grounding procedure. Stan answered "yes" to both questions and admitted that he had simply forgotten and made a mistake. The general manager suggested that he see Joe (a senior electrician) and go over the grounding procedure again. The general manager also emphasized the safety reasons for knowing the procedure.

As Stan was leaving the office, he turned with a puzzled look on his face and asked, "Aren't you going to chew me out?"

The general manager responded, "No. I could if it would make you feel any better, but I chew people out when they *don't* take initiative, not when they *do*. Do you plan on making the mistake again?"

The employee responded emphatically, "No way. Now I know what I did wrong and I won't do it again."

"Fine," said the general manager. "That's all that needs to be said."

This general manager was leading in a way that encouraged employee initiative, skill development, and self-leadership. Consistent with the SuperLeadership perspective, he served as a model and a source of encouragement, guidance, and reinforcement. Over time, many incidents involving this kind of leadership behavior led to a culture largely based on effective employee self-leadership. During his tenure in the plant, he was frequently amazed by the creative improvements employees made in task procedures. He always made it a point to praise these modifications. Most of all, productivity in the foundry continually increased while he was general manager.

Reprimand is usually the opposite of what needs to be done to develop productive thought patterns in others. One objective of the

SuperLeader is to encourage constructive self-confidence as an important part of the transition to self-leadership, but reprimand induces guilt and depression and diminishes self-confidence. On the other hand, if a SuperLeader treats a mistake as a learning opportunity, then employee self-esteem can be enhanced. After all, one sign of self-confidence is an individual's objectively realizing that he has "made every mistake in the book" and has the experience and confidence to handle surprising situations.

In our research, we have discovered many incidents where Super-Leaders are required to deal with subordinates' mistakes. In our profiles of both Joe Paterno and MacGregor, we discuss how they have dealt with mistakes. SuperLeaders, while not liking or encouraging it, invariably see a mistake as an opportunity for learning—"learn from mistakes." We suspect these executives are able to recall how important the opportunity to make mistakes was in their own self-leadership development.

In summary, we recognize that reprimand is sometimes a necessary element in a SuperLeader's repertoire of behaviors, especially with new employees or chronic underperformers. But the most important lesson to remember is that the careless use of reprimand can be very discouraging to employees who are in the "reaching out" stage in their transition to self-leadership. The main focus should be to treat a mistake as a learning opportunity, to provide positive acceptance of the person despite the mistake, and to remember how the opportunity to make mistakes was a critical element in the SuperLeader's own development. Following these tips will result in a *constructive* reprimand that will influence long-term effectiveness.

SuperLeaders . . . invariably see a mistake as an opportunity for learning.

The following incident, observed during our research on self-managing work teams (see chapter 9), illustrates this kind of constructive orientation.

Late one afternoon, a young male employee entered the quality-control laboratory. He was a production worker from one of the small assembly teams. He went to a chemical work bench and quickly performed a "spot test" on a piece of material. At the end of the test, he came to the coordinator (leader) and said, "I think we've got trouble. The chemistry seems to be wrong on X part." With encouragement from the coordinator, several other pieces were randomly selected from the production area and also tested. The problem seemed to be pervasive and a significant portion of the day's production had to be scrapped. Immediately, a "fix" was initiated to bring the chemistry back within tolerance. Incidentally, the young worker stayed two hours beyond his regular quitting time to help solve the problem.

In itself, there is nothing unusual about an employee making a quality check. But in this case, the individual was an hourly production worker, not a quality-control technician, who "sensed" something was wrong because "the color wasn't just right." He had the initiative and the self-developed skill to conduct the test. This example of team members observing their own output and making judgments about the value of that output saved the company a small but significant amount of money by correcting the problem early on and by removing the defective material from subsequent production operations.

During the entire episode, the coordinator reinforced the alertness of the team (and especially of the employee who performed the test) in catching this problem and encouraged such initiative. Privately, he expressed to us his distress that the mistake had been made. Interestingly, he refrained from laying blame and instead concentrated on praising the team for spotting the problem. Later a manager said to us, "You know, it's bad enough when we make a mistake and lose a quarter of a day's production. But think how much more extensive it would have been if he hadn't caught the problem. We probably would have had to scrap several days' production of the full assembly."

PROFILES IN SUPERLEADERSHIP:
RENE MCPHERSON

Most observers of U.S. industries decry the state of so-called rustbelt manufacturing businesses. The decline of basic manufacturing industries in America through the 1970s and 1980s is well documented. One exception is a company that has prospered in the face of significant foreign competition: Dana Corporation.

The transformation of Dana from a large, stodgy auto-parts manufacturer into a model of productivity is generally credited to Rene McPherson, CEO at Dana in the late 1960s and 1970s. During his twelve years as a top executive at Dana, general revenues quintupled to $2.6 billion and earnings per share improved an average of 15 percent per year. At a time when other U.S. executives were not yet aware of the foreign challenge, productivity at Dana, adjusted for inflation, doubled. The company's performance has continued to improve since McPherson's retirement in 1979. Sales per employee have quadrupled from 1970 through 1986. Over the last five years, dividends have increased at about 8 percent per year. Analysts continue to see Dana's future as very promising.[1]

THE ARCHITECT OF CHANGE

McPherson's outstanding performance at Dana has been widely recognized. He was chosen as one of America's chief executive officers of the year by *Financial World* in 1978; he was honored with the Alumni Achievement Award of Harvard Business School in 1981; and, more recently, he was inducted into *Fortune*'s U.S. Business Hall of Fame. Arthur M. Louis described him in *Fortune* as "feisty, profane, and outrageously opinionated,"[2] and some of those qualities came through in the interview conducted for this profile.[3]

McPherson's awareness of the importance of people began early in his life. "My father was a real big influence. . . . He was . . . a great people person." His experience continued during his World War II service in the Pacific, where he won the Distinguished Flying Cross. Within two weeks of his assignment as assistant squadron operations officer, the operations officer was stricken with appendicitis: "I got thrown into very deep water and I had to swim quickly!" These circumstances provided McPherson with an early opportunity to assume responsibility and learn self-leadership by doing.

After the war was over and he had graduated from Harvard Business School, McPherson entered Dana in 1952 under the guiding hand of John Martin, a firm believer in developing people's potential. McPherson had broad early experience, serving in both sales and manufacturing. One of his most important assignments was that of manager of the Auburn Clutch plant in Indiana.

At the Auburn plant, McPherson soon became known for his nontraditional behavior. He frequently asked the question, "What do you think?" He was constantly seeking advice and suggestions from the workers. In the rather traditional, autocratic Dana of that time, McPherson's superiors seemed somewhat ill at ease with his actions. Nevertheless, they accepted his tactics because he was consistently turning in superior results. He described the keystone of his approach: "I tried to spend a lot of time on the floor, because that's where the action is."[4]

He frequently asked the question, "What do you think?"

McPherson credits John Martin with giving him the opportunity to hone his self-leadership skills. "He did a marvelous job with a bunch of us—of stuffing us into various kinds of jobs, and then he more or less didn't mess with you. . . . You handled it on your own, and if you didn't, well, that was part of the training he was giving you. He wasn't gonna baby anybody, but he was sure gonna give you a crack at it." Part of his participative style was learned from Martin: "He was great at the four most important words in business, 'What do you think?' " Obviously, Martin served as a self-leadership model for McPherson.

From his position as plant manager at Auburn, McPherson became plant manager of a Canadian division that seemed about to go under. The plant had suffered six consecutive years of losses. Again, he was forever soliciting the advice of workers on how to improve the efficiency of the plant. "If you don't have the foot soldiers with you, you're not going to win the damned battle."[5] His effort was a great success: the plant turned a profit in his first year. Most of all, the assignment was another opportunity to hone his "What do you think?" style of leadership.

McPherson's rise at Dana was rapid. In 1966, he was selected as executive vice-president, where the bureaucracy chafed him. The president at that time, according to McPherson, had "a big hots for staff," which McPherson characterized as "a lot of BS." He stated, "You don't need staff; you need to work with the line guys directly." Remembering his own line days, he stated, "I didn't like a bunch of staff guys coming and telling me what I had to do! . . . I was responsible, and I was gonna run it." He felt the centralization and staff orientation at Dana stifled initiative. He was concerned with giving responsibility to the people who needed it.

McPHERSON AS CEO

McPherson was appointed president in 1968, and chairman and CEO of Dana in 1972. One of his first concerns as president was to simplify operations at Dana. The most famous story is about one of his first actions: eliminating the procedures manuals.

According to one account, the procedures manual had risen to a height of $22\frac{1}{2}$ inches. McPherson replaced it with a one-page policy statement. The following are some excerpts from this statement:

- We are dedicated to the belief that our people are our most important asset.
- We believe that people respond to recognition, freedom to participate, and the opportunity to develop.
- We believe that people should be involved in setting their own goals and judging their own performance. The people who know best how the job should be done are the ones doing it.

- We endorse productivity plans which allow people to share in the rewards of the productivity gains.
- We believe that on-the-job training is an effective method of learning.
- We believe our people should move across product, division, and organizational lines.
- We encourage professional and personal development of all Dana people.
- Commitment is a key element of the Dana Management Style.
- We discourage conformity, uniformity, and centralization.
- Responsibility should be pushed as far into the organization as possible.
- We believe in task forces rather than permanent staff functions.
- We do not believe in company-wide procedures.
- This organizational environment stimulates initiative and innovation.
- It is the job of all managers to keep Dana people informed. We believe [in] direct communication with all of our people.

Clearly, this policy statement contains strong elements of self-leadership. While an almost idealistic philosophy, the statement is an excellent framework from which SuperLeadership can be inspired.

"We discourage conformity, uniformity, and centralization."

For the most part, the initial reaction to this one-page policy statement was positive. However, to quote McPherson, "If you were the kind of person who needed a security blanket and liked to suck your thumb, then you were a little anxious about it. If you were a 'going Jessie' and you knew what needed to be done . . . you thought it was the best goddam thing that happened since you came to the company."

McPherson stresses placing responsibility where it is needed—at the individual level. "Nobody was gonna tell you how to act. *You* were gonna decide that."

On occasion in following this new philosophy, McPherson had to swallow some of his own words. "I was giving a guy [hell] one day at one of his plants and I told him [it] was baloney. The guy looked me right in the eye and said, 'Listen, we like it, and we're responsible. When you threw away the corporate book, you threw away your opportunity to tell me I can use it or I don't have to use it. I like it and I'm going to continue to use it.' I just . . . looked him right back in the eye and said, 'You're a no good son of a bitch—and you're right!—and I'm wrong! Adios!"

Even when not agreeing with specific actions of subordinates, he still tried to promote their self-leadership abilities and to develop their personal responsibility for their own spheres of action. By doing this, he provided a model for others. He wanted both division and plant managers to push responsibility down as far as possible within the hierarchy.

McPherson also eliminated unnecessary staff in order to enhance the responsibility of line managers. In fact, this elimination effort was quite dramatic. Initially, the staff was cut from over 400 to approximately 150. Later the figure dropped to below 100.[6] With the elimination of over three-fourths of the corporate staff positions, he signaled to the rest of the organization that individuals could take on greater responsibility and develop their own methods. He set the wheels of SuperLeadership in motion.

With his division general managers, in particular, he put his ideas about autonomy in place. He began with the abolition of the traditional budgetary policy, which he felt was too concerned with detail and had corporate headquarters deciding on petty matters. With McPherson's new procedure, budgets from above were abolished. Division general managers were given a lump sum and told to spend it however they wanted.

When asked about this radical departure from traditional budgetary concepts, McPherson replied, "You can control a business in one of two ways: You can institute a kind of martial law, with troops stationed in each hamlet or village standing guard; or, you can sit back and let each village be self-governing. . . . What we are after is to help that person [the division manager] to be [his own] money manager."[7]

> "You can [station troops] in each hamlet or village standing guard; or, you can sit back and let each village be self-governing."

Of course, division general managers were not left entirely on their own. Each general manager reported to headquarters to give a presentation on his division. During these presentations, they stated what they had aimed to do last year, and what they had actually accomplished. Then they would state what they were going to do in the coming year. "Then we would decide," said McPherson, "based on how well we thought you could manage, how much dough you were gonna get." The concept of self-leadership was clearly present: "We didn't tell the guys what they were gonna do—they came in and told us."

This process was clearly not a love-in. It was painstaking and created considerable stress for the general managers. Indeed, some called it "hell week." Nevertheless, this procedure was instrumental in promoting responsibility and accountability at the divisional level.

McPherson saw what this procedure accomplished. "The guys that were really good quickly showed up and the guys that were really bad quickly showed up. That was really quick. The really bad ones didn't last very long—in that job—now we didn't go fire 'em, we just put 'em in a place where they could run something they could run." To McPherson, this procedure meant that top management was not doing things by fiat: "You weren't saying, 'Hey, I'm the president and I'm so much smarter than you dumb bastards that here's what we're gonna do.'" There was "no place to hide." Actions were brought out into the open, and if help was needed, it was given.

One key to the development of self-leadership is to provide the opportunity for people to grow. From the first, McPherson was committed to providing self-development educational opportunities to Dana employees. He uses the following analogy to stress the importance of education: "You can't take a knife, or an axe, or a hatchet, and use it and not sharpen it. . . . It's the very same thing with people." His emphasis on executive education is an example of what an organization can do to develop the self-leadership capabilities of employees.

McPherson was the inspiration behind the founding of Dana University in 1969. But Dana U. was not a mandatory training program. "If you were responsible as a plant manager or a division manager and you didn't want to send anybody, you didn't have to. . . . If you wanted to send somebody, you had to pay tuition, and you had to provide a fill-in person. If you needed it, you used it, and if you didn't need it, you didn't use it."

He also believes in cross-functional experience as a developmental opportunity. "Who knows what you can manage and where you can go? Just because you've got a financial background doesn't mean you gotta be a financial person, etc. My feeling is that all of us can do lots of things." Clearly, he is optimistic about people.

"All of us can do lots of things."

RENE McPHERSON: SUPERLEADER

Most of all, self-responsibility is a recurrent theme in McPherson's rhetoric. Self-responsibility is what he so earnestly tried to develop in others. He stressed the importance of people: "You've got to get out there and tell your people that you think they're important. You've got to say it, say it, say it, and then act it, act it, act it. And you can magnify the effect by making sure the people around you—the ones you promote—do it too."[8] He has left a meaningful legacy for Dana Corporation. He has transformed a top-heavy, bureaucratic, torpid organization into one of the most successful and competitive manufacturing businesses in the United States today. Self-leadership was a key ingredient: Rene McPherson had a special capacity to lead others to lead themselves.

"You can magnify the effect by making sure the people around you . . . do it too."

8

Creating Self-Leadership Systems: Organizational Culture

A major factor in developing SuperLeadership is the challenge of designing an integrated organizational environment that is conducive to high performance. Organizations will find it difficult to obtain initiative and innovation from employees without providing a pervasive environment that facilitates those elements of self-leadership.

For most of this book, we have focused on the one-on-one relationship between an executive and a subordinate: How can an executive lead that subordinate to lead him/herself? For an organization, however, the best results derive from a total integrated system that is deliberately intended to encourage, support, and reinforce self-leadership *throughout* the system. Of course, this is an issue that mainly falls within the responsibility of top management. Nevertheless, we hope managers will read this chapter with the intention of concentrating on their own responsibility—creating a self-leadership culture within their own departments. In this chapter and the next, we address this issue of self-leadership systems through the ideas of (1) organizational culture, (2) designing sociotechnical systems, and (3) teamwork.

CREATING A SELF-LEADERSHIP ORGANIZATIONAL CULTURE

"Joe! Get the XLC order using the Y process and then report back to me for further instructions," Frank Young, the newly employed department manager, curtly directed one of his employees. "And we need it *now,* so get your rear in gear!" Frank had just joined the company after six years in the military. Joe left with a scowl on his face.

"Take it easy," a quiet voice suggested to Frank after Joe had left. Frank turned to see Fred Harris, another department manager, standing near him with a friendly smile on his face. "You're working too hard, Frank, or at least you're overmanaging," Fred added.

"Pardon me?" Frank wondered what Fred meant.

"Haven't you gotten the word yet? We don't operate that way around here under Phil Smith, our V.P. As he often says, 'We're not the military.' I've noticed you supervising your employees very closely since you came on board last week, and sometimes you're pretty harsh. Phil is committed to getting our workers to learn how to manage themselves. He says it's our job to help him create a cultural value system in this division, in which everyone sees himself as an important resource and a self-manager."

"Are you joking?" Frank asked suspiciously, thinking Fred was simply trying to pull his leg since he was the new guy on the block.

"I know it may sound strange at first," Fred responded. "When I first heard Phil describing his vision of every employee as a manager, I thought it sounded impractical and idealistic. But, you know, it's working. People here *do* behave differently than any other place I've been, and they perform damn well. They seem to have a different set of values and beliefs about working and the role of management. Frank, you're in a different world here; a manager's job is to help employees to manage themselves, not to manage them closely—not to tell them what to do. After all, people have the potential to manage their own jobs much more closely than we can. I know it takes some getting used to, but I'll help you as much as I can. Our employees are used to a more subtle style of managing, where we depend on them to come through on their own. If you get too authoritarian, you're headed for trouble. Once you learn the basics and how well they work, you'll like it. In fact, it makes our job easier."

Recently, one concept that has received great attention is organizational culture. For years, we have known that moving from one *national* culture to another brings many significant changes in a person's manner and style of living. More recently the powerful influences of distinct *organizational* cultures have been recognized by both organization scholars and executives. Organizations evolve their own unique pattern of values, folklore, rituals, traditions, style, and meaning, all of which significantly influence the behavior of organization members. An organization's culture could be termed a *psychological environment*—the mental or cognitive expectations that guide behavior.

Some experts have gone so far as to argue that strong, distinct corporate cultures may be the key to organizational survival and success.[1] The unique importance of culture is made evident by the manner in which several prominent organizations are recognized: Digital Equipment's emphasis on innovation that creates freedom with responsibility, IBM's "IBM means service" orientation, GE's "progress is our most important product," 3M's new product "bootlegging," and so forth. The values and visions captured within the culture of an organization provide a unique kind of control mechanism—one that creates meaning, purpose, and commitment for employees.

Further, the various ingredients of corporate cultures can be important and powerful tools for weaving a fabric of high performance—of excellence at work. The notion of culture can be a crucial factor in facilitating successful implementation of corporate strategies. Indeed, an organizational culture will either support or hinder an organization's progress. When organizations make strategic shifts, their own unique culture is typically a great source of strength or weakness. Successful entry into a highly competitive market calling for aggressive risk-taking behavior, for example, may be difficult if there is a tradition of thoughtful, controlled, low-risk action in the firm. How ready was the AT&T culture, for example, to take on the demanding competition of a nonregulated environment? *Business Week* argued that if new strategies violate employees' fundamental beliefs about their roles in the company or about the traditions upon which the organization's culture is based, then failure is assured.[2]

The values and visions captured within the culture of an organization provide . . . meaning, purpose, and commitment for employees.

An interesting example of the demotivating influence of an over-controlling culture is the Skylab 3 mission, launched on November 16, 1973. After more than a month in space, the highly trained and disciplined astronauts "turned off the radio and refused to talk with Houston Mission Control." This action has been characterized as the first strike in space.[3]

While the reasons leading to this action are complex, much of the cultural philosophy of ground controllers can be inferred from a quote from a prominent NASA official, described as a "tough, energetic flight director . . . [who] was proud of the amount of control he could achieve."

"We send up about six feet of instructions to the astronauts' teleprinter every day—at least 42 separate instructions telling them where to point the solar telescope and which scientific instruments to use. We lay out the whole day for them, and they . . . normally follow it to a T! What we've done is learned how to maximize what you can get out of a man in one day!" Not surprisingly, this quote preceded the strike.

Obviously, this philosophy assumes a minimum of autonomy in space and further assumes that the maximum productivity can be gained by driving astronauts as if they were machines. It has the faint echoes of Fredrick Taylor and the thousands of American managers of the past who believed that they could attain maximum productivity by treating workers in a similar manner. One result has been the quality crisis of shoddy workmanship in American industry. The lack of self-leadership at NASA resulted in a strike in space.

SuperLeadership at the top requires the creation of positive organizational cultures within which self-leadership can flourish. Such environments consist of a host of factors, some observable and concrete, others more subtle and symbolic. Overarching organizational values and goals that are part of a distinct corporate culture are just as important as the physical materials that are necessary for task performance. Training and development efforts that equip employees with both task-performance and self-leadership capabilities are important means of stimulating cultures based on leading others to lead themselves.

The SuperLeader's challenge is not limited to direct leadership; the SuperLeader must also foster an integrated world in which self-leadership can survive and grow, in which self-leadership becomes an exciting, motivating, and accepted way of life.

The SuperLeader's challenge is . . . [to] foster an integrated world . . . in which self-leadership becomes an exciting, motivating, and accepted way of life.

Most everyone is familiar with the unique culture that has been created at Disney World. A trip there is like walking into a different world full of fantasy and wonder. Disney, Inc., is also noted for its success in establishing a behind-the-scenes organization that sustains this world for the guests (they are not referred to by the colder term *customers*). Through experience, Disney guests come to have very high expectations regarding how they will be treated. During a recent visit to Disney World, one of the authors imagined what it would be like if the culture were violated by even one employee. Allow us to illustrate the point by creating a fictive amusement park called Imagination World.

You have just arrived at Imagination World with high expectations of a day of carefree fun. You immediately proceed to a ride that especially excites you. After waiting in line for what seems an awfully long time, you begin to feel your excitement waning and some growing impatience, but you reassure yourself that the exhilaration of the ride will be well worth the wait. Finally, as you near the head of the line, you hear an Imagination World employee curtly announce that the ride is closed and rudely instruct (not ask) everyone to turn around and leave the way they came. No apology or explanation is offered. Scattered questions from the group are met only with the announcement repeated again by the employee in a voice that reflects growing irritation that his directions are not being promptly followed.

This rather cold treatment may not seem that unusual for other settings, but at Imagination World? Along with the rest of the grumbling and angry mob of people, you find yourself fuming and now feeling like a very dissatisfied customer. You don't feel anything like a valued guest as you are herded out with no reward or consolation for your wait. Your trip to the land of fantasy is darkened, not so much by the mechanical failure of a sophisticated ride—that's bound to happen once in a while—but mainly by the inappropriate, inconsiderate behavior of a single employee. During the remainder of the day you are treated courteously by other employees but you are never quite able to shake the effect of this rude treatment. You make a summary judgment about the kind of organization you have just experienced and decide this will be your last visit to Imagination World.

Culture weaves a delicate but powerful fabric. Undoubtedly, Disney, Inc., is one of the most successful companies in the world in successfully weaving the type of fabric that translates into a totally effective enterprise. Not surprisingly, an organizational culture can only be as strong as its weakest link, the single employee who meets the customer, so the self-leadership of each and every employee is of the utmost importance: even one violation of an otherwise remarkable culture can stand out as a particularly ugly stain on what was once a handsome piece of cloth.

Self-Leadership and Human-Resource Systems

Designing a culture that facilitates self-leadership can be addressed at different levels. The most ambitious approach within a single organization is to view the challenge from an overarching strategic human-resource management perspective. Strategic management is a way of viewing organizations that has shown some potential in recent years. More specifically, strategic design of entire human-resource systems that foster effective self-leadership is indeed an ambitious and, it would seem, remarkably potent idea. The meshing of organizational structures, technologies, control systems, management styles, corporate cultures, training and development programs, and so forth, all of which bring out the best in people, is an exciting challenge.

The notion of strategic management of human resources is relatively new to organizations. Many major corporations have now recognized this challenge and are currently addressing it with some vigor. A case in point is 3M Corporation. Long noted for its remarkable ability to develop and market profitable product innovations, 3M recently undertook a course of action intended to build the management of its human resources into its strategic planning process—perhaps its most ambitious innovation yet and one that could assure its ability to innovate in the future.[4]

The essence of the plan, as described by Christopher Wheeler, vice-president of human resources at 3M, is "to get human-resource managers to think more like line managers and line managers to think more like human-resource managers." The goal is to establish a strategic partnership between line managers and human-resource managers so that human-resource decisions are an integral part of the strategic planning process, not just an afterthought. Consequently, the classic line-staff relationship between line and personnel managers could be replaced by a new spirit of cooperation and teamwork. This fundamental change in the corporate culture has the potential to change the thought patterns of managers throughout the organization and to equip them with the knowledge and ability to practice greater self-leadership in making human-resource decisions. Organizational ventures such as this do indeed represent a new era of management practice. The development of human-resource management strategies designed to bring out the self-leadership capability of the work force is an important factor in cultural change and a major organizational opportunity of the future.

One example is the culture that has evolved at Merck & Co. under the leadership of its chairman, P. Roy Vagelos. *Business Week* has declared Merck "The Miracle Company" because of its remarkable success in the prescription drug industry. Merck is known as an organization that gives its scientists extraordinary freedom. According to Alfred Alberts, a Merck scientist, "There is no Merck way of doing it. Or, maybe there is a Merck way: it's going out there and letting the best people find the best way. And then taking those people and putting everything together. That's the nitty-gritty of getting a drug from discovery to marketplace."[5] Like 3M, Merck encourages so-called underground projects—those not officially sanctioned by the company.

Overall, the point is clear: top-level strategic management need not and should not restrict itself to traditional concerns such as the economy, market opportunities, financial and product mixes, and the like. More specifically, successful SuperLeadership depends on the strategic creation of overarching cultural systems within which people can truly become self-leaders. Creating such environments will energize people and provide them with substitutes for bureaucratic control that can be flexibly adapted to varying situations. Yet the self-leadership culture provides stability and integration of effort and an environment where human potential can be fully released. Within such systems, human initiative, creativity, determination, and inspiration can unfold.

The development of human-resource management strategies designed to bring out the self-leadership capability of the work force is an important . . . organizational opportunity of the future.

SuperLeadership and Culture

From a SuperLeadership view, culture becomes an important and legitimate means to exert leadership. Culture can be thought of as an evolution of acceptable responses that have worked in the *past*— patterns that were guided by the norms, values, and beliefs that existed during top managers' rise to power.[6] But a true SuperLeader will develop an ability to recognize the culturally relevant needs of employees *today*—not yesterday—and devote significant effort to deliberately orchestrate an organizational culture for high performance and development of people. Consider the following case:

> Thursday evening, 7:30 P.M. In his office on the seventh floor, Michael G. Smith, new CEO of Avant-Garde Computer, Inc. (AGC), examines the last sales report. The message is depressing: sales have leveled off in the past year. AGC is a small, innovative young company

located in Silicon Valley. Founded eight years ago, AGC specializes in engineering graphics design software. The founder, an engineer himself, had successfully marketed two highly specialized software packages for mechanical and electronic design.

The founder (now retired) depended heavily on the two chief engineers who now head the two main divisions of the company. Both engineers are deeply experienced and firmly committed to the present strategy of mechanical and electronic design graphics. Further, both of them are known as "autocrats" who keep a firm hand on the younger engineers within their divisions. For the last three years, turnover among the younger engineers has been increasing. Michael Smith knows from transcripts of exit interviews that most of them are leaving because the chief engineers exercised detailed control over their activities.

Two years ago, the need for capital became acute, so the founder sold AGC to a very large multinational corporation. Michael Smith has been appointed CEO by the parent corporation. He recognizes the difficulty of AGC's current situation, but he believes a change of strategy can revive the company. His strategy would be to broaden AGC's market by adapting and offering its graphics products to other end-user specialists besides engineers and to add a consulting service to orient clients to graphics applications. He foresees, however, that AGC's chief engineers would not be thrilled by his view of the future since they are consumed by the engineering applications. Further, he needs to do something about the turnover of the younger engineers. Quite honestly, he really does not know how to introduce these major strategic changes without losing the valuable experience of the two chief engineers. In this case, Michael Smith clearly recognizes the need for a cultural change. Now his challenge is to effectively facilitate such a change to enable the organization to meet its current needs, which differ from those it faced in the past. [7]

The basic SuperLeadership elements that have been discussed in previous chapters are very relevant in meeting this challenge. The SuperLeader can model, encourage, provide guidance for, and reinforce the kinds of behaviors that will help create a positive cultural pattern. Our view, consistent with the SuperLeadership philosophy, is that this cultural pattern should be centered on employee self-leadership: the SuperLeader will facilitate a culture that not only allows but is founded upon the fundamental belief that effective self-leadership is critical for success—a culture that recognizes the unique needs, strengths, and contributions of each individual and facilitates the fullest development of the potential of each person. Most of all, a SuperLeader is a positive self-leadership model for others and helps employees to be models for one another. Furthermore, the SuperLeader will make it clear that such self-leadership behavior is not only acceptable but expected. To accomplish this, initiative, creativity, responsibility, and distinctiveness should be encouraged, reinforced, and viewed as the typical model of behavior.

The SuperLeader will facilitate a culture that . . . is founded upon the fundamental belief that effective self-leadership is critical for success.

Without any guidelines or integration of effort, a kind of anarchy would exist that would preclude common purpose and high performance. At the other extreme, rigid bureaucratic controls can stifle the initiative, creativity, and commitment required for excellence. Embedded in culture are the shared values, beliefs, and visions that provide the integrating mechanism that allows excitement and synergy at work to flourish; to use Peters's and Waterman's terms, "loose-tight controls" are what's needed.[8] In their leadership roles, SuperLeaders create a culture that facilitates self-leadership and allows the vast potential of the work force to flow.

In his more recent book, *The Renewal Factor*, Robert Waterman expanded on this theme. He discusses the simultaneous provision of direction and the passing on of power to the work force. Managers at successful organizations he calls "renewing companies" define the boundaries, and their subordinates figure out the best way to do the job within those boundaries. He calls this management style an astonishing combination of direction and empowerment. The manager gives up tight control in order to gain more control over the end results.[9]

One way of viewing this challenge is to think of culture in action-oriented terms. One concept, the psychological "script," is especially helpful. [10] Simply stated, a script is a mentally stored list of appropriate behavioral responses (often in specific sequence) that apply to specific situations. For example, attending church or dining at a formal restaurant call for certain appropriate behaviors known to all. The knowledge of these expected behaviors is stored in a person's mind.

In a restaurant, for example, a person waits to be seated at a table, reads the menu and orders her food, places her napkin on her lap and eats her food in the correct order (salad, then entrée, and so on), waits for the bill, tips a specific percentage of the total bill, pays the bill, and so forth, all in an orderly manner. Likewise, attending a business meeting, conducting a performance review with a subordinate, and giving directions all call for appropriate scripts. The typical interactions between managers and subordinates are especially guided by organizational scripts.

In fact, we would argue that an organizational culture is a system of interrelated and generally expected scripts for both behaving and thinking. If we use this perspective, then SuperLeadership involves modeling, encouraging, guiding, facilitating, and reinforcing desirable scripts. These scripts can be both specific (constructive ways of contributing to problem-solving meetings based on an individual's unique strengths and character) and general (viewing and dealing with work challenges or shared visions regarding the overarching goals of a person's work team as constructive opportunities). Most of all, the SuperLeader will model, encourage, reinforce, and otherwise facilitate scripts that translate self-leadership philosophy, values, and beliefs into effective action—scripts for taking initiative, setting personal goals, building in natural rewards, establishing constructive thought patterns, and so forth. By diffusing self-leadership scripts throughout the organization, the SuperLeader can facilitate a powerful culture for self-leadership. Consider the following:

John Scully uses the term *impresario* to describe his efforts to develop a culture at Apple Computer. To us, the characteristics that Scully attributes to an impresario sound very similar to our SuperLeadership ideas for creating self-leadership cultures and functional self-leadership scripts. Scully describes his ideas as follows:

[Impresario] is an important metaphor for inspiring creativity. . . . The impresario must cleverly deal with the creative temperaments of artists. At times he may coach because he knows that creativity is a learning process. . . . He ensures that the setting and stage are conducive to the production. . . . At Apple, we bring together a company of artists. . . .

This is the difference between inspiring . . . and simply motivating people. Virtually all our models of motivation derive from industrial and postindustrial labor. Getting people to reach beyond their best abilities is knowing how to manage creativity.

[Traditional] management and creativity might even be considered antithetical states. While management demands consensus, control, certainty, and the status quo, creativity thrives on the opposite— instinct, uncertainty, freedom, and iconoclasm.

Apple impresarios try to remove all hierarchical obstacles, but they ensure that the resources are there when needed, and they help to build support for the work being done. The impresario . . . allows artists to do their work without having to deal with the structure. . . . We want people to reach ideas they haven't dreamed of yet. . . .

I would worry if there weren't a little bit of anarchy in the organization. It's like arsenic: a little is medicinal, but a lot can kill you. . . . We don't give creative people traditional responsibilities, like being at the office every day from 8 to 5, or check on them for efficiency and punctuality. Instead, they are made accountable for the results of their work. . . . Just as academia offers its people the freedom to structure their own time, we do the same, and yet people work incredibly hard.

The impresario must have a clear grasp of what it is we are all here to do. His artists need both the freedom and the discipline to let their creative ideas take us on incredible unexplored journeys. This need calls for nonbureaucratic organizational scripts that encourage people to believe in creative nontraditional ways. Someday, maybe we'll see more companies searching not for managers and employees, but for impresarios and wizards that act out their organizational roles according to the most innovative organizational scripts. [11]

Top-management SuperLeaders are concerned with developing a self-leadership culture throughout the organization. At lower levels, the challenge for aspiring SuperLeaders is to develop subcultures within their own control that stimulate the unique self-leadership strengths of subordinates. The evolving culture becomes an integrated environment within which diversity, self-leadership, and future excellence are nourished. Again, the SuperLeader musters the strength of ten and more—a strength that is founded on the unique multiple abilities of others rather than on the limited qualities of one person who happens to be called the leader. This challenge is indeed difficult, especially for very large, complex organizations. Nevertheless, faced with a rapidly changing global economy, many U.S. corporations have undertaken a substantial revitalization of their organizational culture. Ford Motor Company is one prominent example (see pages 174–181).

A CONCLUDING COMMENT ABOUT CULTURE AND SUPERLEADERS

Obviously, strategic efforts toward self-leadership organizations are important. But, an employee might object, "Hey—I'm not a CEO. I can't change the total culture of my organization." Indeed, the primary target of this book is the individual executive or aspiring executive. While these individuals are sometimes in a position to influence the overall organizational strategic process, the most important target involves their influence on the subcultures within which their own immediate subordinates perform. Most executives are faced with the challenge of managing only a part within a total organization, but this influence is nevertheless very important.

In a sense, an organization's personality and character are largely manifestations of each of the subcultures that executives and managers spawn within their own areas of responsibility. The Super-Leader will know how to take advantage of this opportunity to create a backdrop for performance that brings out the best in subordinates. Through this effort, the organization's culture as a whole moves in the direction of an integrated self-leadership system.

An organization's personality and character are largely manifestations of each of the subcultures that executives and managers spawn within their own areas of responsibility.

In this chapter we have provided some ideas about how SuperLeaders can create integrated systems that are fertile for self-leadership. As Warren Bennis, a leading leadership scholar, has stated, "When strategies, processes or cultures change, the key to improvement remains leadership."[12] Sometimes, as we read our own writing, the words make this task seem easy. But it's not. The key task, from an overall organizational viewpoint, is to move toward self-leadership and all its benefits without (as one colleague put it) "going off in twenty-six directions at once." Achieving this objective is challenging, and it begins and ends with managers moving toward self-leadership within their own spheres of control.

For a SuperLeader to achieve long-term lasting success in stimulating self-leadership in others, significant attention should be given to establishing and maintaining a constructive overall self-leadership system. The character and personality of larger organizational cultures are born from the aggregate of the many smaller cultures that are spawned throughout the firm. Positive subcultures emphasizing the self-leadership of every person can generate a true culture in which individuals can be encouraged to lead themselves.

PROFILES IN SUPERLEADERSHIP: FORD MOTOR COMPANY—A LEADERSHIP CULTURE IN EVOLUTION

In Automobile Town, U.S.A., usually known as Detroit, there once was a company noted for its emphasis on hardball internal politics, featuring periodic "king of the hill" leadership battles. It was a company noted for clashes between strong personalities. The executive-suite battleground had been stained with the career blood of losers who found themselves casualties, not because they lacked talent or ability, but because of struggles emanating from the old-style, power-oriented leadership. This leadership style could not tolerate strong followers, let alone other independent, strong-willed leaders within the same territory. That leadership seemed to measure its potency by the degree to which it could arbitrarily alter others' lives.

In some ways, this company was the antithesis of the leadership philosophy advocated in this book. Number-two and apparently destined to always be eating the dust of a larger, stronger, and apparently more effective competitor, the company was losing a billion dollars a year just a few years ago and seemed to be completely out of touch with its work force and its customers. The company is Ford Motor Company.

But in this profile, we will discuss another firm, though it has the same name, that is attempting to deemphasize high-image, top-down leadership. Instead, the new emphasis is on the soldiers that wage the battle. This new company is placing a strategic spotlight on employee involvement and participative management. Leadership today—at least Ford's ideal of leadership—is founded upon a set of guiding principles that encourages people to operate with freedom and autonomy within a common vision. The current theme encourages managers to act in partnership with the work force rather than to command its obedience and respect. It is also a company that recently has enjoyed large gains in its market share, an improved cost and profit performance, and acclaim for its new stylish and efficient products; and in recent months it has been kicking up more than its share of dust for the competition to chew on. The name of this company, a firm struggling to meet the challenge of operating according to principles of SuperLeadership, is the same—but it's the new and improved Ford Motor Company.

A NEW ERA OF LEADERSHIP AT FORD

Perhaps most people haven't heard that much about the newly evolving Ford. We wouldn't be that surprised. We get the impression that if too many people could easily name Ford's chairman of the board and president Ford would be disappointed. Indeed, Donald E. Petersen (Chairman and CEO) and Harold Pohling (President) appear to be surprisingly content to maintain rather low profiles. "We don't want stars," says Petersen. "Being a part of a team is a much more productive environment. I feel very comfortable with the lack of spotlight and limelight." He explains that Ford officials decided that "through people we are going to have our best chance to make profits."[1]

Petersen himself represents an interesting new kind of leadership model for the company. His low-key image reflects an obvious willingness to deemphasize his own importance in the leadership of the company, and he expects others to follow his example. "Everyone with legitimate input to your decision should have a chance to be heard," he pointed out. "And when the decision is made, it must be explained, so that dissenters don't feel ignored."[2]

Much of Petersen's commitment to participative management stems from his aversion to the fear and envy that were rampant at Ford in his early days: "Those days built into me a strong desire to see things work differently, a strong desire to stop all the fighting, backbiting, and working to prove the other guy wrong."[3]

As an example of the positive benefits of the new form of leadership at Ford, Jack Telnack, Ford's chief of design, told the following story: Petersen, president at the time, looked over some preliminary designs and then asked Telnack if that was the kind of car he himself would like to drive. After some thought, Telnack decided to answer honestly: "Absolutely not. I wouldn't want that car parked in my driveway."

Petersen responded by telling him to design something he would be proud of. The now highly successful "jellybean" cars (the Taurus and other rounded models) resulted. For Telnack, after years of very autocratic Ford leadership, his chance had finally come, and he responded with one of the most innovative and successful designs seen in the automotive industry.[4]

SOME SPECIFIC INGREDIENTS IN THE FORD EVOLUTION

In making this striking culture change, Ford has introduced several specific strategies. First, it has undertaken several changes that might seem a bit obvious in terms of adhering to sound business practice: an increased emphasis on quality, responsiveness to the customer, and improved cost efficiency (becoming "leaner but meaner"). But these are not the ingredients of success that we will emphasize. Rather, we are more interested in the behind-the-scenes efforts that we believe are crucial to Ford's long-term improvements. In particular, we are referring to Ford's participative management and employee involvement (PMEI) program, its "Mission, Values, and Guiding Principles," and its emphasis on training people to contribute their best and to help others to do the same.

In recent months Ford has devoted significant time and resources toward increasing the participation and commitment of every employee on the Ford team. We had an opportunity to observe one of the many workshops that have been conducted for various Ford managers. The three-day session, focusing on participative management and employee involvement, consisted partly of training in conflict management, positive feedback, team development, and so forth, to enhance leadership. But perhaps more important, it afforded managers a chance to be at ease and just get excited about the prospect of fully using the abilities of Ford employees. Clearly, many participants saw the training as instrumental in breaking down the traditional power-based roadblocks by enhancing the idea that every person is a valuable, exciting resource waiting to be tapped. The final event of this program ran well into the evening, with tongue-in-cheek awards and an uninhibited rah-rah ceremony that sent participants off, apparently reenergized and with a renewed perspective on the value of expecting people to contribute their own ideas and talents.

Invariably our discussions with people in different parts of the company regarding leadership turned to the emphasis being placed on PMEI. Ford has been making significant reductions in its white-collar work force, which may seem antithetical to an enlightened human-resource philosophy. Yet Ford management seems to recognize that the future success of the company depends on effective utilization of its people. As Ford management gets smaller in numbers, involvement and participation of all people at all levels must greatly increase for the company to succeed.

As this process unfolds, a significant factor in maintaining cohesiveness and coordination within the company is a common set of values and principles referred to as "Mission, Values, and Guiding Principles." Petersen and Pohling have felt strongly about this integrating statement, as demonstrated by the significant time they have devoted to its development and communication. (A copy of the statement is presented on page 178.) Our experience at Ford underscores the importance of this document.

A reading of the statement makes Ford's emphasis on people at all levels of the company obvious. Note in particular the portion of the document relating to people: "Our people are the source of our strength. They provide our intelligence and determine our reputation and vitality. Involvement and team work are our core human values." Petersen and Pohling, together, have expressed their strong commitment to this message on a videotape that has been widely shown throughout Ford.

THE STRUGGLE OF TRANSITION

The transition to a SuperLeadership pattern of management at Ford has not been easy and is not yet completed. Some employees don't know how to serve as followers (that is, self-leaders) under a participative management system. Moreover, some managers have not been able to make the transition. In one case, for example, an individual in

FORD

MISSION

Ford Motor Company is a worldwide leader in automotive and auto-related products and services as well as in newer industries such as aerospace, communications, and financial services. Our mission is to improve continually our products and services to meet our customers' needs, allowing us to prosper as a business and to provide a reasonable return for our stockholders, the owners of our business.

VALUES

How we accomplish our mission is as important as the mission itself. Fundamental to success for the Company are these basic values:

People—Our people are the source of our strength. They provide our corporate intelligence and determine our reputation and vitality. Involvement and teamwork are our core human values.

Products—Our products are the end result of our efforts, and they should be the best in serving customers worldwide. As our products are viewed, so are we viewed.

Profits—Profits are the ultimate measure of how efficiently we provide customers with the best products for their needs. Profits are required to survive and grow.

GUIDING PRINCIPLES

Quality comes first—To achieve customer satisfaction, the quality of our products and services must be our number one priorlty.

Customers are the focus of everything we do—Our work must be done with our customers in mind, providing better products and services than our competition.

Continuous improvement is essential to our success—We must strive for excellence in everything we do: in our products, in their safety and value—and in our services, our human relations, our competitiveness, and our profitability.

Employee involvement is our way of life—We are a team. We must treat each other with trust and respect.

Dealers and suppliers are our partners—The Company must maintain mutually beneficial relationships with dealers, suppliers, and our other business associates.

Integrity is never compromised—The conduct of our Company worldwide must be pursued in a manner that is socially responsible and commands respect for its integrity and for its positive contributions to society. Our doors are open to men and women alike without discrimination and without regard to ethnic origin or personal beliefs.

Ford's "Mission, Values, and Guiding Principles"

sales and marketing opted for early retirement when his boss insisted he change his autocratic style. For him, the transition was just too much to swallow. Joe Kordick, the head of Ford's parts and service division, mandates that his managers manage participatively. He has pointed out that many managers, having learned and succeeded in the old environment, are trying to adjust to the new style. Some are making it and some aren't. [5]

(We note an interesting paradox here—the use of nonparticipative leadership at the top to instill a more participative leadership pattern throughout the organization. It's almost as if top management were issuing an eleventh commandment—"Thou shalt be a participative leader." Indeed, we have seen this contradiction in more than one organization.)

One story of a successful transition can be found at the Ford Batavia, Ohio, plant, which manufactures automotive transaxles. [6] Interestingly, Batavia produces a product identical to that produced by a Mazda plant in Japan. Mazda furnishes about 30 percent of the automatic transaxles used by Ford.

A few years ago, Ford was considering closing the plant because its product could not compete in quality and productivity with that of Mazda. Today, products from the Batavia plant are considered superior to those made by Mazda. What were the reasons for this amazing turnaround?

The ingredients include better labor-management relations and statistical quality control. But teamwork and employee involvement seemed to be the most critical factor. In December 1987, there were thirty-six employee-involvement groups. Six months after the team concept started in 1985, the plant was making parts more cheaply than Mazda. Who said American workers can't compete with Japanese workers?

In our own experience, we have observed human-resource executives from many parts of Ford spend time examining and discussing the self-leadership concept. In one off-site meeting, it was quite apparent to us that the struggle reaches right to the roots of each individual's philosophy of leadership. One individual who spoke at the meeting, for example, had difficulties accepting the notion of self-leadership, explaining that leadership *requires* that someone influence someone else (a top-down viewpoint), that there is no such thing as leading one's self. Another manager exclaimed, "If it's any good, someone else would have done it before and written it up!" To us, this statement indicated a severe aversion to risk taking and innovation.

To be fair, however, most of the participants at this meeting were open-minded and were sincerely struggling with the challenge of translating ambiguous philosophies of leadership into everyday, on-the-job behavior. Most seemed to accept the overall logic of self-leadership. Yet their main challenge seemed to be understanding the specifics of how individual managers can actually implement self-leadership among their subordinates. (By the way, observing this struggle added to our motivation for completing this book.) In general, the meeting reflected Ford's struggle with its transition to a new leadership style. Individual executives spoke with considerable emotion on different ways to meet the challenge, and many differing views were expressed. Most of all, the majority of attendees seemed determined to avoid falling in the rut of viewing leadership as the old top-down style of management.

At the end of the two-day session, a task force was established to study the leadership issue and to pursue a commonly agreed-upon perspective; since then, it has met several times. Ford has indeed been struggling with this leadership transition, but clearly leadership that relies on the full use of human resources is taken quite seriously; the company seems committed to using the minds and abilities of everybody at all levels.

A CONCLUDING COMMENT

In many ways, Ford serves as an interesting case of large-scale Super-Leadership. Despite the fact that SuperLeadership in general does not, and at Ford did not, produce overnight cultural change, Ford is clearly challenged by its new leadership perspectives. The pragmatic difficulties of massive organizational change that Ford is encountering are the real reasons that the company serves as such a useful example. Movement toward a self-leadership culture involves hard work, patience, and some risk. Perhaps the greatest risk is that only a halfhearted attempt at involving employees might be made. A sincere commitment to the concept of leading others to lead themselves is needed for the process to really work. Allowing a few employees to sit in quality circles every week or so is only a baby step—it's not going to get the job done. Rather, the concept needs to permeate the whole corporate philosophy and values and especially needs to be modeled by the actions of managers throughout the company.

This is the kind of challenge that Ford seems to have undertaken. It is in a real cultural transition and its journey is still far from over. Indeed, its recent successes may lead to a false sense of security and stability. To expect absolute completion at any time may be unrealistic. Rather, a continuing pursuit of the target may be the reality of leadership that enables people to be effective self-leaders. After all, people are very dynamic creatures. Ford's leadership seems committed to successfully diffusing self-leadership throughout the company. The payoffs already seem to be unfolding.

9

Creating Self-Leadership Systems: Sociotechnical Design and Teams

Effective self-leadership systems require more than the psychological support provided by organizational culture. Cultural patterns also need to be supported by physical systems that are designed to facilitate rather than retard self-leadership.

SOCIOTECHNICAL SYSTEMS

The concept of sociotechnical design is useful in viewing this issue. A fundamental assumption of sociotechnical design is that the technical system must be designed to complement and facilitate the desired social system, and the social system should be consistent with the technical system. From a SuperLeadership perspective, this means that technical and physical design should encourage self-leadership as much as possible. Note that in earlier chapters we discussed the notion of the self-design of tasks as an important element of self-leadership.

An individual is significantly limited, however, in designing his own tasks if the physical technology is too pervasive in locking in a single way of accomplishing the task. The concept of the self-designed task implies at least some discretion in how the work is accomplished. The micromovements required in a traditional assembly-line system are a classic example of a technology that removes much discretion and self-leadership potential from a task.

Part of SuperLeadership involves assuring that the physical requirements and existing technology support a self-leadership philosophy. In a manufacturing system, for example, the necessary equipment and machinery, materials and supplies, power sources, maintenance tools and the like must be available for workers to perform their tasks. In addition, if the technology employed requires that some workers are dependent on others before their work can be performed (in assembly lines, for example), work must flow adequately between work stations to enable continued performance. Better still, in-process "buffers" (small inventory reserves) might be used to establish "territories" within which some self-leadership might be possible. Also, the SuperLeader must make the necessary expertise available to assure that the equipment or work processes or both can be maintained and adjusted as the situation requires. This could involve a maintenance technician in a manufacturing plant, a service manager with knowledge and authority to handle customer exceptions in a service company, and employees given especially extensive cross-skill training to extend their abilities to meet their own needs.

While these points may seem obvious, they are important enough to be reiterated. Employees cannot exercise self-leadership if they don't have what they need to perform or if the technology does not permit self-leadership. No matter how developed the self-leadership ability of a production worker, the product cannot be assembled without parts, tools, necessary maintenance, and so on. For a Super-Leader to capitalize on the strength of others, then, he must establish and maintain an environment that assures that task requirements are provided.

Each situation will determine the extent to which this context must be managed by the SuperLeader and to what degree employees can be trained and allowed to do this for themselves. Employees are usually in the best position to know how current requirements can be best met and when adjustments to these production requirements are needed. Modeling, encouraging, guiding, and reinforcing initiative in this regard can help assure the long-term health of the work system.

Employees also need to have the necessary skills required for performance. These skill requirements can be divided into two general categories: task skills and self-leadership skills. Task skills involve the knowledge necessary for completing the tasks themselves. Sociotechnical designs that intend to capitalize on employee self-leadership typically require a much broader repertoire of task skills for each employee. Cross-skill training and job rotation are typical.

Employees are usually in the best position to know . . . when adjustments . . . are needed.

Self-leadership skills enable employees to direct their own effort, to persist in the face of adversity, to create and maintain personal motivation, and to continually renew a constructive and innovative pattern of thinking. Employees that develop these two types of skills to a high degree become very valuable resources; they are indeed pillars upon which a SuperLeader can be supported.

Training is critical to develop *both* task and self-leadership skills. This training may come from formal organizational training programs (such as the modeling-based programs discussed on pages 94–98), or it may be facilitated through more traditional, less sophisticated means, such as on-the-job training. For example, 3M Company, noted for its creative and well-developed work force, long relied on a saying dating back to the years that McKnight was at the helm: "All development is self-development." The challenge to SuperLeadership is to assure a technical and physical environment that encourages employees to develop themselves.

The SuperLeader's success is dependent on the skill level of subordinates. Instead of issuing forceful, unwavering commands and closely monitoring the forces in the heat of battle, the SuperLeader should help individuals to be well equipped before each battle begins. Their skill is a necessary element. By being and providing effective models, and encouraging, guiding, and reinforcing task and personal excellence in followers, SuperLeaders will one day find themselves surrounded by capable leaders in their own right. In this dynamic context, positive self-leadership can flourish and the potential for progress is awesome. Indeed, workers will often develop into a dynamic team in which members become models and catalysts for each other.

Instead of issuing forceful, unwavering commands . . . in the heat of battle, the SuperLeader should help individuals to be well equipped before each battle begins.

One of the more interesting examples of contemporary sociotechnical design that facilitates team-oriented self-leadership is the Volvo automobile assembly method. Volvo has considerable experience with team-assembly concepts, which were pioneered at its Kalmar plant. Further, the automobile-assembly approach has been completely scrapped in the design of the new $315 million plant Volvo is constructing at Uddevalla. The key organizational philosophy at this plant is the work team, and the technical system has been designed to match that organizational concept.

One of the technical elements that facilitates the team concept is the computer-controlled carriers that ferry cars under assembly around the plant. Work teams of about twenty people are responsible for putting together entire units of the car, which are assembled within specially designed areas that support the team's social system. Typically, each worker does a series of tasks. "I want the people in a team to be able to go home at night and really say, 'I built that car,'" said Peter Gyllenhammar, Volvo's chairman. [1]

Volvo claims that not only are employees more satisfied but quality, productivity, and bottom-line profits have improved.

SELF-MANAGING TEAMS

Closely connected to sociotechnical design is the self-managing team approach, which has had a slow start in the United States. More recent media interest seems to indicate that the idea is about to take off. The dramatic success of the team approach at the GM-Toyota joint venture in Fremont, California, has been instructive to the U.S. automotive industry in general. Indeed, one of the more public issues of the GM-UAW negotiations in the summer of 1987 was GM's desire to move the total corporation to the team concept.

Top-management teams were also important to Tom Watson, Jr., former CEO of IBM. "My most important contribution to IBM was my ability to pick strong and intelligent men and then hold the team together. . . . I knew I couldn't match all of them intellectually, but I thought that if I used fully every capability that I had, I could stay even with them."[2]

Often one of the interesting indicators of a self-leadership culture is the presence of quite a few teams. The types of teams (not all work groups are called that) include product teams, top-executive teams, ad hoc teams, and even shop-floor self-managing teams. Of course, teams usually require a good deal of self-leadership to function correctly.

Like many Americans, David Packard, cofounder of Hewlett-Packard, learned respect for teams through his athletic experiences. "I liked basketball and track," he recalls. "You learn a lot of things in athletics and they're very important in your later career. . . . You . . . develop a sense of the importance of teamwork . . . whatever you do."[3]

A RESEARCH ANALYSIS OF SELF-MANAGING TEAMS

One of the most interesting aspects of our research program over the past ten years has been our direct observations of self-managing teams. The following is a report of our observations of a particular manufacturing plant that uses self-managing teams. Most of this information was reported in our academic research paper, "Leading Workers to Lead Themselves: The External Leadership of Self-Managing Work Teams."[4]

Estimates suggest that two to three hundred manufacturing plants in the United States use some derivative of a highly participative team approach.[5] In addition, other, nonmanufacturing organizations rely on some variation of this approach, like the insurance firm studied by Charles Manz and Harold Angle[6] and a financial investment firm we recently studied. These groups, called autonomous or self-managed work groups, are mainly characterized by an attempt to create a high degree of decision-making autonomy and behavioral control at the work-group level. Consequently, a much greater emphasis is placed on control from within rather than from outside the group. There is some debate about whether these teams are established to improve productivity or simply the quality of the employee's worklife, but it seems clear that management decision makers who take this approach at least have implicit goals of improved productivity, better-quality products, reduced conflict, or all three.

Researchers have had limited access to organizations that use the team approach, and sometimes when they have been given access it is with the proviso that there be no publicity or writing about it. As a result, relatively little research has been published about self-managing teams. We were fortunate in our study to have open access to a manufacturing plant organized according to a self-managing-team work system that had been in place for several years.

Description of the Team System

The nonunionized small-parts plant we studied is located in the southern part of the United States. It is owned by a large corporation and employs approximately 320 workers. The plant has been in existence since the early 1970s and was organized from the very beginning according to a self-managing-team concept. The technology used in the plant can be described as small-parts production or assembly, and it is generally based on a type of assembly-line system. Each work group is assigned a system of closely related tasks, many of which are small assembly-line operations. Teams are generally distinct from each other, both physically and by in-process inventory buffers.

The organizational structure has three distinct hierarchical levels. Upper plant management (called the support team) handles many traditional plant-management responsibilities (for example, planning overall plant production schedules, dealing with client firms, and so on). The support team is also formally responsible for the supervision of coordinators. The support team generally plays a supportive rather than directive role in the plant's operation and attempts to operate as a team. The work-team coordinators, external leaders who are assigned overall responsibility for one or more teams, occupy the next hierarchical level. The final level is the self-managing work teams themselves. The size of the teams ranges from approximately three to nineteen members, although most included eight to twelve. Within each team, an elected team leader also has leadership responsibilities and receives higher pay than other group members. For the most part, this individual does the same physical work as the other employees.

The work system generally places more responsibility on employees than do typical manufacturing environments. The general philosophy is self-control or self-management. Work teams are assigned a wide range of tasks and responsibilities, including preparation of an annual budget, keeping records of the hours they worked, recording quality-control statistics (subject to audit), making intragroup job assignments, and participating in assessment of the job performance of fellow group members. Teams engage in various problem-solving activities that include handling scheduling, equipment, and process problems as well as group-member problem behaviors such as absenteeism. Weekly scheduled and ad hoc meetings serve as problem-solving forums in which such issues are addressed.

The scheduled weekly meetings are typically held away from the production area. Teams have been trained in conducting meetings and in group problem solving. Problems are frequently raised for open discussion during these meetings. Usually, the elected team leader will organize and conduct the meeting, but other team members are provided with the opportunity to speak freely. The external coordinator or members of the support team are often invited to work with the self-managing team in dealing with specific issues and problems but do not attend on a routine basis. A coordinator might attend a team meeting, for example, to help members work out a particularly difficult quality-control problem. Our observations of a number of these meetings revealed a relatively sophisticated level of discussion and problem solving (that is, in terms of the technical nature of the discussions and their persistent emphasis on reaching a solution) that focused on improving work performance as well as on the various concerns of individual team members.

The pay system at the plant is based on the expertise level of employees. The level of pay for an individual employee is based on the number of tasks he can competently perform. When employees feel they have mastered a given job, they are tested on that job. In order to reach the highest pay level, an employee must learn all of the jobs of two work groups. This pay system is similar to that used in a pet-foods plant studied by Richard E. Walton and in a paint production plant studied by Ernesto J. Poza and M. Lynne Markus.[7]

Another distinguished characteristic of this work system is its noticeable lack of status symbols. The plant manager's office, for example, can be and frequently is used for group meetings without advance permission. There is no assigned parking, and there is a single cafeteria for all employees.

Self-Managing Conversations[8]

Many of the self-management activities take place during team meetings, which normally serve as problem-solving forums. Each team has at least one regularly scheduled half-hour team meeting each week. In addition, special meetings are called to deal with specific problems. All meetings are held on company time, and employees are paid their regular wages while attending.

These team meetings proved to be a rich source of information about the culture of the plant. We attended many of both the routine and special meetings over several weeks. To preserve normal conditions, we did not record conversations but instead took careful notes. In our previous research, we had become skilled at systematically categorizing verbal behavior in organizational situations. It was only natural, therefore, that we should give special attention to the nature of the verbal behavior within these self-managed work groups. We asked ourselves: What do they say? What do they talk about? Do they deal with serious productivity issues, or do they just fool around? How is their conversation linked with the operations of the plant?

We noted various categories of verbal behavior during our visits:

1. Rewards.
2. Reprimands.
3. Task assignments.
4. Work scheduling.
5. Production goal setting and performance feedback.
6. Routine announcements.
7. Problem resolution.
8. Discussion of communication problems.
9. Performance evaluations.
10. Team membership.

Our purpose is to provide a categorization of team verbal behavior, to explain the particular categories, and to give some specific examples that we witnessed.

Rewards and Reprimands. Exchanges between team members occurred rather frequently. A verbal reward is a compliment, a thank-you, or praise given in response to a useful or helpful action. Sometimes the exchange was a quiet one-on-one interaction: "Bobby, thanks for helping me with that No. 1 machine last night." At other times, verbal rewards might be given in front of the whole team, and these rewards were frequently delivered by the team leader: "We owe a special thanks to Emily for making sure that the [X] materials were ready last Monday. We would have had to shut down if she hadn't looked ahead and gotten what we needed."

We believe that verbal rewards were particularly important in building esprit de corps. It reinforced helping behavior within teams and promoted the practice of working together to achieve objectives.

The counterpoint to verbal rewards was verbal reprimands. In this behavior, one team member would direct displeasure or criticism toward one or more fellow team members. At this plant, both positive rewards and criticism were technically designated as "feedback." A verbal reprimand was called "negative feedback."

We observed an especially dramatic incident of verbal reprimand. At a regular team meeting, after several items of routine business were completed, the team leader addressed one of the members: "Jerry, we want to talk to you now about your absenteeism." He then went on to recount Jerry's record of absenteeism. The leader had a record of dates on which Jerry had been absent. He asked Jerry if he had anything to say about the absenteeism. Jerry briefly talked about his wife's illness. The team leader then went on to talk about the effect of absenteeism on the other team members—how others had to work harder because of Jerry's absences and how the absences were hurting team performance. He stated unambiguously that Jerry's absences were "unacceptable. We won't allow it to continue." He said that if he were absent one more time, Jerry would face a formal disciplinary charge that would be entered into the record. The team leader concluded by asking Jerry about his intentions. Jerry replied, "I guess I've been absent about as much as I can get away with. I guess I better come to work."

Verbal rewards were particularly important in building esprit de corps.

This was an interesting case of group self-discipline. In our discussions with many managers who have not had direct experience with self-managing work groups, the question of group self-discipline is the most controversial. Many managers believe that teams are incapable of disciplining their own members, and this is their major reservation about the concept of self-managing work groups. Yet we have seen this self-discipline take place in several different organizations, and we believe that, with the proper nurturance, such a disciplinary system can succeed. Indeed, we believe that peer pressure can be an effective form of employee control.

Task Assignments and Work Scheduling. We also observed several incidents of allocation of task assignments. In self-managed work groups, the decision of who does which job is made by the group itself, not by an outside supervisor. We observed many different patterns of task allocation among different groups. Some made relatively permanent task assignments on the basis of seniority. Others traded jobs on almost an hour-by-hour basis and still others on a daily or weekly basis, so that each person would have an equal share of both the "dog" jobs and the "gravy" jobs.

This exercise of control over their own jobs had a significant effect on employees' motivation. We sometimes observed employees negotiating with other team members about job allocation. Most of the time, this was handled without substantial conflict, but we observed one incident where emotions ran high. In this case, a six-man team was split across three shifts. A dispute arose over which shift had the responsibility for completing a particularly dirty and physically demanding job. There was no agreement. Finally, the coordinator virtually locked the team members in a room and demanded that they remain there until they worked out a solution. "I could make the decision for them," he told us, "but it will be a better decision and they will do a better job if they work it out among themselves."

This incident was atypical in its emotional intensity, but it was representative of the way issues were worked out at the plant. If a problem existed, the usual procedure was to get those involved to sit down and work it out themselves. Hard feelings and bruised egos sometimes resulted, but in the long run solutions seemed to be better and had a greater chance of enduring because they were worked out by the participants themselves and not imposed from the outside.

Many incidents revolved around issues of production scheduling, that is, what specific product should be produced at what particular time. Because of decreasing product demand, this plant had recently undergone a reduction in total production volume—without an employee layoff. One response to this crisis was a significant attempt to reduce in-process inventories. Of course, less inventory meant less room for mistakes, less flexibility if a particular part is not ready, and, in general, a more intense problem of managing the day-to-day, and indeed the hour-by-hour, production.

We observed an interesting conversation revolving around this issue. One employee was vigorously complaining about the trouble caused by the lack of buffer inventories. He asked why inventories had been cut so low. A fellow team member replied: "Do you know what the cost of interest is these days? For every piece that we have in inventory, we have to pay a finance charge, man! That comes straight out of profits. We have to keep inventories low if our business is going to make a profit!" He was referring to his own team when he used the word *business*.

These conversations about production scheduling saved the company a significant amount of money, we believe. In a traditional plant, these problems would be resolved by foremen and general foremen. If a production section ran out of material or parts, it would merely cease operations until the foreman got the necessary parts. In this plant, shortages severe enough to shut down production were rare because team members anticipated problems and took corrective action before production stopped.

Shortages severe enough to shut down production were rare because team members anticipated problems and took corrective action before production stopped.

Production Goal Setting and Performance Feedback. Conversations among team members often revolved around production goal setting and performance feedback. At this plant, the overall plant production goal or schedule is determined not locally but by corporate and division requirements, so for the most part the employees do not participate in setting overall goal levels. Nevertheless, they are very much involved in deciding how these overall levels are to be achieved and are also involved in nonproduction goal setting. Here is one conversation we observed about making a weekly production quota: "We won't have materials to run [product X] on Wednesday. We won't be able to meet our goal this week." "Why don't we shift over to [product Y] on Wednesday, and build up a bank for next week," a second team member replied. "We'll be short of [X] this week, but we can get a jump on [Y] for next week, and then we can make up [X] next week."

Note that the important factor here is that the team itself had discretionary authority to shift product mixes within certain time limits, and it used its leeway to overcome short-term difficulties.

We also observed goal setting in other areas, especially in quality and safety, as in this example: "Our rejection rate last month was 5.8 percent. We need to get it down to below 5 percent for this month. How are we going to do it?"

Again, note that this problem was raised *within* the team and was not an exhortation from a foreman or supervisor.

There was constant feedback. In addition to the personal feedback discussed under verbal rewards and reprimands, teams were provided with daily, weekly, monthly, and quarterly quantitative feedback. Each team maintained charts of quantity, quality, and safety performance. Frequently, we heard reports like "We made 3,948 units yesterday. We got ahead about 10 percent." Here is another interesting comment: "Have you heard about the safety results? The plant is now in the top one-third of the company."

Charts were everywhere. Formal charts posted on walls showed long-term trends in performance. However, there were also sloppier informal charts on hooks and clipboards and posted near machines. It seemed obvious to us that feedback was a critical aspect of the information sharing at this plant.

Routine Announcements and Problem Resolution. Routine announcements were also a significant part of the team conversations, as in this example: "The Christmas party will be on Monday the 20th. Give George your $3 if you are planning on coming."

Significant amounts of time were spent on the resolution of special problems. For instance, we observed an interesting incident revolving around the solution of a quality problem. A meeting had been called by a coordinator to discuss a certain quality deficiency. Four members from two different teams were present with the coordinator and a quality-control technician. The coordinator presented the problem, citing statistics that showed a gradual rise in the reject rate over several weeks. He asked, "What's the problem? What can we do to correct it?"

From our viewpoint, the meeting started slowly. No one had an immediate solution. But the coordinator was patient, and he listened carefully, encouraging the workers when they spoke. After five minutes, the meeting seemed to become more productive. Over the next half hour, several causes of the problem were suggested, and several "fixes" were proposed. Near the end, the group listed the proposed solutions according to ease of implementation and agreed to begin applying them in an attempt to eliminate the problem. Afterward, we asked the coordinator whether he had actually learned anything new or was just going through the motions for the sake of participation. "Sure," he replied. "I wasn't aware of many of the ideas they brought out. But most of all, they've now taken it on as their problem, and they will do whatever has to be done to solve it."

Note that both of these incidents concerning special problems involved quality. Although the self-managed work groups were not quality circles per se, they devoted much of their efforts to solving quality problems. Self-managed work groups really go beyond quality circles: they address quality issues continually, not just during weekly meetings, and are invested with significantly more authority to implement solutions.

Although the self-managed work groups were not quality circles per se, they devoted much of their efforts to solving quality problems.

Discussion of Communication Problems. We observed many incidents involving communication problems that arose between teams as well as within teams. For example, one team might complain about the quality of the product produced earlier in the production process by another team. One solution we saw was the temporary exchange of team members. Working with the other team for a week or so resulted in an improved shared understanding of why particular problems occurred, why certain procedures were important, and how negligence could affect other workers.

Performance Evaluations and Team Membership. While we did not directly observe performance evaluations for pay raises, we did observe conversations about these evaluations. For example, in a team meeting a member said to the team leader: "How about running a performance test on the [Z] machine? I think I'm ready." The reply was, "OK, I'll try to schedule it this week." These evaluations were on-the-job task performance demonstrations to determine whether a worker could perform all aspects of a job. They were generally conducted by a coordinator, the team leader, and a fellow team member, usually one more senior than the person being tested.

We also observed discussions about entry into and exit from the team. During our visits, we attempted to determine rules for assignment of employees to teams. We did not discover a specific set of rules. A typical explanation was, "Well, we just work it out." We did observe one incident during a team meeting that addressed this issue. Because of lower production levels, this team had been asked to reduce its numbers by one person. That person would be assigned to a temporary "construction" team that was being formed to undertake repair and cleanup work. The team leader presented the issue to the group and asked, "How should we handle it?" The first reply was, "Well, unless someone wants to go, we should do it by seniority." The man with the least seniority then spoke up: "Well, that's me, and I don't want to go." The team leader asked, "Does anyone want to go?" One person asked, "Would they be working outside? Is there any carpentry work?" Eventually, this person volunteered to move to the construction team since he wanted to be outside and to do some craft work.

Summary. Overall, the verbal behavior proved to be a rich indication of both attitudes and behavior in the plant. While verbal behavior inevitably reflected some amount of self-concern and was sometimes trivial, the organizational commitment and motivation of these employees were among the highest we have observed.

But what is the connection between conversation and productivity? What is there about what people say that translates into bottom-line results? Why is talk more than just talk?

Part of the reason that conversations get turned into productivity is *information sharing* and part is influence on employee *motivation*.

If any executive is asked what his major problem is, the chances are good that the reply would be something like this: "Communication. Our communication is not what it should be. We just never seem to have the right information at the right place at the right time." Inadequate communication often means inadequate information sharing. More often than not, this problem is the result of a policy of secrecy: tell employees only what they need to know to do their jobs. But there frequently is a significant difference between what a manager thinks an employee needs to know and what the employee actually needs to know. The result is that the employee often does not really have the optimal information needed to perform the job.

At the plant where we observed the self-managed work groups, a strong sharing philosophy prevailed: Management's viewpoint seemed to be to share virtually all information that was not considered personal. One reason given was that management was not in a good position to judge what specific information might be relevant. Only the individual employee and the work group itself were in a position to know just what information was important and what was not.

The net result was a climate of openness that we found virtually unprecedented in our previous experience. Furthermore, this information sharing provided a basis for employees to engage in proactive problem solving. They did not need to wait for management to present a problem for solution; in many cases, they were able to discover and correct problems at a relatively early stage. This took place through the verbal behavior of the employees. For example, an operator spoke up at a team meeting: "We need to replace that bearing this weekend. If it doesn't get done, then that machine will break down next week, and we'll lose a half day of production."

Multiply this one incident by a thousand times, and the net result is a substantial savings in productivity.

Management's viewpoint seemed to be to share virtually all information that was not considered personal.

Conversations also seemed to influence productivity through their influence on individual motivation. Over and over again, we observed instances where individual behavior was perceived as affecting the group: if an individual performed well, then the group as a whole was seen to be the beneficiary; if, on the other hand, an individual fell down, the group was seen to be hurt. The net result was strong peer pressure to contribute to the efforts and performance of the group. Motivation and discipline came from within the group, not from management. Again, this motivation and peer pressure were manifested mainly through group conversations. The positive rewards and the reprimands described earlier are examples.

The important point is that management's role did not seem to be to *directly* provide motivation and discipline to individual employees, as is the case in more traditional plants. Instead, management created a climate in which motivation and discipline came mainly from within the individual employee and from fellow employees. In our opinion, this is the most effective form of motivation and gets translated into bottom-line productivity. People who wish to perform well and achieve are more likely to do so. Conversations within work groups are the means by which this interpersonal influence gets translated into motivation and, ultimately, into bottom-line results.

We do not wish to leave the impression that the plant was a model of tranquility and harmony. On the contrary, in this plant as well as in several other self-managed team settings we have studied, interactions between members of the self-managing teams were sometimes tough and intense. We observed emotional conflict, but the prevailing mode seemed to be to deal with the conflict openly and directly. Overall, the level of motivation and commitment was high.

LEADING SELF-MANAGING TEAMS

An important aspect of our research investigated the leadership of the self-managing teams. Management was interested in understanding the leadership behaviors that facilitated group member self-management. For the most part, this leadership was conducted by the coordinators, the external leaders of the self-managing teams. We think of coordinators, given the self-managed team environment they function in, as a type of SuperLeader—they lead teams to lead themselves.

Coordinator leadership was manifested primarily through minute-by-minute verbal and nonverbal behavior, which we observed at the site. For example, we observed coordinators encouraging teams to engage in self-leadership behaviors, such as self-observation, and self-evaluation. One example is the case we described earlier (see chapter 7, page 152), in which a young production worker, with the encouragement of his coordinator, discovered a quality defect on his own.

We also observed coordinators conducting role-playing exercises with elected team leaders—a form of rehearsal—and encouraging groups to evaluate themselves and to give both positive and negative feedback within the team. In the instance mentioned earlier where a team conducted a formal reprimand of a team member during a team meeting for excessive absenteeism, the coordinator had encouraged this confrontation and worked with team members in rehearsing approaches for the meeting. Our subsequent direct observation revealed a very effective meeting.

In general and consistent with the SuperLeadership perspective, we observed a notable absence of direct commands or instructions from the coordinators to the teams. However, questions (an important tool of guided participation) were used with great frequency. "What is a reasonable scrap rate to shoot for?" (facilitating self-goal-setting); "What will you say to Bill about his absenteeism?" (encouraging rehearsal); "Do you think you can do it?" (eliciting high self-expectation).

Other coordinator behaviors also had self-leadership implications and so were important. For example, we frequently observed coordinators' efforts to encourage group problem solving. Sometimes a special meeting might be suggested to solve a difficult quality or process problem, but the meeting would be carried out by the team itself. In one instance a coordinator used questions to stimulate independent problem solving. An employee informed his coordinator that a piece of equipment had been damaged and asked the coordinator what he should do. The coordinator responded by asking, "What do you think should be done?" After a moment of reflection, the employee indicated what he thought would be appropriate and, with the coordinator's encouragement and reinforcement, proceeded with the repair according to his own plan. Coordinators also used more traditional behaviors, such as communicating between work groups and management and using positive verbal reward.

Overall, we observed a general pattern of behavior that was quite different from our previous experiences in more traditional production plants. The underlying theme of leadership practice was for the coordinators to influence the team and team members to do it themselves rather than for the coordinators to exercise direct control or to do it for the team. An abundance of deliberate, calculated efforts fostered independence rather than allowed the dependence of more traditional work groups.

The underlying theme of leadership practice was for the coordinators to influence the team and team members to do it themselves.

Our detailed research compiled a list of leadership-behavior variables that were relevant in this team context. The table on pages 201 and 202 lists these leadership behaviors and serves as a beginning guide to identifying the appropriate leadership behavior to facilitate team performance.

Some of the leadership behaviors found in this research are similar to those in the existing leadership literature: communicating between a work group and management and between work groups, helping to assure that work groups have the equipment and supplies they need,

Variable Name	Variable Description
Trains inexperienced employees	Leader trains group members on various group jobs.
Encourages group problem solving	Leader encourages the group to solve its own problems.
Encourages within-group job assignments	Leader encourages the group to assign tasks to its members on its own.
Encourages flexible task boundaries	Leader encourages group to be flexible in its work (i.e., to do whatever needs to be done that the work group is capable of).
Positive verbal reward	Leader verbally rewards (i.e., praises) group for desirable performance.
Punitive/corrective behavior	Leader verbally reprimands group for poor performance.
Goal setting	Leader assigns performance goals to the work group.
Expectation of group performance	Leader expects high group performance.
Communicates production schedule	Leader communicates to the group about plant production schedule (including any changes).
Works alongside employees	Leader physically works with group members to help them do their work.
Truthfulness	Leader communicates in a way that is truthful and believable to group members.

Description of Leader Behaviors for Self-Managing Teams
(continued on next page)

Variable Name	Variable Description
Encourages self-reinforcement	Leader encourages work group to be self-reinforcing of high group performance.
Encourages self-criticism	Leader encourages work group to be self-critical of low group performance.
Encourages self–goal setting	Leader encourages work group to set performance goals.
Encourages self-observation/ evaluation	Leader encourages work group to monitor, be aware of, and evaluate level of performance.
Encourages self-expectation	Leader encourages work group to have high expectations for group performance.
Encourages rehearsal	Leader encourages work group to go over an activity and "think it through" before actually performing the activity.
Communicates to/from management	Leader communicates group views to upper management (i.e., support group) and management views to the group.
Facilitates equipment supplies	Leader facilitates obtaining equipment and supplies for the work group.
Communicates between groups	Leader communicates group views to and from other groups.
Encourages within-group communication	Leader encourages open communication among group members, including the exchange of information for learning new jobs.

Description of Leader Behaviors for Self-Managing Teams (cont. from page 201)

training inexperienced employees, and so on. However, a fundamental difference does exist in how leadership functions are carried out, especially in terms of the shift in the source of control from the leader to the follower. The uniqueness of the self-managed team leader's role lies in the commitment to the philosophy that the team should successfully complete necessary leadership functions for itself. The dominant role of the external leader, then, is SuperLeadership—to lead others to lead themselves. This is quite different from the traditional role of the leader.

Widely held notions of traditional leadership seem to revolve around the idea that the leader is someone who does something to influence someone else directly. The assumption is that the power and initiation are vested almost entirely within the leader.

In our research, we compared our results with data from two other studies in which traditional leadership behaviors were emphasized.[9] This comparison is shown in the table on page 204.

The implicit assumptions underlying the set of self-managing group leadership behaviors are quite different from those of the earlier, more traditional behaviors. Instead of a top-down philosophy of control, these behaviors imply a bottom-up perspective. Even the labels of the behaviors indicate that subordinates can perform leadership functions for themselves and that the leader's job is to teach and encourage subordinates to lead themselves effectively. As we observed the leadership practices within the self-managing teams, this fundamental philosophical difference was strongly apparent. In the self-management system, organizing, directing, and monitoring functions—all part of traditional notions of leadership—are largely centered within the team.

SELF-MANAGING TEAMS AND EFFECTIVENESS

Overall, the statistical results of our study indicated that several self-management leadership behaviors were significantly related to overall leadership effectiveness and that these relationships exist even when the effects of more traditional leadership-behavior variables were removed.

TRADITIONAL LEADER BEHAVIORS		SELF-MANAGING LEADER BEHAVIORS
Study 1*	Study 2†	
Initiation: Originates, facilitates, or rejects new ideas.	Emphasizes goals.	Encourages self-reinforcement.
Organization: Defines and structures his or her own work, the work of group members, and the relationships among group members in the performance of work.	Coordinates groups. Provides information. Proposes solutions.	Encourages self-observation/evaluation. Encourages self-expectation. Encourages self-goal setting.
Domination: Restricts the behavior of individuals or the group in action, decision making, or freedom of expression.	Specifies problems.	Encourages rehearsal.
Production: Sets levels of effort or achievement or prods members for greater effort.	Exercises influence. Talks frequently.	Encourages self-criticism.
Recognition: Expresses approval or disapproval of group-member behavior.		
Integration: Subordinates individual behavior, encourages pleasant group atmosphere, reduces conflict among members, and promotes individual adjustment to the group.		
Communication: Provides information to subordinates, seeks information from them, facilitates information exchange, shows awareness of affairs pertaining to the group.		

*Taken from Schriesheim, House, and Kerr (1976).[9]
†Taken from Lord, Foti, and DeVader (1984).

Comparison of Traditional Leader Behaviors with Self-Managing Leader Behaviors

In other research, Daniel Denison compared manufacturing plants using self-managing teams with plants using a more traditional organizational design. He found systematic differences in the perceived control. Workers in self-managing teams believed they had more control than their counterparts from the more traditional plants. Interestingly, perceived control by the middle managers at both plants showed no differences. In essence, lower-level workers from the team plants experienced higher self-control without lower perceived control by the middle managers. [10]

Fully developed teams seem to have a remarkable capacity to instill enthusiasm and motivation in team members. Santos Martinez, a team member at the highly successful New United Motor Manufacturing Inc. (a joint venture between GM and Toyota at Fremont, California, often called Nummi for short), describes his team experience this way: "My responsibility now is to the team, which works together like a family to solve problems and do the job. And no one places blame when something goes wrong. We all take responsibility, and, therefore, no one ever wants to let a team member down. It sounds so simple, but you really [have to work the] system to understand." [11]

While we do not have specific quantitative data to ascertain whether the system we studied was effective as a whole, informal conversations with corporate officials indicated productivity gains "significantly greater than 20 percent" when compared to other plants of the same technology using more traditional management methods. Our discussions with management also revealed similar positive comparisons regarding quality, turnover, and worker satisfaction. In the case of turnover, for example, in response to our inquiry, a manager in the plant counted on the fingers of one hand the employees who had chosen to leave. In fact, the corporation we studied is currently engaged in an extensive effort to extend this team system throughout its organization.

Officials indicated productivity gains "significantly greater than 20 percent."

SUMMARY: LEADERSHIP AND SELF-MANAGING TEAMS

First, our visits to this plant were very instructive regarding the potential of people to work together productively. A point to emphasize here is that this plant is not a Japanese operation, so we do not have the difficulty of sorting out the separate effects of culture and managerial organization and style. From evidence available at this plant, it is apparent that American workers can respond responsibly and productively to self-leadership programs. In listening to their day-to-day conversations, we heard the message of their competence and commitment loud and clear.

Overall, our study of this organization and several we have studied since then suggests that there is a legitimate role for external leaders of self-managing teams and that it differs considerably from the traditional leadership role. In general, our data suggest the following: (1) the self-management leadership behaviors (derived from self-leadership theory) generally represent important indicators of external-leadership effectiveness in team situations; (2) there is some evidence that these leader behaviors have a significant additional importance over and above the more traditional leadership or sociotechnical system leadership behaviors; (3) an important means by which these self-management leadership behaviors are expressed is through one-on-one individual communication with team members, especially internal team leaders; and (4) the most important self-management leadership behaviors are encouraging self-reinforcement and encouraging self-observation and evaluation.

The SuperLeadership behaviors and other relevant leadership behaviors identified in this research provide a beginning for exploring and understanding what external leaders actually do in a context characterized by a strong self-management philosophy. Also, we believe these behaviors have potential for allowing insight into other situations, including those in traditional organizations where a self-management philosophy is not overtly embraced. Clearly, additional study is needed to further validate and better understand this list of behaviors. Currently, we are involved in researching self-managed teams in a wide range of industries and work settings. Ultimately, such a line of research could provide the insight needed to meet the challenge of leading those who are supposed to be self-leading and for providing badly needed guidelines for selecting and training external leaders of self-managing teams. We believe that the continued study of this particular type of application will contribute greatly to the understanding and application of SuperLeadership principles in modern organizations.

PROFILES IN SUPERLEADERSHIP: MACGREGOR[1]

This is a true story that is almost too good to believe: it concerns a man who not only earns accolades as the company's most highly touted plant manager but also perfects his golf game on company time. His secret: raising delegation to a fine art.

My encounter with MacGregor came about during the course of a study of the extent to which operating managers actually *use* participative management techniques in their dealings with subordinates.

MacGregor, who at the time was manager of one of the largest refineries in the country, was the last of more than 100 managers I interviewed in the course of the study.

The switchboard operator answered with the name of the refinery. When I asked for MacGregor's office, a male voice almost instantly said, "Hello." I then asked for MacGregor, whereupon the voice responded, "This is he." I should have recognized at once that this was no ordinary manager; he answered his own phone instantly, as though he had been waiting for it to ring. To my question about when it would be convenient for me to come see him, he replied, "Anytime." I said, "Would today be all right?" His response was, "Today, tomorrow, or Wednesday would be OK; or you could come Thursday, except don't come between 10:00 A.M. and noon; or you could come Friday or next week—anytime." I replied feebly, "I just want to fit in with your plans." Then he said, "You are just not getting the message; it makes no difference to me when you come. I have nothing on the books except to play golf and see you. Come in anytime—I don't have to be notified in advance, so I'll be seeing you one of these days," and he then hung up. I was dumbfounded. Here was a highly placed executive with apparently nothing to do except play golf and talk to visitors.

I took MacGregor at his word and drove over immediately to see him without any further announcement of my visit. MacGregor's office, in a small building at one corner of the refinery, adjoined that of his secretary—who, when I arrived, was knitting busily and, without dropping a stitch, said to me, "You must be Mr. Carlisle; he's in there," indicating MacGregor's office with a glance at a connecting door.

MacGregor's office was large and had a big window overlooking the refinery, a conference table with eight chairs arranged around it (one of which, at the head, was more comfortable and imposing than the rest), an engineer's file cabinet with a series of wide drawers, two easy chairs, a sofa, a coffee table with a phone on it, and a desk. The desk had been shoved all the way into a corner; there was no way a chair could be slipped in behind it, and it was covered with technical journals. A lamp stood on the desk, but its plug was not connected to an outlet. There was no phone on the desk. MacGregor, a tall, slender man with a tanned face, stood by the window peering absently into space. He turned slowly when I entered his office and said, "You must be Carlisle. The head office told me you wanted to talk to me about the way we run things here. Sit down on the sofa and fire away."

MacGREGOR'S MODUS OPERANDI

"Do you hold regular meetings with your subordinates?" I asked.

"Yes, I do," he replied.

"How often?" I asked.

"Once a week, on Thursdays, between 10:00 A.M. and noon; that's why I couldn't see you then," was his response.

"What sorts of things do you discuss?" I queried, following my interview guide.

"My subordinates tell me about the decisions they've made during the past week," he explained.

"Then you believe in participative decision making," I commented.

"No—as a matter of fact, I don't," said MacGregor.

"Then why hold the meetings?" I asked. "Why not just tell your people about the operating decisions you've made and let them know how to carry them out?"

"Oh, I don't make their decisions for them and I just don't believe in participating in the decisions they should be making, either; we hold the weekly meeting so that I can keep informed on what they're doing and how. The meeting also gives me a chance to appraise their technical and managerial abilities," he explained. "I used to make all the operating decisions myself; but I quit doing that a few years ago when I discovered my golf game was going to hell because I didn't have enough time to practice. Now that I've quit making other people's decisions, my game is back where it should be."

"You don't make operating decisions any more?" I asked in astonishment.

"No," he replied. Sensing my incredulity, he added, "Obviously you don't believe me. Why not ask one of my subordinates? Which one do you want to talk to?"

"I haven't any idea; I don't even know how many subordinates you have, let alone their names. You choose one," I suggested.

"No, I wouldn't do that—for two reasons. First, I don't make decisions, and second, when my subordinate confirms that I don't make decisions, you'll say that it's a put-up job, so here is a list of my eight immediate subordinates, the people who report directly to me. Choose one name from it and I'll call him and you can talk to him," said MacGregor.

"OK—Johnson, then. I'll talk to him if he's free," said I.

"I'm sure he's able to talk to you. I'll call him and tell him you're on the way over." Reaching for the phone, he determined that Johnson wasn't doing anything, either, and would be happy to have someone to talk to.

SUBORDINATES' VIEWS OF MacGREGOR

I walked over to Johnson's unit and found him to be in his early thirties. After a couple of minutes of casual conversation, I discovered that MacGregor and all eight of his subordinates were chemical engineers. Johnson said, "I suppose MacGregor gave you that bit about his not making decisions, didn't he? That man is a gas."

"It isn't true though, is it? He does make decisions, doesn't he?" I asked.

"No, he doesn't; everything he told you is true. He simply decided not to get involved in decisions that his subordinates are being paid to make. So he stopped making them, and they tell me he plays a lot of golf in the time he saves," said Johnson.

Then I asked Johnson whether he tried to get MacGregor to make a decision and his response was:

"Only once. I had been on the job for only about a week when I ran into an operating problem I couldn't solve, so I phoned MacGregor. He answered the phone with that sleepy 'Hello' of his. I told him who I was and that I had a problem. His response was instantaneous: 'Good, that's what you're being paid to do: solve problems,' and then he hung up. I was dumbfounded. I didn't really know any of the people I was working with, so because I didn't think I had any other alternative, I called him back, got the same sleepy 'Hello,' and again identified myself. He replied sharply, 'I thought I told you that you were paid to solve problems. Do you think that I should do your job as well as my own?' When I insisted on seeing him about my problem, he answered, 'I don't know how you expect me to help you. You have a technical problem and I don't go into the refinery any more; I used to, but my shirts kept getting dirty from the visits and my wife doesn't like washing all the grime out of them, so I pretty much stick in my office. Ask one of the other men. They're all in touch with what goes on out there.'

"I didn't know which one to consult, so I insisted again on seeing him. He finally agreed—grudgingly—to see me right away, so I went over to his office and there he was in his characteristic looking-out-the-window posture. When I sat down, he started the dirty-shirt routine—but when he saw that I was determined to involve him in my problems, he sat down on the sofa in front of his coffee table and, pen in hand, prepared to write on a pad of paper. He asked me to state precisely what the problem was and he wrote down exactly what I said. Then he asked what the conditions for its solution were. I replied that I didn't know what he meant by that question. His response was, 'If you don't know what conditions have to be satisfied for a solution to be reached, how do you know when you've solved the problem?' I told him I'd never thought of approaching a problem that way and he replied, 'Then you'd better start. I'll work through this one with you *this* time, but don't expect me to do your problem solving for you because that's *your* job, not mine.'

"I stumbled through the conditions that would have to be satisfied by the solution. Then he asked me what alternative approaches I could think of. I gave him the first one I could think of—let's call it X—and he wrote it down and asked me what would happen if I did X. I replied with my answer—let's call it A. Then he asked me how A compared with the conditions I had established for the solution of the problem. I replied that it did not meet them. MacGregor told me that I'd have to think of another. I came up with Y, which I said would yield result B, and this still fell short of the solution conditions. After more prodding from MacGregor, I came up with Z, which I said would have C as a result; although this clearly came a lot closer to the conditions I had established for the solution than any of the others I'd suggested, it still did not satisfy all of them. MacGregor then asked me if I could combine any of the approaches I'd suggested. I replied I could do X and Z and then saw that the resultant A plus C would indeed satisfy all the solution conditions I had set up previously. When I thanked Mac-Gregor, he replied, 'What for? Get the hell out of my office; you could have done that bit of problem solving perfectly well without wasting my time. Next time you really can't solve a problem on your own, ask the Thursday man and tell me about it at the Thursday meeting.' "

I asked Johnson about Mr. MacGregor's reference to the Thursday man.

"He's the guy who runs the Thursday meeting when MacGregor is away from the plant. I'm the Thursday man now. My predecessor left here about two months ago."

"Where did he go? Did he quit the company?" I asked.

"God, no. He got a refinery of his own. That's what happens to a lot of Thursday men. After the kind of experience we get coping with everyone's problems and MacGregor's refusal to do what he perceives as his subordinates' work, we don't need an operating superior any more and we're ready for our own refineries. Incidentally, most of the people at our level have adopted MacGregor's managerial method in dealing with the foremen who report to us and we are reaping the same kinds of benefits that he does. The foremen are a lot more self-reliant, and we don't have to do their work for them."

I went back to see MacGregor. His secretary was still knitting. The garment she was working on was considerably more advanced than it was on my first visit. She motioned me into MacGregor's office with her head, again not dropping a stitch. MacGregor was in his traditional office posture, looking vacantly out of the window. He turned and asked, "Well, now do you believe that I don't make any decisions?"

I said, "No, that could have been just a fluke." He suggested I see another subordinate and asked me to pick another name from the list. I picked Peterson, who, when phoned to see whether he was available, said that he had nothing to do. So I went to Peterson's office.

Peterson was in his late twenties. He asked me what I thought of MacGregor. I said I found him most unusual. Peterson replied, "Yes, he's a gas." Peterson's story paralleled Johnson's. MacGregor refused to make decisions related to the work of his subordinates. When Peterson got into a situation he could not deal with, he said he called one of the other supervisors, usually Johnson, and together they worked it out. At the Thursday meetings, he reported on the decision and gave credit to his helper. "If I hadn't," he added, "I probably wouldn't get help from that quarter again."

In reply to a query on what the Thursday meetings were like, he said, "Well, we all sit around that big conference table in MacGregor's office. He sits at the head like a thinned-down Buddha, and we go around the table talking about the decisions we've made and, if we got help, who helped us. The other guys occasionally make comments— especially if the particular decision being discussed was like one they had had to make themselves at some point or if it had some direct effect on their own operations." MacGregor had said very little at these past few meetings, according to Peterson, but he did pass on any new developments that he heard about at the head office.

HEAD-OFFICE ASSESSMENT OF MacGREGOR

By the time I had finished with Johnson and Peterson, it was time for lunch. I decided I'd go downtown and stop in at the head office to try to find out their assessment of MacGregor and his operation. I visited the operations chief for the corporation. I had wanted to thank him for his willingness to go along with my study, anyway. When I told him I had met MacGregor, his immediate response was, "Isn't he a gas?" I muttered something about having heard that comment before and asked him about the efficiency of MacGregor's operation in comparison with that of other refineries in the corporation. His response was instantaneous. "Oh, MacGregor has by far the most efficient producing unit."

"Is that because he has the newest equipment?" I asked.

"No. As a matter of fact he has the oldest in the corporation. His was the first refinery we built."

"Does MacGregor have a lot of turnover among his subordinates?"

"A great deal," he replied.

Thinking I had found a chink in the MacGregor armor, I asked, "What happens to them; can't they take his system?"

"On the contrary," said the operations chief. "Most of them go on to assignments as refinery managers. After all, under MacGregor's method of supervision, they are used to working on their own."

MORE POINTERS ON MacGREGOR'S STYLE OF MANAGING

"How do they run their own operations—like MacGregor's?" I asked.

"You guessed it. More and more of our operations are using his system."

I went back to the refinery with a few last questions for MacGregor.

"Now let me focus a bit more on your role as refinery manager. You say you don't make decisions. Suppose a subordinate told you at a Thursday meeting about a decision he'd made and you were convinced that it was a mistake. What would you do about it?"

"How much would the mistake cost me?"

"Oh, I don't know," I answered.

"Can't tell you, then. It would depend on how much it would cost."

"Say, $3,000," I suggested.

"That's easy, I'd let him make it," said MacGregor. I sensed I'd hit the upper limit before MacGregor either would have moved in himself or, more likely, would have suggested that the subordinate discuss it with the Thursday man and then report back to him on their joint decision.

"When was the last time you let a subordinate make a mistake of that magnitude?" I asked skeptically.

"About four weeks ago," said MacGregor.

"You let someone who works for you make such a serious mistake? Why did you do that?"

"Three reasons," said MacGregor. "First, I was only 99.44 percent sure it would be a mistake and if it hadn't turned out to be one, I'd have felt pretty foolish. Second, I thought that making a mistake like this one would be such a tremendous learning experience for him that he'd never make another like that one again. I felt it would do him more good than signing him up for most of the management-development courses that are available. Third, this is a profit center. It was early in the budget year and I felt that we could afford it."

"What was the result?" I asked.

"It *was* a mistake—and I heard about it in short order from the controller downtown by phone." (I realized suddenly that during the whole time I had been in the office, neither MacGregor's phone nor his secretary's had rung.)

"The controller said, 'MacGregor how could you let a stupid mistake like that last one slip through?' "

"What did you say?"

"Well, I figured a good attack is the best defense. I asked him which refinery in the corporation was the most efficient. He replied, 'You know yours is. That has nothing to do with it.' I told him that it had everything to do with it. I added that my people learn from their mistakes and until the rest of the plants in the organization started operating at the same degree of efficiency as this one, I wasn't going to waste my time talking to clerks. Then I hung up."

"What happened?"

"Well, relations were a bit strained for a while—but they know I'm probably the best refinery manager in the business and I can get another job anytime, so it blew over pretty quickly," he said, not without a degree of self-satisfaction.

MacGregor's Control Systems

"Peterson told me you have quite a control system here. How does it work?" I asked.

"Very simply," said MacGregor. "On Wednesdays at 2:00 P.M., my subordinates and I get the printout from the computer, which shows the production men their output against quota and the maintenance superintendent his costs to date against the budget. If there is an unfavorable gap between the two, they call me about 3:00 P.M. and the conversation goes something like this: 'Mr. MacGregor, I know I have a problem and this is what I'm going to do about it.' If their solution will work, I tell them to go ahead. If not, I tell them so and then they go and work on it some more and then call back. If the new one will work, I tell them to go ahead with it. If not, I suggest they get in touch with one of the other men, work it out together, and then call me and tell me how they are going to deal with it. If that doesn't work, I refer them to the Thursday man. That way, I don't get involved in making operating decisions.

"I used to have a smaller refinery than this one where I found myself frantically busy all the time—answering the phone constantly and continually doing my subordinates' problem solving for them. They were always more than willing to let me do their work because it was easier than doing it themselves and also because, if the solution did not

215

work out, then I was to blame. Can't fault them for trying that. But when I came here, I resolved to get myself out of that kind of rat race and set about designing this system. I worked out a computer-based production control system in conjunction with a set of quotas I negotiate each year with each of my operating people and a cost budget with the maintenance man. Then I arranged for Wednesday reports. Sometimes it takes a bit of time to renegotiate these quotas—and I've been known to use peer pressure to get them to a reasonable level—but these performance objectives really have to be accepted by the individual before they have any legitimacy or motivational value for him. I chose Wednesday because if a problem did develop, I'd still have time to act on my own if my subordinates couldn't come up with a solution. You see, our production week ends Saturday night. I don't want my head to fall in the basket because of their inability to make good decisions, so I minimized the risk this way.

"I can't even remember when I've had to get directly involved myself with their work. I do a lot of reading related to my work. That's why, when they call me with solutions, I can usually tell accurately whether or not their proposals are going to work out. That's my job as I see it—not doing subordinates' work but, rather, exercising supervision. A lot of managers feel that they have to keep proving to their people that they know more about their subordinates' jobs than the subordinates themselves by doing their work for them. I refuse to do that anymore."

INTERPRETING THE CASE

We were especially pleased to receive permission to reprint portions of the article "MacGregor" by Professor Arthur Elliott Carlisle of the University of Massachusetts, because the character, MacGregor, illustrates SuperLeadership in several interesting ways. In general, MacGregor is committed to a leadership philosophy that depends for its success on developing effective subordinates.

MacGregor doesn't just encourage his subordinates to work independently (to be self-leaders); he absolutely insists on it. As a consequence, his employees demonstrate an unusual ability to work on their own in a highly effective and responsible manner.

More specifically, MacGregor relies on his own tailor-made versions of many of the strategies we have presented in this book. To begin with, he is an excellent *model* for his subordinates. He demonstrates through his own behavior a commitment to self-leadership and to solving his own problems. Further, his dramatically unique style of leading others is, in turn, being adopted by his managers for dealing with their own subordinates. This style centers on fostering subordinate growth and independence by facilitating their full abilities to solve their own problems and to make their own decisions. One clear measure of MacGregor's long-term success is that his subordinates often go on to be highly effective managers of their own refineries.

MacGregor also provides the necessary *guidance* for his employees to grow in their self-leading capability, though sometimes this nondirective external influence seems to be provided grudgingly. The incident in which Johnson tried to get MacGregor to solve a problem for him is a case in point. When MacGregor realized that Johnson was not going to make the decision without some guidance, he finally agreed to help. But the guidance he provided left the responsibility and final control with Johnson and was still intended to contribute to his self-leadership growth. Through a series of questions (much like we have suggested for the process of guided participation), Mac-Gregor drew out Johnson's ideas and facilitated his skill at independent problem solving. After helping Johnson to reach a solution, MacGregor instructed him to solve his own problems in the future.

MacGregor also *reinforces* his subordinates for their independent efforts. In particular, he makes it a practice to recognize and give credit to his employees for their self-led accomplishments in their weekly Thursday meetings. Further, he is very committed to *goal setting*. Indeed, his control system largely centers around helping his employees to establish their own challenging performance objectives and providing concrete feedback on their progress. Again, however, he insists that his subordinates reach these goals by means of their own decisions and efforts.

MacGregor also displays a willingness to occasionally use *reprimand*, a problematic strategy within the SuperLeadership framework. But his use of reprimands is not based on task failures or mistakes but is mainly directed at resistance to performing one's own responsibilities. In fact, MacGregor views mistakes, even relatively costly ones, as an investment in his subordinates' learning and growth. He is apparently quite willing to provide verbal negative feedback, however, to those employees who try to get him to "perform their jobs."

Finally, MacGregor has clearly facilitated the development of a high-performance *culture based on self-leadership.* Employees recognize taking personal responsibility, working independently, and exercising self-control as strongly entrenched cultural norms. Over time self-leadership became the normal way of doing things within MacGregor's work unit. His refinery has become a model for others in the company and his leadership style, a model for aspiring SuperLeaders.

10

Creating Exceptional Self-Leaders through SuperLeadership

We have now presented the fundamental elements of SuperLeadership and have provided several case examples that illustrate specific aspects of the overall model. Our objective in this chapter is to pull it all together by giving an overview of the comprehensive framework of SuperLeadership. Thus, while the previous chapters introduced and illustrated the pieces, mainly drawing from real-life examples, the following discussion will assemble the overall picture. Our intent is to provide a process for creating exceptional self-leaders through SuperLeadership.

SUPERLEADERSHIP: A COMPREHENSIVE FRAMEWORK

It should be clear by now that we are addressing a different approach to leadership, radically unlike many of the classic stereotypes of strong leadership. The cases we have presented provide only glimpses of the many ways that the SuperLeadership approach has been pursued by current and past leaders in many different facets of society.

Let us reiterate that SuperLeadership is a process that can be *learned*, that it is not restricted to a few "special" individuals that are born with an unusual capability. Granted, some seem to have more to learn than others. But in the end, a person's recognition of a need to improve and work toward a new, more powerful leadership style may well cause an "initially deficient" leader to become truly exceptional.

We have specifically discussed several separate ingredients of SuperLeadership including modeling and encouraging self-leadership; providing and facilitating the establishment of goals for self-leadership progress; guiding the development of self-leadership in others; reinforcing effective self-leadership when it does occur; and creating and nurturing systems that allow self-leadership practice to flourish. The figure on page 221 brings these separate components together in an organized framework with self-leadership at the core. The logic is that each SuperLeadership component is essential to the development of the self-leadership system within each employee. The potential payoffs include increased employee performance and innovation flowing from enhanced commitment, motivation, and employee capability. A brief summary of the primary SuperLeadership components follows.

Each SuperLeadership component is essential to the development of the self-leadership system within each employee.

Modeling is the first and, in many ways, the most important step toward SuperLeadership. Before executives can reasonably expect to successfully lead others, they must learn to effectively lead themselves. After all, a leader's own self-leadership behavior serves as a powerful model for followers. The example a leader sets can overshadow most other ways that information is transmitted to followers about appropriate behavior. For the modeling process to operate effectively, it needs to be managed. Leaders can effectively influence

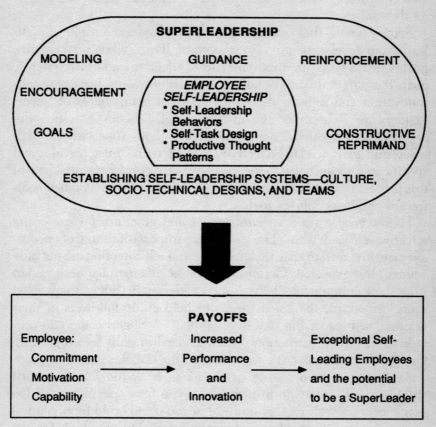

The SuperLeadership Approach

others through modeling if they are viewed as credible and display the desired behaviors in a vivid and detailed manner. Followers also need the opportunity to practice or rehearse, either physically or mentally, the self-leadership behaviors they observe in order to effectively retain them. Also, when effective self-leadership is modeled by the leader, followers need both the freedom to exercise self-leadership in their own environment and the incentives to use the self-leadership behavior themselves.

Setting *goals* that are specifically focused on employee self-leadership development is also important. Thus, while performance goals will always be an important part of effective leadership systems, goals that target initiative, taking responsibility, and mastering self-motivation and self-direction are important components of Super-Leadership. Remember the employees at Lincoln Electric who are evaluated on their "ability to work without supervision." Self-leadership goals need to be set that are challenging but achievable and specific and meaningful to the followers. Further, an essential part of this process is the transition, over time, from manager-assigned goals toward employee self-set goals.

Followers also need *encouragement* and *guidance* for exercising effective self-leadership. The leader is an important source of encouragement and reassurance that initiative and self-direction are not only wanted, but expected. Communication of this message becomes an important component of the SuperLeader's job. But perhaps even more important, the leader needs to help guide followers in their personal self-leadership skill development. A SuperLeader can provide some direct instruction on self-leadership skills for employees. One of the most effective ways that a SuperLeader can offer guidance, however, is by using questions such as the following that stimulate self-leadership thinking: "Do you have specific goals? Do you know how well you are doing? Do you try to build more natural enjoyment and motivation into your work? Do you look for the positive, challenging aspects of your work?"

Also, the leader needs to be adept at using *rewards* and *reprimands*. However, the primary focus of this process changes. Instead of concentrating solely on task performance, the SuperLeader shifts the emphasis to self-leadership behavior. Subordinates are rewarded for exercising initiative and for effectively using self-leadership strategies such as self-set goals, self-observation, and self-reward. In addition, especially in transition, the tolerance level for failure needs to be carefully reconsidered. The transition from external control to self-control is bound to contain some rough spots. Commitment to effective employee self-leadership requires patience. In fact, the whole process of using reprimands must be balanced against the goal of developing followers as self-leaders. An inevitable objective is to develop subordinates so that they become their own primary source of leadership criticism, and constructive feedback.

Developing individual self-leaders will—in the aggregate—create the desired end of an overall *self-leadership culture*. To some degree, this process should unfold naturally. But the SuperLeader also needs to be sensitive to the primary elements that make up the other parts of overall self-leadership systems and manage this process. Followers who are expected to become dynamic self-leaders require important ingredients such as adequate equipment and resources, complimentary design of both social and technical systems, necessary task and self-leadership skills, and enough autonomy to exercise their potential. The SuperLeader's example, guidance, and reinforcement can all contribute to the development of values and expectations that support this end. In the process, the *appropriate work scripts* and *patterns of thinking* that followers adopt for playing their parts in the work unit's performance are rewritten so that their potential can be more fully mined. Eventually, self-leadership can become the norm instead of the exception. Members of the culture become important sources of encouragement and reinforcement for both themselves and one another.

Ideally, the SuperLeader comes to be surrounded by strong people, self-leaders in their own rights, who pursue exceptional achievement because they love it. The SuperLeader's strength is greatly enhanced since it is drawn from the strength of many people who have been allowed to grow, flourish, and become important contributors. As tight control is relinquished and self-leadership is nurtured, the power for progress is unleashed and the potential to be a SuperLeader is established.

Self-leadership can become the norm instead of the exception.

SEARCHING NOT FOR HEROIC LEADERS
BUT FOR HERO MAKERS

Throughout this book, we have been describing a framework for SuperLeadership. A framework, however, is not much good if it serves no useful purpose. We believe that SuperLeadership offers the most viable mechanism for establishing exceptional subordinates (self-leaders) in the workplace in this modern age. True excellence can be achieved by facilitating the self-leadership system that operates within each person—by challenging each person to reach deep inside for the best each has to offer. Employee compliance is not enough. Leading others to lead themselves is the key to tapping the intelligence, the spirit, the creativity, the commitment, and, most of all, the tremendous, unique potential of each individual.

Our perspective is straightforward. Those executives, or for that matter, any aspiring SuperLeaders, can choose no better strategy than nurturing and harvesting the vast capabilities of those who surround them. SuperLeadership means tapping into a power that transcends the imagination of employee capability. This book has indeed been written for those who wish to become SuperLeaders by discovering how to lead others to lead themselves.

The pursuit of high achievement, at least in spirit if not in action, has enjoyed a resurgence in our society. The difficulties and threats to our self-esteem have been striking: declining achievement-test scores of our children, erosion of the stability and health of our family structures, frightening surges in crime, the apparent collapse in the foundations of international sanity that terrorism suggests.

The notion of excellence is not only refreshing, but a badly needed tonic. And in delivering this tonic to the general public, few efforts have received more attention than that of Tom Peters and Robert Waterman, Jr., in their book *In Search of Excellence*. While some might quibble about its content or scientific precision, few would argue about the impact of their work. In their introduction they point out that good management practice is not the sole possession of the Japanese, and that American companies can reap much good from treating people well, allowing them to excell, and encouraging them to produce quality products. They further suggest that small motivated groups replace scale efficiencies, that committed champions substitute for carefully planned R&D efforts, and that thick rule books be thrown out in favor of allowing everyone to contribute. [1] Since that first book, Peters sometimes seems more pessimistic, but in his more recent book, *The Renewal Factor*, Waterman continues to be upbeat. He especially points to companies like Ford as examples of companies that have undergone a substantial change for the better. [2]

Leading others to lead themselves is the key to tapping the intelligence, the spirit, the creativity, the commitment, and, most of all, the tremendous, unique potential of each individual.

To us, the message is clear: excellence is achievable, but only if leaders are dedicated to tapping the vast potential within each individual. Most of all, this does *not* mean that more so-called charismatic or transformational leaders are needed to influence followers to comply with and carry out the vision of the leader. Rather, the vision itself needs to reflect and draw upon the vast resources contained within individual employees. The currently popular notion that excellent leaders should be visionary and charismatic may be a trap if taken too far.

Indeed, it is time to transcend the notion of leaders as heroes and to focus instead on leaders as hero makers. Is the spotlight on the leader, or on the achievements of the followers? If you want to be a great leader of others, first learn to lead yourself. Then encourage and help others to do the same and reward them when they break the bounds of dependency. All the while, you will be creating a culture of exceptional achievement based on exceptional self-leaders. That's the simple message of this book. True SuperLeadership is *not* about attracting the admiration of others with great charisma and vision. That approach only increases the attention on the leader at the expense of the followers. Instead, the object is to develop so-called followers into dynamic self-leaders that are inspired by their own potential and effectiveness.

It is time to transcend the notion of leaders as heroes and to focus instead on leaders as hero makers.

In fact, the so-called charismatic or transformational leaders might be today's smoothed-out version of the dictatorial, autocratic leaders of past generations—leaders who bend the will of others to their own, not by threat or fear, but by capitalizing on an artificial sense of the leader's greatness or superiority. Visionary, charismatic leaders who possess a broad view of the organization and its environment can be very important, especially in the short term or in crisis and particularly in disorganized cases where the organizational culture has lost its direction and sense of competence. Iacocca did wonders at Chrysler after it reached the brink of collapse. But in the long run, overemphasizing the charismatic leader can foster a dependence that can actually weaken the system. How will Chrysler fare when Iacocca is gone?

Is the spotlight on the leader, or on the achievements of the followers?

The Iacoccas of the world need to gradually turn the spotlight from themselves to individual employees. Developing effective self-leaders is the key that will assure an organization's optimal, long-term viability. Leadership—SuperLeadership—founded on effective employee self-leadership creates a resilient performance system that can stand on its own when the leader is gone. Visionary leadership based on charisma can create a system that may not be able to function in the absence of the leader—one that collapses like a house of cards when the leader moves on. With charismatic leadership, the power and vision are vested in the leader, so the followers can become as empty vessels. With SuperLeadership, the power and the vision rest in the followers. The so-called followers stand as strong pillars of self-leadership that support the overall system for the long haul.

We are talking about a new sort of awesome leader, a SuperLeader. . . . To discover this new breed of leader, a person must simply look *not* at the leader, but at the followers. SuperLeaders have SuperFollowers.

In the end, we are talking about a new sort of awesome leader, a SuperLeader, one that turns leadership inside out, upside down, and literally on its ear. To discover this new breed of leader, a person must simply look *not* at the leader, but at the followers. SuperLeaders have SuperFollowers who are dynamic self-leaders. And these ideas are not new—they have existed for ages. Perhaps they were most effectively expressed in a poem by Lao-tzu, a sixth-century B.C. Chinese philosopher. We previously quoted some of these words in our preface. So as a fitting close to our book, we end as we began by offering these words as a gift to you, the SuperLeaders of tomorrow.

> *A leader is best*
> *When people barely know he exists,*
> *Not so good when people obey and acclaim him,*
> *Worse when they despise him.*
> *But of a good leader, who talks little,*
> *When his work is done, his aim fulfilled,*
> *They will say:*
> *We did it ourselves.*
> —LAO-TZU

Notes

Preface

1. "Wal-Mart: The Model Discounter," *Dun's Business Month* (December 1982), pp. 60–61.
2. "Determination—Not Talent—Found to Be Key to Success," *Los Angeles Times*, in *The Minneapolis Star and Tribune* (February 17, 1985), pp. 17a–18a.

Chapter 1

1. Charles C. Manz and Roger Grothe, "Is the Workforce Vanguard to the 21st Century a QWL Deficient Prone Generation?" (unpublished working paper, 1988).
2. Robert E. Kelley, *The Gold-Collar Worker* (New York: Addison-Wesley, 1985).
3. See, for example, Edward E. Lawler III and J. G. Rhode, *Information and Control in Organizations* (Pacific Palisades, CA: Goodyear, 1976).
4. See, for example, Edward L. Deci, *Intrinsic Motivation* (New York: Plenum, 1975).
5. Dave Hage, "How Do Managers Learn to Manage?: Honeywell Uses Study to Look for Answers," *Minneapolis Star and Tribune* (March 18, 1985), p. 1M.
6. John Naisbitt, *Megatrends* (New York: Warner Books, Inc., 1982).
7. Thomas J. Peters and Robert H. Waterman, Jr., *In Search of Excellence* (New York: Harper & Row, 1982), p. 86.
8. D. Quinn Mills, "The Evolving Independent Executive: Bridging the Corporate Generation Gap," *The New York Times* (April 7, 1975), p. F3.

Chapter 2

1. Chapters two and three in this book are inspired by two works by Charles C. Manz: *The Art of Self-Leadership* (Englewood Cliffs, NJ: Prentice Hall, 1983) and "Improving Performance Through Self-Leadership," *National Productivity Review* (Summer 1983), pp. 288–297.
2. This example is based on an article by Charles C. Manz and Charles A. Snyder,

229

"Systematic Self-Management: How Resourceful Entrepreneurs Meet Business Challenges and Survive," *Management Review* (October 1983), pp. 68–73.

3. Lee Iacocca with William Novak, *Iacocca: An Autobiography* (New York: Bantam Books, 1984), p. 47.
4. Private videotaped interview taken from the historical files of Hewlett-Packard, taped August 26, 1980.
5. Iacocca, p. 32.
6. Ibid, p. 32.
7. This example is based on reports from Fred Luthans and Tim Davis in "Behavioral Self-Management (BSM): The Missing Link in Managerial Effectiveness," *Organizational Dynamics*, 8 (1979), pp. 42–60.

Chapter 3

1. The concept of natural rewards is very similar to the idea of intrinsic rewards. For one viewpoint on intrinsic rewards, see Edward L. Deci, *Intrinsic Motivation* (New York: Plenum, 1975).
2. Hans Selye, *Stress Without Distress* (New York: Signet, 1974).
3. See, for example, Martin L. Hoffman, "Is Altruism Part of Human Nature?" *Journal of Personality and Social Psychology*, 40 (1981), pp. 121–37.
4. See, for example, Albert Ellis, *A New Guide to Rational Living* (Englewood Cliffs, NJ: Prentice Hall, 1975).
5. For a detailed procedure for succeeding in this belief-challenging process, see David D. Burns, *Feeling Good: The New Mood Therapy* (New York: William Morrow and Company, Inc., 1980).
6. Donald Meichenbaum and Roy Cameron, "The Clinical Potential of Modifying What Clients Say to Themselves," in M. J. Mahoney and C. E. Thoreson, eds., *Self-Control: Power to the Person* (Monterey, CA: Brooks-Cole Publishing Co., 1974). Also for a very practical recent treatment of self-talk applications, see Shad Helmstetter, *What to Say When You Talk to Yourself* (New York: Pocket Books, 1986).
7. Daniel Goleman, "Research Affirms Power of Positive Thinking," *The New York Times* (February 3, 1987), p. 15N.
8. Ibid.
9. Charles C. Manz, Dennis Adsit, Sam Campbell, Margie Mathison-Hance, "Managerial Thought Patterns and Performance: A Study of Perceptual Patterns of Performance Hindrances for Higher and Lower Performing Managers," *Human Relations*, 41 (1988), pp. 447–65.

Profiles in SuperLeadership: William L. McKnight of 3M Company

1. Note that many of the quotes recorded in this case were collected firsthand through multiple interviews and observations recorded at 3M's headquarters in St. Paul as part of a study of 3M's Human Resource Management Systems and Practices. For more information on this study, see H. L. Angle, C. C. Manz, and A. H. Van de Ven,

"Integrating Human Resource Management and Corporate Strategy: A Preview of the 3M Story," *Human Resource Management*, 24 (1985), pp. 51–68.

2. Minnesota Mining and Manufacturing Company, *Our Story So Far: Notes from the First 75 Years of 3M Company* (St. Paul, MN: Minnesota Mining and Manufacturing Company, 1977).

3. Ibid, p. 12.

4. Ibid, p. 127.

5. Ibid, p. 130.

6. For more detail on William McKnight's life and leadership style, see M. H. Comfort, *William L. McKnight, Industrialist* (Minneapolis, MN: T. S. Denison and Co., Inc., 1962).

Chapter 4

1. Kahlil Gibran, *The Prophet* (New York: Alfred A. Knopf, 1923) pp. 64–65.

2. We originally described this procedure in our article "Self-Management as a Substitute for Leadership: A Social Learning Theory Perspective," *Academy of Management Review*, 5 (1980), pp. 361–67. This procedure is inspired by the work of D. Meichenbaum and R. Cameron in their article "The Clinical Potential of Modifying What Clients Say to Themselves," in M. J. Mahoney and C. E. Thoreson, eds., *Self-Control: Power to the Person* (Monterey, CA: Brooks-Cole Publishing Co., 1974).

3. Warren Bennis, "The 4 Competencies of Leadership," *Training and Development Journal* (August 1984), pp. 14–19.

4. For a more detailed discussion regarding the amount of participation to allow subordinates under differing circumstances, see Victor H. Vroom and Phillip W. Yetton, *Leadership and Decision Making* (Pittsburgh, PA: University of Pittsburgh Press, 1973).

5. Robert E. Kelley, *The Gold-Collar Worker* (New York: Addison-Wesley, 1985).

6. William Serrin, "The Way That Works at Lincoln," *The New York Times* (January 15, 1984), pp. iii–4.

7. For a thorough discussion of a reciprocal view of influence, see Albert Bandura, *Social Foundations of Thought and Action: A Social Cognitive Theory* (Englewood Cliffs, NJ: Prentice Hall, 1986).

8. Serrin, pp. iii–4.

Profiles in SuperLeadership: Joe Paterno

1. Most of the Paterno quotes are taken from a personal interview conducted by Henry P. Sims, Jr., in Paterno's office in the summer of 1985. Other quotes, indicated by footnotes, are taken from Mervin D. Hyman and Gordon S. White, Jr., *Joe Paterno: Football My Way* (New York: Collier Books, 1971).

2. Hyman and White, p. 138.

3. Ibid, p. 45.

4. Ibid, p. 45.

5. Ibid, p. 44.
6. Ibid, p. 13.
7. Ibid, p. 45.
8. Ibid, p. 56.
9. Ibid, p. 14.
10. Ibid, p. 46.
11. Ibid, pp. 266–67.
12. Ibid, p. 45.
13. Ibid, p. 138.
14. Ibid, p. 268.

Chapter 5

1. Quote from a letter to the editor in *Business Week* (November 26, 1984), p. 9.
2. For more detail on these parts of the modeling process, see Albert Bandura, *Social Foundations of Thought and Action: A Social Cognitive Theory* (Englewood Cliffs, NJ: Prentice Hall, 1986), chapter 2, and Charles C. Manz and Henry P. Sims, Jr., "Vicarious Learning: The Influence of Modeling on Organizational Behavior," *Academy of Management Review,* 6 (1981), pp. 105–13.
3. Gary P. Latham and Lisa M. Saari, "Applications of Social Learning Theory to Training Supervisors Through Behavioral Modeling," *Journal of Applied Psychology,* 64 (1979), pp. 239–46.
4. See Charles C. Manz and Henry P. Sims, Jr., "Beyond Imitation: Complex Behavioral and Affective Linkages Resulting from Exposure to Leadership Training Models," *Journal of Applied Psychology,* 71 (1986), pp. 571–78, for another modeling-based leadership training experiment and for a review of some of the research in this area.

Profiles in SuperLeadership: General Dwight D. Eisenhower

1. Some of the text in this profile is drawn from the master's research paper ("Five-Star Manager: The Leadership Style of General Dwight D. Eisenhower," The Pennsylvania State University, May, 1985) written by Joan C. Everett under the direction of Dr. Henry P. Sims, Jr. We thank Ms. Everett for her enthusiastic interest in this project and for her permission to use the results of her research for this profile.
2. Dwight D. Eisenhower, *At Ease: Stories I Tell to Friends* (New York: Doubleday & Company, Inc., 1967), p. 119.
3. Ibid, p. 214.
4. Stephen E. Ambrose, *Eisenhower: Soldier, General of the Army, President-Elect 1890–1952* (New York: Simon and Schuster, 1983), p. 134.
5. Peter Lyon, *Eisenhower: Portrait of the Hero* (Boston: Little, Brown, and Company, 1974), p. 102.
6. Ambrose, p. 294.
7. Ibid, p. 122.

8. Ibid, p. 129.
9. Lyon, p. 201.
10. Stephen E. Ambrose, *The Supreme Commander: The War Years of General Dwight D. Eisenhower* (New York: Doubleday & Company, Inc., 1970), p. 213.
11. Eisenhower, pp. 141–42.
12. Ibid, p. 214.
13. Ambrose, *Eisenhower*, p. 134.
14. Eisenhower, p. 243.
15. Ambrose, *The Supreme Commander*, p. 55.
16. Eisenhower, p. 254.
17. Ambrose, *Eisenhower*, pp. 219–20.
18. Ibid, p. 227.
19. Ambrose, *The Supreme Commander*, p. 168.

Chapter 6

1. Gary Latham and Edwin Locke, "Goal Setting: A Motivational Technique that Works," *Organizational Dynamics* (Autumn 1979), pp. 68–80.
2. Private videotaped interview taken from the historical files of Hewlett-Packard, taped March 18, 1981.
3. Martin Berger, "Learning to Slow Down," *The New York Times Magazine* (September 16, 1984), p. 106.
4. This case on learning to speak was inspired by Michael T. Motley's article, "Taking the Terror Out of Talk," *Psychology Today* (January 1988), pp. 46–49.

Profiles in SuperLeadership: Dr. Ruth Randall

1. This material was developed using the following sources:
   • A research project of a Minnesota School District (data in the study was gathered through multiple interviews with relevant stakeholders and constituents in the school district; archival review of school district documents; and newspaper articles).
   • N. Roberts, "Transforming Leadership: Sources, Processes and Consequences," *SMRC Discussion Paper Series* (Minneapolis: Strategic Management Research Center, University of Minnesota, 1984).
   • Two interviews with Dr. Ruth Randall.
   • A short case centering on Ruth Randall drafted by Janet Dukerich, an assistant professor at New York University.
2. Roberts, p. 20.

Chapter 7

1. Kenneth Blanchard, *Minneapolis Star and Tribune* (May 27, 1987), sec. B, p. 6.

Profiles in SuperLeadership: Rene McPherson

1. See, for example, William Cahill, "Overhaul Job," *Barrons* (June 1986), pp. 55–57.
2. Arthur M. Louis, "The U.S. Business Hall of Fame," *Fortune* (April 14, 1986), p. 108.
3. Unless otherwise indicated, the quotes in this profile were taken from a telephone interview with Mr. McPherson conducted in 1987 by Mr. Craig Pearce, under the guidance of Henry P. Sims, Jr. In addition, some of the text in the profile was written by Mr. Pearce as part of his senior honor thesis ("Leading Others to Lead Themselves: The Epitome of Management," The Pennsylvania State University, 1987) under the direction of Dr. Sims. The authors wish to thank Mr. Pearce for his enthusiastic interest in this project and his permission to use the results of his research.
4. Louis, p. 108.
5. Ibid, p. 108.
6. Geoffery Foster, "Dana's Strange Disciplines," *Management Today* (September 1976), pp. 59–63.
7. Stanley W. Gustafson, "Hell Week—Or How Dana Makes Its Managers Money Conscious," *Management Review* (March 1974), pp. 18ff.
8. Richard Meyer, "Managing Is More Than Magic," *Quest*, no. 1 (1983), p. 20.

Chapter 8

1. T. E. Deal and A. A. Kennedy, *Corporate Culture* (Reading, MA: Addison-Wesley, 1982); and H. Schwartz and S. M. Davis, "Matching Corporate Culture and Business Strategy," *Organizational Dynamics* (Spring 1981), pp. 30–48.
2. "Corporate Culture," *Business Week* (October 27, 1980), p. 148.
3. These quotes were taken from the case "Strike in Space," by Balbaky and McCaskey, Harvard Business School, #1–481–008, copyright 1980 by the President and Fellows of Harvard College, and was based on the account by Henry F. S. Cooper, Jr., *A House in Space* (New York: Holt, Rinehart & Winston, 1976).
4. For a more thorough discussion of this strategic human-resource innovation, see H. L. Angle, C. C. Manz, and A. H. Van de Ven, "Integrating Human Resource Management and Corporate Strategy: A Preview of the 3M Story," *Human Resources Management*, 24 (1985), pp. 51–68.
5. "The Miracle Company," *Business Week* (October 19, 1987), pp. 84–90.
6. H. Schwartz and S. M. Davis, "Matching Corporate Culture and Business Strategy," *Organizational Dynamics* (Spring 1981).
7. This case is adapted from E. Pitre and H. P. Sims, Jr., "The Thinking Organization," *National Productivity Review* (Autumn 1987), pp. 340–47.
8. Peters and Waterman, *In Search of Excellence*.
9. Robert H. Waterman, Jr., *The Renewal Factor* (New York: Bantam Books, Inc., 1987).

10. For a more thorough discussion of scripts, see R. P. Abelson, "Psychological Status of the Script Concept," *American Psychologist*, 36 (1981), pp. 715–29.
11. John Sculley, "Sculley's Lessons from Inside Apple," *Fortune* (September 14, 1987), pp. 108–18.
12. Warren Bennis, "The 4 Competencies of Leadership," *Training and Development Journal* (August 1984), pp. 14–19.

Profiles in SuperLeadership: Ford Motor Company—A Leadership Culture in Evolution

1. "A Better Idea?: Ford's Leaders Push Radical Shift in Culture As Competition Grows," *The Clip Sheet* (reprinted from the *Wall Street Journal*) (December 3, 1985).
2. "Ford's Idea Machine—A Once Troubled Giant Discovers a Recipe for Recovery: Change Everything," *Newsweek* (November 24, 1986), p. 66.
3. Brian Dumaine, "A Humble Hero Drives Ford to the Top," *Fortune* (January 4, 1988), pp. 24–25.
4. "Ford's Idea Machine," *Newsweek*, p. 66.
5. Ibid.
6. Frank Swoboda, "Ford Plant Reverses to Outdo Import," *The Washington Post* (December 26, 1987), p. A1.

Chapter 9

1. Steve Lohr, "Volvo Plans to Abandon Assembly Line, Use Work Teams," *Minneapolis Star and Tribune* (July 25, 1987), p. 38.
2. Tom Watson, "The Greatest Capitalist in History," *Fortune* (August 31, 1987), p. 29.
3. Private videotaped interview taken from the historical files of Hewlett-Packard, taped August 26, 1980.
4. Charles C. Manz and Henry P. Sims, Jr., "Leading Workers to Lead Themselves: The External Leadership of Self-Managing Work Teams," *Administrative Science Quarterly*, 32 (1987), pp. 106–29.
5. This information is based on our informal conversation with Edward Lawler, and on Richard E. Walton, "From Control to Commitment in the Workplace," *Harvard Business Review*, 63 (1985), pp. 76–84.
6. Charles C. Manz and Harold Angle, "Can Group Self-Management Mean a Loss of Personal Control: Triangulating on a Paradox," *Group and Organization Studies*, 11 (1986), pp. 309–34.
7. Richard E. Walton, "Work Innovations at Topeka After Six Years," *Journal of Applied Behavioral Science*, 13 (1977), pp. 422–33; Ernesto J. Poza and M. Lynne Markus, "Success Story: The Team Approach to Work Restructuring," *Organizational Dynamics* (Winter 1980), pp. 3–25.

8. This section is based in part on Henry P. Sims, Jr., and Charles C. Manz, "Conversations within Self-Managed Work Groups," *National Productivity Review*, 1 (1982), pp. 261–69.
9. Chester A. Schriesheim, Robert J. House, and Steven Kerr, "Leader Initiating Structure: A Reconciliation of Discrepant Research Results and Some Empirical Tests," *Organizational Behavior and Human Performance*, 15 (1976), pp. 297–321; Robert G. Lord, R. J. Foti, and C. L. DeVader, "A Test of Leadership Categorization Theory: Internal Structure, Information Processing, and Leadership Perceptions," *Organizational Behavior and Human Performance*, 34 (1984), pp. 343–78.
10. Daniel Roland Denison, "Sociotechnical Design and Self-Managing Work Groups: The Impact on Control," *Journal of Occupational Behavior*, 3 (1982), pp. 297–314.
11. Rick Madrid, "New Attitudes, New Ambitions Imprint New United Motor," *GM Today*, 11 (October 11, 1985), p. 4.

Profiles in SuperLeadership: MacGregor

1. This case is excerpted, with permission of the author, from the article "MacGregor" by Arthur Elliott Carlisle, *Organizational Dynamics*, 5 (Summer 1976), pp. 50–62.

Chapter 10

1. Thomas J. Peters and Robert H. Waterman, Jr., *In Search of Excellence* (New York: Harper & Row, 1982), p. xxv.
2. Robert H. Waterman, Jr., *The Renewal Factor* (New York: Bantam Books, Inc., 1987).

Index